Winston
Churchill

Winston Churchill

Personal accounts of the great leader at war

Michael Paterson

David and Charles

For my wife, Sarah

A DAVID & CHARLES BOOK
David & Charles is a subsidiary of F+W (UK) Ltd.,
an F+W Publications Inc. company

First published in the UK in 2005

Distributed in North America
by F+W Publications, Inc.
4700 East Galbraith Road
Cincinnati, OH 45236
1-800-289-0963

A catalogue record for this book is available from the British Library.

ISBN 0 7153 1964 7 hardback

Printed in Great Britain by Antony Rowe Limited, Wiltshire
for David & Charles
Brunel House   Newton Abbot   Devon

Commissioning Editor Ruth Binney
Desk Editor Lewis Birchon
Head of Design Alison Myer
Production Director Roger Lane

Visit our website at www.davidandcharles.co.uk

David & Charles books are available from all good bookshops; alternatively you
can contact our Orderline on (0)1626 334555 or write to us at FREEPOST EX2 110,
David & Charles Direct, Newton Abbot, TQ12 4ZZ (no stamp required UK mainland).

CONTENTS

FOREWORD

Why another book about Sir Winston Churchill? There is certainly no doubting the public interest in the man. Hardly a day goes by without a reference in the newspapers or an appearance on television, but Churchill must also be one of the most chronicled, reported and written about figures of all time.

This book is not attempting to be another general biography. It aims to show how Churchill the war leader was shaped by his own experiences of war. He is remembered now as an orator, a writer, and a politician, but his training was a soldier and his nature was to admire nothing more than courage under fire.

Churchill wrote a lot about himself and his military exploits. Most of his literary works are accounts of the conflicts in which he played a role, and he retained a lifelong interest in military campaigns and commanders. This book highlights the accounts and impressions of those who came into contact with him during his formative years and his wartime premiership. It lets us hear the voices of Churchill's superiors, fellow officers, subordinates and secretaries, thereby suggesting fresh perspectives on familiar episodes and new insights into Churchill's character. Through the use of regimental histories and other contemporary accounts, it paints a vivid picture of what it was like for Churchill to train and serve as a soldier in the last days of Queen Victoria's Empire.

There is no doubt that Churchill enjoyed his military career, even if he always saw it as a springboard to political success. The army may have been in his blood, for he was certainly aware of his Marlborough lineage, but it was also his university: it taught him to fight and to lead, and it provided him with adventure and a wealth of material for his lucrative writing career. Churchill may have successfully forged his sword in a despatch box in 1900, but his links to the service remained strong. When politics turned sour for him in 1915, over the failure of the Dardanelles Campaign, he returned to his first profession and experienced modern warfare at first hand during a six-month stint in the trenches.

In 1929, after becoming Chancellor of Bristol University, Churchill told the assembled students that he had not been thought clever enough for an academic career but, 'was put to be trained in technical matters of a military college, and almost immediately afterwards things opened out very quickly into action and adventure'. This book is not just another biography; it is a book about the shaping of Winston Churchill.

Allen Packwood
Director
Churchill Archives Centre

INTRODUCTION

Blandon churchyard in Oxfordshire, where Sir Winston Churchill is buried, was described at the time of his funeral:

> **Standing on a slight hill above a picturesque huddle of limestone cottages and narrow, twisting streets the church of St. Martin is the most prominent feature in a village of 400 people. It is typical of the man that after the pomp and glory of a state funeral in London, he should have chosen to lie in the bosom of the humblest country village.**

Years afterwards an American travel writer, pausing there, remarked on the plainness of this resting place. Contrasting it with his own country's tradition of creating vast memorial libraries for even the most obscure of presidents, he considered Churchill's monuments – this simple grave and a statue outside Parliament – an admirable show of restraint.

He was entirely wrong, for Churchill – the most 'presidential' of prime ministers – does not lack conspicuous commemoration. Indeed, only Queen Victoria, Prince Albert and the Duke of Wellington have had more things named after them. An international scholarship and a building at the Royal Military Academy, for instance, are named after him. His most conspicuous monument is the Cambridge college named in his honour and founded five years before his death (he himself planted the first tree in the grounds). Within it is the Churchill Archives Centre, guardian of his personal papers and the only equivalent in Britain of the great presidential libraries in the United States, though it is on a more modest scale.

Few things associated with Winston Churchill merit the adjective 'modest', for his personality, his achievements and his place in the national memory are greater than those of anyone in recent history. He is as instantly recognizable a historical figure as Hitler or Napoleon or Queen Elizabeth I. He remains one of the most quoted of English statesmen or writers, whose scalding wit, florid imagery and neat turn of phrase can still amuse and inspire though the context in which he spoke may be long forgotten. The shadow he casts is still so lengthy that, in the autumn of 2002, British television viewers voted him 'the greatest Briton of all time', comfortably outdistancing the heroes of war, politics, science and literature – even including, to the surprise of many people, Shakespeare.

This status was, of course, earned by his leadership in World War II, and specifically by his defiant resistance to Hitler in 1940. It survived his rejection at the ballot box five years later and his long physical and mental decline. By the time of his death he was regarded as a secular saint and his funeral, with its gun-carriage and marching troops and dockland cranes bowing in salute, seemed entirely fitting. It is sometimes implied that the granting of a state funeral to a Commoner was a unique honour, though in fact the same tribute had been paid to the *previous* century's greatest Briton, the Duke of Wellington, in 1852 and to the altogether less illustrious William Ewart Gladstone in 1898. In all these instances, the passing of an elderly public figure was hailed as the end of an era, but in Churchill's case this was resoundingly true. His stature on the world stage had ensured for Britain a degree of influence that her economic and military resources had ceased to deserve. Though the country would go on to find other forms of greatness, he had personified a Victorian aristocratic confidence that was no longer sustainable. His departure from the scene seemed to expose a threadbare grandeur that the splendid ceremonial of his obsequies could not conceal. Small wonder that Charles de Gaulle wrote, on hearing of his death: 'From today onward, Britain is no longer a great power.'

My own connection with Winston Churchill dates from his death on that bleak January Sunday in 1965. I recall the sombre mood of the grown-ups over lunch that day, and my older brother, then aged ten, intoning portentously, 'This is a sad day for Britain.' I was one of the legions of British children who were presented with commemorative coins – the Churchill crown – by grandparents with the solemn injunction, 'Now look after this carefully, it will be worth a lot of money one day.' Unfortunately for all of us, the Royal Mint had produced 19 million of the things. As a result they are still so common that they can be bought, four decades later, for 50 pence – only twice their face value.

In spite of this disappointment, I have followed the progress of the Churchill legend ever since. Naturally, he is seen as a symbol of Britain; apart from the shrines at Chartwell and the Cabinet War Rooms, a number of tourism-related establishments have used his name. He has equal potency as a symbol of reliability and of unshakeable determination; his image is used by an insurance company, and he even appears on a poster addressed to the physically impaired: 'Winston Churchill had a speech impediment,' announces a caption next to the bowler-hatted, bulldog features, before going on to explain: 'Disability can be overcome' – a valid observation, since he became one of history's great orators, and an intriguing reflection of his universality. For a host of reasons, he can inspire on many different levels. He is one of Britain's national treasures though he also belongs, without question, to the wider world.

His life – especially his military life – merits close study, and as the details of his career become more clear, the clichés that litter the public imagination can be swept away: Churchill was not slow or stupid at school; virtually nobody (with the notable exception of his father) who had dealings with him in his youth thought him unpromising. As a young officer he was not universally hated by those at the top of the army. The cavalry charge in which he rode at Omdurman was not the last such action in British history. The horseman who captured him as he fled from the wreck of the armoured train in South Africa was not the Boer leader, General Louis Botha; it was not Churchill who, in World War II, invented the term 'commando' to describe special forces, nor did he coin the phrase 'iron curtain' in its aftermath. And so the list goes on until his death, after which, as we have seen, he was not the only Commoner to be granted a state funeral.

The character that emerges from this clutter of misapprehensions is more complex, more vulnerable and more engaging than we are perhaps used to imagining. For all his spectacular gifts, he was no 'darling of the gods'. The superficial but fantastic glitter of his life – the influential contacts that helped to launch his careers in politics and journalism, the immensely lucrative writing that lifted him permanently above the ruck of everyday existence (so that he never visited a shop or had any idea how to use public transport) giving him a staff of servants and the best of whatever he wanted – these things were balanced by years of frustration, unpopularity and seemingly permanent eclipse. All his life, Churchill battled with depression. Even during his adventurous years as a soldier and correspondent, he had a sense of lost opportunity and wasted time. Though happily married, he was often deeply stressful to live with; Clementine Churchill was very much to be admired, but I suspect that few women would have wanted to trade places with her.

This book principally examines one aspect of Churchill's life – his career as a soldier and war-leader spanning the 50 years from 1895, when he joined the Spanish forces in Cuba, to the defeat of Hitler in 1945 – though it would be impossible to do this without also looking at his lives as politician and writer, and without examining in some detail his formative years. He possessed a genius for strategic thinking that became evident early in his life and influenced his approach to government; he was always a soldier dealing in politics more than a politician playing soldier. Though experience of savage fighting on three continents left him in no doubt about the vileness of war, he retained all his life the sense of boyish adventure that had caused him to choose the military profession. What he found fascinating in war were the drama of huge events; the clash of ideas, ideologies and national wills; the possibilities for affecting and directing and driving the destinies of nations; the challenge of living up to – and making – history. Unlike most people, he was comfortable wielding power in such grave and terrifying circumstances; he had somehow expected, all his life, to do this.

Once, when told that yet another book was being written about his life, he grunted, 'There's nothing much in *that* field left unploughed.' Yet as Norman McGowan, who was one of his valets, remarked, 'The man is of such a grandiose and complex character that one yearns to know more.' Many people want to find out what it was like to live such a crowded and exciting and useful life, to command such a range of abilities, to wield such immense power and then to lose it, to be a leading actor in one of history's great dramas, to be a national monument. Churchill's unconcealed weaknesses – his enjoyment of luxury, and indulgence in smoking and drinking and gambling, his habitual lateness and frequent sulks, his irascibility and self-centredness – fortunately make him more human, as does his love of fish and butterflies, dogs and cats and pigs. They make it possible to relate to him, and without these things he would have been too distant.

Even without his accomplishments as politician, writer, artist and statesman, Churchill would merit our attention (and the writing of books about him) because of his military career. This was unique in British history for the width and depth of the expertise he accumulated. No one else in the British Government in 1940 could boast the experience that he had of fighting, planning and leading in war.

He had been a lieutenant in the cavalry, a major and a colonel in the infantry. As First Lord of the Admiralty (1911–15 and 1939–40) he was twice in charge of the Royal Navy, and as Secretary of State for Air (1919–21) he was responsible for the Royal Air Force in its early years. As Minister of Munitions (1917–18) he held responsibility for supplying the armies that fought in France at the end of World War I. As Secretary of State for War (1919–21) he implemented Britain's response to the threat of Communism.

He was *de facto* leader of the nation's war effort, and as Premier and Minister of Defence between 1940 and 1945 he almost entirely ignored domestic political issues in order to assume the role of commander-in-chief of Britain's armed forces. As well as an understanding of military matters that was based on personal experience, he had both studied and written extensively in the field of military history, thereby expanding his knowledge well beyond that of most of those who commanded the armies and fleets.

Naturally he made mistakes, and understandably he was regarded as a meddling amateur by military professionals. Nonetheless it was his personality, with his unparalleled range of knowledge and experience, that did more than anything else to ensure Allied victory in World War II.

Churchill's story divides between two centuries, and they have required different approaches. The colonial campaigns in which he participated between 1895 and 1900 are largely unfamiliar to a modern audience, and so their origins, nature and significance have to be explained in some detail. The major events of the two world wars, by contrast, are well known to most readers. The amount of source material relating to these conflicts is naturally much greater. Coverage must therefore be less intensive, less analytical and more wide-ranging.

Having read huge amounts of books and documents about Churchill's life in general and his military career in particular, I have tried to present the views of him that are less well known, especially through the voices of those whose lives he touched. I hope a picture will emerge that differs from the myths which have grown around him and which, in a number of cases, he perpetuated himself. Some of these accounts have not previously been published; others have seen the light of day but have been forgotten for a generation; while some, though well known, are too illuminating to be left out. I very much hope that they will add to your understanding and appreciation of this unique Englishman.

There are a great many people whom I would like to thank for various forms of assistance with this book. First and foremost my wife Sarah, to whose tireless endeavours no gratitude could hope to do justice, and to my friend Sandy Malcolm, whose way with computers did so much to redeem my own incompetence.

At David and Charles I would like to thank Miranda Spicer, Ruth Binney, Alison Myer, Lewis Birchon – and Margaret Harris who, if there were a Nobel Prize for Patience, would be on her way to Stockholm. Val Porter also deserves my gratitude for editing the text with sympathy and humour.

In the Churchill Archives Centre at Churchill College, Cambridge, I would like to acknowledge the kindness of Allen Packwood and the cheerful, friendly and very efficient assistance of Ieuan Hopkins, Sandra Marsh and Louise King.

The staff at the Imperial War Museum have also been extremely helpful, and I thank Tony Richards, Justin Saddington and Kate Martin of the Department of Documents, as well as Jane Rosen, Amanda Robertson and Andrew Colquhoun of the Department of Printed Books.

At Harrow School, the Archivist Mrs Rita Boswell Griggs and the Librarian, Mrs. Margaret Knight, were extremely courteous and hospitable during my several visits to the Hill.

In addition I would like to express gratitude to Ms Mary Elliot and Mr John Powell of the Queen's Royal Irish Hussars Museum at the Redoubt Fortress, Eastbourne, for their help with the finer points of 4th Hussars uniform; to Mr Len Sellars, founding editor of *The Royal Naval Division Journal*; to Mr James Opie of Bonham's auctioneers who shared his expertise regarding Victorian toy soldiers and to Mrs June Jamieson who similarly shared her collection of newspapers relating to Churchill; to Lt Col Wayne Warlow, LF, and to the staff of Lock and Co, hatters of St James' Street.

Finally, I would like to thank all those who gave permission for the quoting of their own – or others' – memories and opinions. Responsibility for any errors in the text is, of course, mine alone.

Michael Paterson

1
THE PUBLIC FIGURE: SOLDIER AND STATESMAN

For nearly 70 of his 90 years, Winston Churchill was a public figure. His life was so lengthy and involved so many different offices, circumstances and fields of action that inevitably a vast amount was said and written about him by people of all sorts – heads of state, strikers, parliamentarians, housewives, voters . . . At some time in the first half of the 20th century every person in the United Kingdom, and millions more in the wider world, was affected by something he said or did. Many of them have left us their views.

These divide fairly evenly between admiration and censure, but it is his heroic side to which we are more accustomed. His role in World War II made him one of the greatest figures in British, indeed world, history and this stature is reflected in much that was said about him during the last quarter-century of his life. At several stages his achievements were paraded before the public in broadcast or published eulogies: when he became Prime Minister in 1940; when his career seemed over in 1945; at his 80th birthday in 1954 and his 90th a decade later; and at his death on 24 January 1965.

Invariably Churchill was described as a 'giant', or as a 'towering figure' who 'bestrode' the world or his time or his environment. Both before and after he died, the litany of praise went on. The *Daily Mail*'s description of him as 'the greatest man of our time' (echoed by the 90th birthday card from a child in Mexico, addressed simply to 'The Greatest Man in the World', which reached him) was exceeded by the Conservative Party ('the greatest man on earth, the greatest statesman in the world'), which was in turn outdone by a Canadian Premier, Louis St Laurent: 'He was one of the greatest men the world has known.' Perhaps the loftiest heights of elegance were attained by America's Adlai Stevenson:

> Like the grandeur and power of masterpieces of art and music, Churchill's life uplifts our hearts and fills us with fresh revelation of the scale and reach of human achievement . . . our world is thus

No politician in a democracy has ever had such a wealth of personal symbols – gestures, garments, habits or sayings – as Churchill. His personality intrigued, amused and inspired the British people whether or not they voted for him.

the poorer [for his passing], our political dialogue diminished and the sources of public inspiration run more thinly for all of us.

At his funeral in St Paul's Cathedral, London, the Australian Prime Minister Sir Robert Menzies highlighted the significance of his conduct at one of history's fateful moments:

In the whole of recorded history this was, I believe, the one occasion when one man, with one imagination, with one fire burning in him, and with one unrivalled capacity for conveying it to others, won a crucial victory not only for the Forces (for there were many heroes in those days) but for the very spirit of human freedom . . .

Even a representative of his Cold War adversary, the London correspondent of the Soviet newspaper *Izvestia*, paid backhanded tribute when he died.

Melor Strua wrote: 'Sir Winston was a great enemy of Russia . . . but it is better to have a great enemy than a small and foolish one.'

There is no question that he deserved these grand sentiments. He would not have disagreed with any of them, since he had maintained a similar view of himself all his life. He was, however, blessed with a sense of humour that enabled him to react to flattery with self-mocking irony. When once asked by a small boy if he really was 'the greatest man in the whole wide world', Churchill snapped: 'Of course I'm the greatest man in the whole wide world. Now buzz off.'

This widespread adulation was, of course, the reward for his leadership in 1940, and it lasted for the rest of his life. Yet Churchill's 'Finest Hour' was a relatively short chapter in the very long story of a soldier and statesman, and his well-merited lustre can obscure the distrust, derision and frank dislike with which he was regarded, for considerable periods, by sections of the public. As another Prime Minister, Sir Harold Wilson, said, 'He has probably been the target of more concentrated parliamentary invective than any other member of any parliamentary age.'

The author and Churchill contemporary Charles Eade, editor of a book of tributes to him, said:

> He has gloried in triumphs such as few men have achieved and he
> has suffered defeats, disappointments, humiliations and derision
> in a measure seldom experienced by any other man in public
> life. He has been mocked and isolated in Parliament and yet has
> lived to see his critics hail him as the greatest parliamentarian
> of modern times – possibly of all time. He was cheered as the
> architect of victory in the greatest war in history and then hurled
> from office by the very people he had led through the terror to
> triumph . . .

Critics might even be found within his own family. When he was young he was, for some years, heir to the Marlborough title because his cousin, the 9th Duke, had no wife and so no children. A few months after the Duke married, the new, American-born Duchess was interrogated by her mother-in-law:

> . . . fixing her cold grey eyes upon me she said: 'Your first duty
> is to have a child and it must be a son, because it would be
> intolerable to have that little upstart Winston become Duke. Are
> you in the family way?

A headstrong child, a bumptious schoolboy, an indecently ambitious soldier, writer and politician, Winston must have been utterly insufferable, and he was frequently at odds with those around him. His maddening self-assurance could provoke a particularly virulent exasperation, and when he entered politics a wider audience came to know and to share this.

As a young Member of Parliament, Churchill seemed to have inherited the instability and the gift for troublemaking that had represented the worse side of his father, Lord Randolph. By deserting the Conservatives in 1904 for the Liberals, Winston gained a nickname, 'the Blenheim Rat', and a reputation for treachery that followed him all the way to 1940. The debacle of Gallipoli in 1915 earned him, quite undeservedly, a parallel opprobrium: a name for rashness, bad judgement and extravagance with lives that proved equally difficult to live down. Suffragettes never forgave him for his determined opposition. His perceived heavy-handedness in dealing with strikes while Home Secretary in 1910–11 was compounded when, as Chancellor of the Exchequer, his policies precipitated the General Strike of 1926. His name was anathema in working-class homes for a generation. For considerable periods during his ministerial career, he had to be assigned a Scotland Yard detective for protection, in an era before such measures were seen as routine for senior politicians.

Even after his wartime surge in popularity, Churchill's detractors had plenty of ammunition. He was overwhelmingly rejected at the polls as an unsuitable peacetime prime minister before hostilities had ended and, after he recaptured Downing Street in 1951, was accused (with justification) of clinging on blindly to the premiership when his powers were clearly on the wane. Someone even viewed him with such venom that they killed all his pet carp by tossing a hand-grenade into the pond at Chartwell.

Yet even Churchill's enemies were compelled to respect his unalterable belief in his destiny and his refusal to be crushed by massive reverses, disappointments or misfortunes. Throughout his personal, military and political life he showed the same determination to succeed, in spite of the odds, that he expressed on behalf of the British people in 1940. Though plagued by depression throughout much of his life, he could swiftly recover both humour and energy. His unofficial motto, 'KBO' ('Keep Buggering On'), summed up an indomitable spirit with which people could identify, whether they voted for him or not.

THE CHURCHILL 'TRADEMARKS'

What were the components of Churchill's perceived 'image' – the trademark habits, sayings, gestures and accoutrements that became imprinted on the public mind? He had more of these than any British, or American, politician before or since, and all were the outgrowth of his personality and inclinations rather than the creation of advisers or image-makers.

Physically he was not prepossessing. Stocky, and just under five foot seven though seeming shorter because of a pronounced forward stoop, he was not handsome at any stage of his life. His broad face, which remained pink and cherubic in maturity, was marked by bright blue eyes, a pug nose and a crooked, thick-lipped mouth. His hair was reddish-brown and did not lose its colour until his last years. His body was almost hairless (he briefly tried to grow a moustache during the Boer War, but it is all but invisible in photographs) and his skin was pale, sensitive (hence his numerous large sun hats) and prone to freckles. His speech impediment is frequently mentioned in descriptions of him. It was not a lisp or a stammer. It was that slurring of the letter 's' for which only speech therapists must have a term, and he tried to cure it as a young man by repeating the phrase 'the Spanish ships I cannot see for they are not in sight'. In no sense a serious hindrance, it is recognizable to anyone who has heard the actor James Stewart or the British politician Tony Benn ('the Shpanish shipsh I cannot shee . . .').

In dress, Churchill's preferences gradually created a personal style that became increasingly marked. As a young man he looked decidedly unkempt, so much so that on more than one occasion when out riding with his mother he was mistaken for her groom. From the time he entered Parliament in 1901 he began to dress fashionably in frock-coats, and adopted the type of polka-dot bow-tie that had been favoured by Lord Randolph. It was to become a lifelong trademark (the pattern is still known to West End shirtmakers as 'Churchill Spot'). From about the same period dates the hefty gold 'Albert' watch-chain that looped so conspicuously across his waistcoat. In 1908 he acquired his most lasting accessory when he received a gold-topped cane as a wedding present from King Edward VII. This, which had 'W.S.C., Turf Club' engraved on it, appears endlessly in pictures of him for he used it until his death, not least for hoisting his hat on when making morale-boosting wartime visits to bombed-out cities or military units.

A streak of eccentric and ebullient raffishness was expressed in some other aspects of his dress. He was known, for instance, to wear pink silk underwear, though this was largely because of his sensitive skin. Throughout his young and middle years he wore an astrakhan-collared overcoat, a garment that was then associated with the vulgar world of the theatre. He frequently wore two-tone, button-sided boots until about the time he became Prime Minister, when he adopted black shoes with zips instead of laces, to facilitate quick dressing. He was also seen, when photographed at home, wearing velvet slippers with his initials embroidered on the toes – a not uncommon upper-class affectation.

His hats were an important aspect of Churchill's individuality throughout his life. His son Randolph was to say, 'My father never met a hat he didn't like.' In addition to a wealth of official headgear – busbies, topees, silk top hats, cocked hats – that he wore in military and ceremonial contexts, he possessed a multitude of Stetsons and Homburgs in which he was often photographed. Once, when staying at a country house that caught fire in the night, he even managed to equip himself with a brass fireman's helmet and, clad in this and his dressing-gown, gave orders to the fire brigade. Hats had been seen to symbolize him since 1910 when a photographer snapped him wearing one, put on by accident, that was far too small. For decades afterwards he was depicted in newspaper cartoons with a huge, balding head crowned by a tiny hat in any style or shape that occurred to the artist.

When Churchill was wartime Premier, the hat that became most familiar was a curious tall-crowned, square-topped bowler. This was called a 'Cambridge'. First seen in 1865, it was popular in the 1870s and 1880s – the years of Churchill's childhood. By World War I it was virtually extinct and by 1940 it seemed an absurd anachronism. This, too, was a long-standing trademark, worn since his early years in politics. It gave him greater height, and may have helped to make him conspicuous in crowds. His valet, Norman McGowan, describing his reluctance to replace familiar old garments with more up-to-date ones, wrote:

> While talking about the way that my Guv'nor kept to well tried and long-owned clothes, I am reminded of the interest his hat aroused when he was in Washington in January, 1952.
>
> It was that very characteristic piece of headgear which some people referred to as a 'sawn-off stove pipe' and is in fact known as a Cambridge hat. All sorts of mens shops in the United States hurriedly made enquiries from American manufacturers as to where they could obtain them, and on being told that they were essentially English, cables came to London, where agents eventually discovered the source of my Guv'nor's purchases, a famous hatters in St James' Street.
>
> The interesting thing was that when the staff turned up the records meticulously kept at this establishment, it was discovered that the last time Mr Churchill had bought one of these hats was in 1919.

Together with the rest of his parliamentary 'uniform' (black morning-coat and waistcoat, striped trousers, bow-tie and walking-stick), this hat gave him the appearance of an old-fashioned country solicitor. This appealed enormously to the British public. Like his flowery and out-of-date rhetoric, his quaint appearance evoked a gentler, older Britain, a sense of long history and ancient certainties, of continuity and survival.

Though he often looked like a Victorian, Churchill could also appear almost futuristic. His famous wartime siren-suit was the one personal symbol that was entirely his own invention. As an amateur bricklayer he had been used to wearing overalls. This was an arguably more formal, but equally practical, variation on the theme. It enabled him to be adequately dressed within seconds if roused from bed by air-raids or urgent news. The no-nonsense, workmanlike appearance of the siren-suit caught another national mood – the desire to grapple with the job in hand and see it through – that was simultaneously the basis of his leadership. The journalist James Laver wrote:

> When a man is as independent as Churchill has always been of the fixed hours of the day and night; when, like Napoleon, a man can sleep for an hour whenever the occasion offers and rouse himself for labour and decision at any point in the twenty-four hours, a kind of 'general purposes' outfit becomes essential. And what could be more suitable than a one-piece garment provided with a sufficiency of pockets, loose enough to provide protection against wintry nights? It was as if he were saying to every factory worker in the country: 'I am on night-shift too.'

His appearance in this garment was, of course, slightly comical. One old friend, Lady Diana Cooper, remarked: 'Winston dresses night and day, and I imagine in bed, in the same little blue workman's boiler suit. He looks exactly like the good little pig building his house with bricks.'

However proletarian their inspiration and whatever the sense of solidarity they engendered, Churchill's siren-suits reflected his own opulent tastes and lifestyle: they were made for him personally, in velvet or worsted, by Turnbull and Asser of Jermyn Street. By the same token his steel helmet, which looked the same as everyone else's, was fitted inside with a velvet band bearing the stamp of Lock & Company, the same St James's Street hatters from which his Cambridge hats were found to have come.

On his first wartime visit to the United States in December 1941 Churchill's siren suit was a matter of great interest to the American press. Despite the cold, he modelled it for them in the White House Rose Garden (see page 271).

He also wore military uniform (he was the only prime minister ever to do so while in office) and this flitted between the Services as occasion demanded. His military wardrobe, which allowed him a suitable degree of martial dignity when dealing with other war leaders and emphasized his soldierly background when among Allied troops, was more than theatrical dressing up. He was appointed (honorary) Colonel of his old regiment, the 4th Hussars, and frequently wore their uniform, notably when witnessing the Rhine Crossings in March 1945 and attending the Potsdam Conference in July of the same year.

Shortly before World War II, Churchill was appointed honorary Air Commodore of a Fighter unit. This was No. 615 (County of Surrey) Squadron of the Auxiliary Air Force. It was based at Kenley, where he himself had had some flying instruction. Like his army colonelcy, this was an official appointment, approved by the King and announced in the *London Gazette*. He took a keen interest in the Squadron's affairs and dined in their mess on several occasions. He therefore had the right to wear RAF officer's uniform (he requested a £40 government clothing allowance to pay for it) and he also sported pilot's wings – to which he was not entitled – appearing in this at the Tehran Conference in 1943 and when welcomed into liberated Paris in November 1944. Both his army and RAF units were proud of their connection with him and were delighted to see him wear their uniforms in illustrious circumstances. On naval occasions, such as his mid-Atlantic meeting with Roosevelt or his visit to the Normandy beaches after D-Day, Churchill wore the brass-buttoned uniform and cap of the Royal Yacht Squadron.

The most widely known of Churchill's peccadilloes was his cigar. This habit was a souvenir of his service in Cuba with Spanish forces in 1895, and it became a lifelong addiction. It has been estimated that he went through cigars at the rate of 4,000 a year and that his lifelong total was therefore a quarter of a million. He was seldom seen without one, though he did not smoke continuously; he might hold an unlit one in his mouth for long periods while lost in thought.

Stocks were held for him in the 'keeps', or basement humidors, at Dunhill's in London, and during the Blitz were moved to a deeper cellar. His fondness was so well publicized that brands were named after him by several manufacturers. Some members of his wartime retinue were even able to turn this vice to profit: during conferences in his headquarters beneath Whitehall, he became highly adept at throwing the butts over his shoulder into a sand-filled fire-bucket. They were retrieved and sold by the Royal Marine sentries who guarded him.

After the war, a different fate befell the remains of Churchillian smokes, as his valet Norman McGowan recollected:

> I never saw the Guv'nor finish a cigar. He used to leave about half in the ash-tray. But those cigar-ends were never wasted. I had special orders about them. No matter where we went – anywhere in the world – I had to collect all the butts and put them in a special box. That box was brought back to Chartwell and the butts were handed to Kearns, one of the gardeners, who used to smoke them in his pipe. And whenever Mr Churchill saw Kearns about the estate he made a point of checking that he was getting his supplies regularly.

Elizabeth Layton, one of his typists, affectionately recalling his smoking habits, mentioned that Sawyers, who was McGowan's wartime predecessor as Churchill's valet:

. . . was the custodian of the famous cigars. Contrary to popular belief, which put the number at anything between thirty and fifty, Mr Churchill did not smoke more than eight or ten cigars a day, but these lasted him all day. Indeed, he never seemed happy for a moment without a cigar between his lips unless it was meal-time. The cigars frequently went out, and vast quantities of large-size matches were used and a certain amount of time consumed in relighting them. They would burn along nicely at first, but then as their smoker's thoughts became fully engaged, their fire would die and they would be used merely as a sort of dummy – until their deficiency was noted and relighting performed. It was no good trying to palm off Mr Churchill with anything but the best cigars, and Sawyers was always scurrying about to keep a sufficiency in store, all smoker's requirements being then in short supply. If some dealers were in the habit of keeping back their best Havana cigars for the P.M., who can blame them? He deserved it. Newcomers to his service might be a little surprised and a little alarmed when, a cigar proving not up to standard, the corpse would be hurled into the fire: old hands knew better than to sit between the Prime Minister and the fireplace, and so avoided the necessity of ducking.

One of the permanent mental pictures I have of Mr Churchill is of the relighting of his cigar. A pause in whatever he was doing: the flame from a very large match jumping up and down, while clouds of blue smoke issued from his mouth: then a hasty shake of the match to extinguish it, and on with the job.

Whatever damage was done to his health by these indulgences was disregarded. Gerald Pawle, who wrote a book on Churchill's wartime travels, remembered that:

> Churchill had smoked cigars all his life. At the age of twenty he had been warned by a doctor that unless he gave up cigars and champagne he would be dead in five years. He had cheerfully ignored this advice at the time, and now, nearly half a century later, he had no intention of denying himself either luxury as long as it remained available.

Churchill's other personal signature was his two-fingered 'V-for-victory' salute. Though this was not unknown before World War II, it originated in German-occupied Europe in 1940. The letter V, surreptitiously painted on walls, became a symbol of resistance and of belief in the ultimate defeat of Hitler. To the French it stood for *victoire*, to the Dutch or Walloons it meant *vrijheid* (freedom). Once adopted by the English-speaking world, it gained wide currency. Churchill used it as a gesture with such regularity that it became inseparable from his public image, notwithstanding that, if made with the back of the hand instead of the palm, it was identical to an older English gesture of unambiguous rudeness. He cheerfully used both forms of the salute, which was often returned in kind. Though naturally he usually made this gesture with his fingers he was capable of exotic variations: on at least one occasion, while bathing off the North African coast, he lay on his back in the surf and formed a 'V' with his legs.

The V-sign so irritated the Nazis that they attempted to hi-jack it. Claiming that it could be an abbreviation of *Viktoria*, an archaic German word for victory long since replaced in their language by the more concise *Sieg*, they hoisted a giant V on to the Eiffel Tower in Paris, where it remained for a short time before widespread derision caused them to remove it.

The gesture has long survived the war. Applied in the arena of politics, it remained Churchill's personal symbol through the rest of his political career. Simple, spontaneous and eloquent, it has seen service with numerous other public figures – most notably, perhaps, President Richard Nixon.

THE CHURCHILLIAN LIFESTYLE

Apart from these specific symbols, Churchill was known to have a comfortable, expensive and extremely self-indulgent lifestyle, and this struck a chord with millions of voters who would have lived in the same manner if they could. He was known to 'enjoy a drink', and was often pictured by hostile commentators (such as the teetotal Hitler) as a drunkard. As with his cigars, he was often to be seen with a glass in his hand, but this did not mean he was imbibing neat alcohol throughout his waking hours. He had developed a pronounced taste for whisky during the Boer War and he continued to enjoy it for the rest of his life. Though he might well begin drinking before mid-morning and continue through the day, the contents of his glass were scarcely a threat to his clarity of mind. His valet Norman McGowan remembers:

> About an hour after breakfast I would place his first whisky and
> soda of the day beside him. For the rest of the day the tumbler
> was never empty, but he drank very slowly, absentmindedly

sipping it from time to time and making each glass last about two hours. It was literally drowned in soda at the outset and as ice cubes had to be in it, which melted long before he had finished, the drink was a very innocuous one.

He drank port and brandy after meals, and consumed his favourite drink, champagne, at a rate of (by his own reckoning) a pint a day. Again this seemed to do him no damage, and he was generous in sharing with others. Churchill's wartime ADC, Commander CR Thompson, remembered:

> So many odd stories have circulated about the Prime Minister's alleged eccentricities in this direction that the truth deserves to be put on record. At home he usually drank a glass of white wine at lunch, champagne at dinner, and then a glass of port or brandy afterwards. As a meal he disliked afternoon tea, and if he had anything at all at that time he would ask for a whisky heavily diluted with ice and water. Cocktails he avoided altogether. He liked to provide champagne for his guests, but as the war went on champagne became more and more difficult to obtain. I therefore suggested that since champagne agreed with him and our stock was running low he might have half a bottle with his meals while his guests were given something more easily obtainable. This was brushed aside. 'What happens if we run out?' I asked. 'Get some more!' he said. He obviously thought the question was slightly ridiculous.

The public was further amused by his unapologetic approach to these appetites ('I have got more out of alcohol than alcohol has got out of me') and by the ease, wit and charm with which he could defend them:

> Montgomery: 'I don't drink and don't smoke and I am one hundred per cent fit.'
>   Churchill: 'I drink and smoke and I am two hundred per cent fit.'

He had a similar approach to food. James C Humes, an author who met him, describes his intake:

> A Churchill breakfast generally consisted of melon, eggs and bacon – followed by a veal cutlet, fried bread with marmalade,

and plenty of coffee and cream. Lunch on the same day might start with a fillet of sole wrapped in smoked salmon and garnished with shrimp, then roast venison stuffed with *pâté de foie gras* and served with a truffle sauce.

Then came dinner, when he really got serious. This is an actual dinner that Sir Winston enjoyed at the Savoy Hotel in his eighty-eighth year: he opened with oysters and champagne, followed by a pea *purée* and a glass of sherry. Then he attacked a poached turbot in cream sauce, washed down with some Poully-Fuisse. The next course was Beef Wellington with a side of carrots and scalloped potatoes, along with a bottle of burgundy. Dessert was *crème brûlée* with a glass of Madiera. And finally, he called for Stilton cheese and a glass of port. After coffee, he concluded the repast with a cigar and brandy.

Though he was able to get through a mountain of business each day, he was famous for his unconventional working habits. Even his opponents in Berlin knew about these, as is shown by this reference in Goebbels' diary:

3 May 1941
A book on Churchill reports that he drinks too much and wears silk underwear. He dictates messages in the bath or in his underpants, a startling image which the Füehrer finds hugely amusing.

Sneering though this is, it is undeniably accurate, for he had a lifelong addiction to bathing. The story is told that when travelling in the Middle East early in his ministerial career, he stopped the train and had hot water from the engine's boiler used to run a bath which, disembarking, he proceeded to take at the track-side in full view of astonished locals. He put the habit to good use, however, as his valet remembered:

As soon as he got into the bath he would start muttering. At first I used to think he was talking to me.
I said: 'Do you want me?'
'I wasn't talking to you, Norman,' he replied, 'I was addressing the House of Commons.'
He sometimes called one of the secretaries to the bathroom door if he thought up a particular point he wanted to have noted down, or he would suddenly jump out of the bath and rush to the

bedroom telephone to make an important call. Quite a number of vital government decisions have been made with Mr. Churchill standing dripping at the bedroom 'phone.

His afternoon naps, which enabled him to continue working until the small hours of the following morning, were just as much a part of his daily ritual. His valet describes how, after lunch:

> . . . he would undress and sleep like a child for two hours.
>
> When enormous pressure of work at the Admiralty during the First World War taxed even his vigour, he started to sleep every afternoon. The effect of this complete break is usually to make two working days out of one – and he literally does twice the amount of work of the average person and exerts himself for twice the length of the conventional eight-hour day.
>
> It was one of the inflexible rules of Mr Churchill's daily routine that he should not miss this rest. When later in my employment he became Prime Minister there was always a bed provided for him in the Houses of Parliament, and, of course, he was always able to get his sleep in before the time came for an important debate . . .
>
> Even on his election tour train there had to be a bed – a big one. It was necessary to tear the side off the coach to get it in . . .

Churchill was known to enjoy luxuriating on yachts or at villas on the Riviera and gambling at Monte Carlo, and his ownership of a racehorse proved popular with the British people. His father had been owner of a horse called Colonist and Churchill, who named his own horse Colonist II, revived Lord Randolph's colours of chocolate and pink. He had always had a fondness for the Turf; as a young man he had astonished a dinner-party audience with his ability to recite the names of all the Derby winners of the past three decades. Once again his valet, Norman McGowan, offers an insight:

> I was with Mr Churchill during the period when he gained considerable fame as the owner of race horses, the most successful being, of course, Colonist II. By the time my Guv'nor sold him in December 1951, he had won thirteen of the twenty-four races for which he was entered and earned more than £22,000 in prize money.
>
> The sports-loving public who, of course, like nothing better

than a flutter on a horse owned by a popular personality, backed Colonist II to a fantastic extent, the amount of money on him bringing the odds down more than the horse's chances really justified. Consequently he was often odds-on favourite, and even those who had backed another horse were pleased when Colonist II came home first.

THE GREAT COMMUNICATOR

These aspects of his personality undoubtedly made him interesting, but much more important were the abilities that enabled him to analyse and persuade, to exercise judgement and leadership or to contribute to culture. Even his severest critics had to acknowledge the astonishing breadth of his talents, and this is a major reason for his continuing fascination. As a politician he held every senior cabinet post except one (Foreign Secretary) . As a parliamentary speaker he was without parallel in his generation, and no one among his successors in the House has earned praise as unstinted as he received. Sir Norman Birkett, a distinguished lawyer who became a Lord Justice of Appeal in 1950, summed up one aspect of his legacy:

> From his lips have come some of the sublimest utterances in the language. Many of his speeches will live as examples of human speech at its highest and best. They will be woven into the fabric of our own history and the history of the world.

That this oratory was used with telling effect precisely when it mattered was the cause of Churchill's greatness. It made him an inspiration even to those for whom he was a flesh-and-blood personality rather than a national symbol. This was expressed, with grace and eloquence, by one of his wartime colleagues, Field Marshal Sir Bernard Montgomery:

> Never has any land found a leader who so matched the hour as did Sir Winston Churchill when he spoke – in words that rang and thundered like the Psalms – we all said 'That is how we shall bear ourselves'.

President John F Kennedy, a statesman of a later generation, added that:

> In the dark days and darker nights when Britain stood alone and most men save Englishmen despaired of England's life,

he mobilized the English language and sent it into battle. The incandescent quality of his words illuminated the courage of his countrymen.

Naturally, there was much more to being a politician than speech-making, and the test of his effectiveness was not just how well he spoke but how he administered the government departments for which he was responsible. Here he had one significant failure: his term as Chancellor of the Exchequer on the eve of the Depression (1925-29) is not regarded as one of his triumphs. He recalled that, when appointed, he had only eight weeks in which to become an authority on economics. Despite expert tuition and his own powerful memory, he never got the hang of what he called 'those damned dots'. The Oxford historian AJP Taylor said of him: 'His erratic finance discredited him in the eyes of more sober politicians and left the Treasury weaker to face a period of real economic difficulty.'

While he might have lacked specialist expertise, his general administration was sound. He had a flair for putting a rocket under complacent civil servants. He seemed to work 24 hours a day and he interfered in all aspects of departmental business – sending memos, demanding reports, interrogating officials. His continuous meddling, and the personal example he set of tireless energy, kept his staffs at a level of perpetual efficiency, and this remained true even when he was well over 70. Viscount Cilcennin, who was First Lord of the Admiralty from 1951 to 1956, gave an instance. Because the First Lord's office was directly across the Horse Guards parade ground from the Prime Minister's study in 10 Downing Street, Churchill was often reminded of the navy:

> Much of Sir Winston's heart still lay with the office he had twice adorned at the beginning of two world wars. In moments of contemplation, when working alone at the Cabinet table, his eye would be caught by the [Lord High Admiral's] flag, and on days which always happened to be particularly busy, the First Sea Lord might receive signals from the Prime Minister. Here is an example:
> 'Pray state, this day, on one side of a sheet of paper, how the Royal Navy is being adapted to meet the conditions of modern warfare.'

While these gifts for management, leadership and communication would be sufficient accomplishment for an ordinary man, Churchill reached out into other fields. He was clearly more than simply a politician who dabbled in writing and military theory. In both of these areas he was a commanding figure who won international acclaim. The Nobel Prize for Literature, awarded to him in 1953, is as great a testimony to his stature as this tribute by Keith Aldritt, a professor of English:

> **As . . . literary historians began to define the canon of English literature over the last hundred years, Churchill's name will stand up with those of the other great prose stylists, such as George Orwell, D.H. Lawrence, T.S. Eliot, Maynard Keynes and Virginia Woolf.**

As a military leader he has been rated even more highly. One historian has come to the conclusion that his demonstrated strategic ability entitles him to be included among 'the great captains of history' – with Julius Caesar, Napoleon and the Duke of Marlborough.

As for the enemy's viewpoint, a wartime book analyzing German propaganda about him comments on the negative view of his naval role in World War I:

> **The Nazis tell us that Churchill did not know much about naval questions, but they have to admit that he showed himself able to arm and direct the greatest navy in the world.**

Churchill was also a relatively accomplished painter, though no one could claim that he deserved to rank with the giants of 20th-century British art – he was no Alfred Munnings or Stanley Spencer. Nevertheless his colourful, boldly rendered and almost always unpeopled landscapes were considered pleasing. He painted for pleasure and as an escape from the burden of responsibility, saying, 'If it weren't for painting I couldn't live; I couldn't bear the strain of things.' Elected to the Royal Academy, he was entitled to exhibit six pictures a year at the Summer Exhibition, and 'sent in' even while Prime Minister. Though his name naturally created interest and added value to his canvases, he had work accepted and sold under pseudonyms: 'Mr Winter' and 'Charles Maurin'. As the latter he held a one-man show in Paris. He once sold a work, 'The Blue Sitting Room, Trent Park, 1934' for 1,250 guineas, and the evidence suggests that he could have earned a comfortable living as a painter. Sir John Rothenstein, the Director of the Tate Gallery, said in 1951:

> Had the fairies struck a paint brush into his hands, instead of
> a pen into one hand and a sword into the other, had he learnt
> while still a boy to draw and paint, and had he dedicated an
> entire laborious lifetime to art, Mr. Churchill would have been
> able to express himself, instead of one small facet. He would have
> painted big pictures.

His verbal gifts might have led him in several other directions. Both the Church and the Bar had been possible future careers for him, but with his exceptional memory he could also have been successful on the stage. Consuelo, Duchess of Marlborough, quotes a friend, Lady Katherine Lambton, as recounting that:

> Sir Laurence Olivier and his wife expressed the wish that Mr.
> Churchill should come to see Richard III which they [were] acting.
>   During the whole play Mr. Churchill recited the words, almost
> putting the actors out. At supper afterward, to the Oliviers'
> immense surprise, he knew the whole of *Henry IV* and *Henry V* by
> heart, and when Sir Laurence Olivier consulted him about how to
> say a certain speech Mr. Churchill gave his rendering and Olivier,
> thinking it better than his own, adopted it.
>   A great statesman, a master historian, a good painter, who
> knows, perhaps also a master actor had the fates so decreed.

This is a record of versatility and achievement unmatched by any politician, or public figure, in British history. If to it is added sporting prowess – Churchill was, after all, a schoolboy fencing champion and member of a cup-winning regimental polo team – his virtuosity is almost overwhelming. Only musical talent (he was a notoriously off-key singer!) is missing.

These attributes might have made Churchill an aloof, Olympian figure, as remotely superior as his near-contemporary Lord Curzon, had they not been balanced by a hefty dose of ordinary humanity. He was, as the playwright and wit Noel Coward put it: 'A great man with more Achilles heels than are usual in a bi-ped.'

Churchill's greatest saving grace was his legendary sense of humour. His remarks, ripostes and observations were cherished, repeated, written down and often published, to reappear decades later and delight the readers of memoirs and histories. He had once said that 'in my belief, you cannot deal with the most serious things in the world unless you also understand the most amusing.'

Others, including Harold Macmillan, one of his successors as Tory leader, agreed that this gave his conversation a very pleasing character and that 'the most endearing thing about him in private talk . . . was his Puckish humour, his tremendous sense of fun, and the quick alternation between grave and gay.'

Churchill said of Field Marshal Montgomery, a brilliant commander but a somewhat smug and humourless personality: 'In retreat indomitable, in advance invincible; in victory insufferable.' And anyone with a mental picture of the haughty General de Gaulle will recognize Churchill's description of him as looking 'like a female llama who had been surprised in her bath'.

He summed up the United States in a single sentence. Once asked by a young woman reporter what he thought of the country, he replied: 'Toilet paper too thin, newspapers too fat.' In 1944, when watching an Allied artillery barrage in Italy and seeing the shells land in the distance, he quipped: 'This is rather like sending a rude letter and being there when it arrives.'

His wit was often displayed in the Commons. One day in 1952, while he was Prime Minister, a Labour member was speaking. Churchill began to doze in his seat on the front bench opposite. As he slipped into oblivion, all eyes left the speaker and watched him. This was such a distraction that the member eventually stopped and cried 'MUST you fall asleep when I am speaking?' Churchill, opening one eye, retorted, 'No, it is purely voluntary.'

And, when told that Field Marshal Montgomery's memoirs had earned more money than his own *History of the English-Speaking Peoples*, he replied: 'I'm not at all surprised that the Field Marshal lived up to the finest tradition of Englishmen, by selling his life as dearly as possible.'

Perhaps more famously, there was this exchange with the MP Nancy Astor, as recounted by his cousin Consuelo Vanderbilt:

> Lady Astor's vivid personality made her many friends, but there were those whose dislike was equally marked. She and Winston Churchill are actuated by a strong antipathy one for the other. It was therefore unfortunate that on one of Lady Astor's visits to Blenheim Winston should have chosen to appear. The expected result of their encounter was not long in coming; after a heated argument on some trivial matter Nancy, with a fervour whose sincerity could not be doubted, shouted 'If I were your wife I would put poison in your coffee!' whereupon

Winston with equal heat and sincerity answered 'And if I were your husband I would drink it.'

As a politician he brought enormous benefits to his country and to the wider world. However difficult, exasperating – even impossible – he may have been at many moments throughout his long life, he was right in his belief that he had an extraordinary destiny and a unique service to perform. 'I have faith in my star,' he had said as a young man. He was wise to believe this.

2
EARLY YEARS

Winston Leonard Spencer Churchill was fated to be a soldier. His antecedents saw to that for, although there was no recent tradition of professional soldiering in his family, he was descended from one of England's greatest military leaders. John Churchill (1650–1722), commanding the forces of Queen Anne in the War of the Spanish Succession, inflicted several crushing defeats on the armies of Louis XIV, and thus saved much of Europe from French domination. In recognition of this the Queen gave him a dukedom and the old royal hunting estate of Woodstock in Oxfordshire. Parliament voted him a sum of money large enough to build a palace, built for him by Vanburgh. It was named in honour of his major victory, in August 1704, near the Bavarian village of Blindheim (corrupted to 'Blenheim').

It was designed as a monument rather than a home. There could be few settings in Britain more calculated to inspire a sense of military endeavour as the path to fame, glory and wealth, and the Duke of Marlborough's ambitious, imaginative descendant cannot have been unaffected by this. As a dwelling, Blenheim is grand and impressive, not practical or comfortable. Its squat bulk, as vast and sprawling as a railway terminus, dominates the surrounding parkland, among the classical follies of which a statue of the First Duke, dressed as a Roman Emperor, looks down on his domain. As overwhelming inside as it is outside, the house contains over 300 rooms.

It was in one of these that Winston Churchill was born in 1874. The date, 30 November, was significant because, being St Andrew's day, there was a ball at Blenheim. His mother attended, against the advice of her doctor, and it was while dancing that her contractions began. She immediately ran for her bedroom but did not get that far. Winston was born in the ground-floor chamber that was serving as a cloakroom. He was two months premature.

Modern visitors to the house who wander through this find a cheerful apartment with rose-patterned wallpaper and a large brass bedstead. As a former Duchess, the New Yorker Consuelo Vanderbilt, recalled, both this room and its neighbours had had a sinister and unwelcoming atmosphere in past generations:

. . . across the hall overlooking a small inner court were rooms
known as Dean Jones's – where, incidentally, Winston Churchill
was born. The Dean had been private chaplain to the first Duke
. . . It seemed strange . . . that he should haunt the ugly apartment
that had been his, but there was no doubt that various people
who slept there were terrified by his appearance . . . So the rooms
remained empty during my reign. They have now become famous
as Winston Churchill's birthplace, and to his other achievements
may be added the fact that it seems he has exorcised a ghost
since no one now mentions having seen Dean Jones; no doubt
disgruntled by his eclipse he no longer haunts the scene.

As the son of a younger son, Winston was unlikely to inherit Blenheim
Palace and he did not grow up there (though he was given a magnificent
start in life by being baptized in the chapel). Nevertheless he would,
from earliest youth, have had a sense that this heritage was his. Through
lengthy visits to his grandparents he would have come to know the
house well, with its great echoing halls, its trophies and banners
and paintings and weaponry, its tapestries depicting his ancestor's
triumphs. Here he would also have absorbed, by osmosis, as it were, the
outlook of the Victorian higher aristocracy, and from the first he moved
comfortably in their world. There were dozens of servants – housemaids,
butlers, footmen and coachmen. Like the automatic deference
of local people and the expectation that it was his destiny to lead
and to dominate, these would have seemed natural to him from early
childhood.

In addition, Winston's parents had status of another sort that influenced
his upbringing and his attitudes, for if he lived much of his adult life in
the limelight, he also grew up in it. Both his father and his mother were
to become major celebrities within a few years of his birth – sufficiently
famous that their photographs would be sold in the shops, and his
schoolfriends would ask him to obtain their autographs. He would have
been used to the idea that through the doors of his parents' home would
pass many of those who mattered in politics, the arts, the armed forces
and society.

LORD RANDOLPH

Winston's father, Lord Randolph Churchill, had met his mother, Jennie
Jerome, at Cowes Regatta in August 1873 aboard a warship, HMS *Ariadne*, at
a ball given for the Prince and Princess of Wales and the Russian Tsarevich.

After a 'whirlwind courtship' that included a good deal of haggling over the financial arrangements for their union, the couple were married at the British Embassy in Paris in April 1874. Lord Randolph, became Conservative MP for the borough of Woodstock according to the wishes of his father, but he and his wife devoted their energies almost entirely to the pleasures of society, spending their lives at race meetings, balls and country houses. These things remained the currency of their lives until, in 1876, scandal forced a significant change in their circumstances.

Lord Randolph had become mixed up in an unpleasant situation concerning his older brother, the Marquis of Blandford, who was romantically involved with the Countess of Aylesford, also a mistress of the Prince of Wales. She became pregnant; her husband was clearly not responsible and, to avoid any suspicion of his own responsibility, the Prince put pressure on Blandford to accept blame by divorcing his wife and marrying the Countess. The Marquis refused, and at that point Lord Randolph stepped in by announcing that he had in his possession the Prince's love letters to Lady Aylesford, which he was prepared to make public. The Prince having challenged him to a duel, Lord Randolph was eventually induced to offer a rather insincere apology but it was too late: the Churchills were ostracized by society.

Prime Minister Benjamin Disraeli suggested a way out of the resulting embarrassment. He offered the Duke of Marlborough the post of Viceroy of Ireland, with Lord Randolph accompanying his father as private secretary. The Duke agreed to the proposal as a means of getting his son out of London.

The exile lasted four years, until Liberals replaced Tories in a general election and Gladstone appointed another Viceroy. During those years, the Randolph Churchills lived in an unpretentious, comfortable home on the edge of Dublin's Phoenix Park. Winston was too young to recall more than a few details of these years, though he dimly remembered the soldiers that route-marched through the park, for it was almost certainly encountering a column of these that caused him to be thrown by a donkey on which he was being taken for a ride. He also remembered the pain of starting to climb the tree of knowledge when a governess was brought in to teach him to read and write and count. This was clearly no enviable task, for his resistance to education began with his first lesson and he once found it necessary to ring for the maid and order: 'Take away Miss Hutchinson. She is very cross.' (Miss Hutchinson, by extraordinary coincidence, was also to be governess to Clement Attlee, Churchill's successor as prime minister.) He imbibed, too, the tension caused by Irish nationalism with its threat of violence.

The years in Ireland had an important effect on Lord Randolph for, cut off from the social rituals that had previously filled his horizon, he decided to take politics seriously. He returned to London as a member of the Opposition, a role for which he was well suited. He possessed gifts of oratory that commanded attention, and he used them to telling effect. His scathing wit and barbed attacks on opponents made entertaining copy and the newspapers began to report extensively on his speeches. He became a thorn in the side of the Government, and scarcely less of a nuisance to the elderly leaders of his own party.

Younger MPs felt that there was little scope for ambition or prospect of attaining the great offices of State. Lord Randolph became a voluble spokesman for this younger generation, relentlessly attacking 'The Old Gang' and suggesting that new faces – naturally and primarily his own – should be appointed to the Shadow Cabinet. He saw himself as a future Prime Minister. The press, and many members of the public, began to see him in this light, too.

Despite his patrician background he had broad appeal with the voters. The Reform Bill of 1867 had extended the franchise to include the top of the working class and Lord Randolph set out to capture these votes. A tireless traveller, jaunty, dandified, humorous and sarcastic, he was an effective debater. His irreverent and sometimes outrageous statements compelled interest and often disguised from audiences the inconsistency of the positions he adopted. One of his nicknames was 'the Music-Hall Cad', and in looking at caricatures it is easy to see why. He is depicted as a dwarfish figure (actually he was taller than his son would be) with a round head, bulging eyes and flaring moustaches. In his well-cut but somewhat loud suit and with his top hat at a rakish angle, he looks the epitome of the upper-class playboy that he still, to a large extent, was.

However boorish his conduct could be, he had very considerable charm when he chose to exercise it. He continued to cultivate grass-roots Conservatism and did this so effectively that he became President of the National Union of Conservative Associations.

Admirers saw him as an idealist; detractors saw him as motivated by a cynical desire to achieve high office using whatever means were available, and it is difficult to argue that self-interest was not behind much that he did. He seemed to be prepared to say anything or argue any cause that would facilitate gaining high office for himself. Asked how he saw his future once he had achieved it, he answered: 'I shall lead the Opposition for five years, then I shall be Prime Minister for five years, then I shall die.'

In 1886 the Tories returned to power, with Salisbury as Prime Minister.

Lord Randolph was briefly Secretary for India, but swiftly moved on to the job of Leader of the House and the post of Chancellor of the Exchequer. He thus became, at 35, the second most important man in the Government, the natural heir to the Premier. He looked forward to many years of glory and achievement and his eldest son, then at prep school, did a brisk trade in his autographs and had to write asking for more.

Six months later Lord Randolph was finished. Disagreeing with his party on the issue of expenditure on the navy, he threatened to resign and Salisbury called his bluff. He was suddenly out of office and there was none of the outcry he had expected from his Parliamentary colleagues or from the party. A single act of hubris, crowning a career in which he had made many enemies, had put an end to his political life. He did not hold office again. In his remaining years he bitterly rejoiced over Conservative defeats and awaited a summons back to power that never came. He had, in any case, become seriously ill with a progressively worsening mental condition that robbed him of his memory and rendered his speeches incoherent.

Much of his time was spent in foreign travel, as he and his wife sought diversion in change of scene, embarking on an exhausting tour of the world. He died at his mother's home on 24 January, 1895, while his son was a cadet at Sandhurst.

Lord Randolph's influence on Winston was overwhelming, the more so because he had appeared so distant. Not only did Winston commit to memory some of his father's speeches, and copy his dress and many of his mannerisms and opinions; he also sought to pick up his father's thwarted political career and carry it on to new glories. He developed a fierce ambition (just as Lord Randolph had when ousted from society) to push himself to the heights for the sake of vindication, but he felt that time was not on his side. Lord Randolph had died at the age of 46 and throughout his early manhood Winston worked on the assumption that he too might not live longer than that. This was a potent reason for his relentless drive to make his mark in the world and achieve high office as fast as possible. From the time he entered Parliament at 25, he expected to have only two decades in which to reach the top.

JENNIE CHURCHILL

Winston's mother was an altogether more interesting personality than his father, and the influence she exerted on her son, directly and through her friends, was even more important. An American of mixed Huguenot, Iroquois Indian and English descent (her forebears had crossed the Atlantic from the Isle of Wight in 1710, and one ancestor had been an officer in Washington's army), she was the middle daughter of the sporting and flamboyant New York financier Leonard Jerome. Jennie had grown up in Manhattan and in Paris; she spent several years in the French capital amid the glitter and elegance of the Second Empire, and was a protégé of the Empress Eugenie. With the fall of the Bonaparte regime in 1870 Jennie and her family, like the Empress, fled to England. There they adapted to the social life of the British upper classes and there, three years later, she met her husband.

She was one of numerous young American women – a veritable invasion – who came to Britain to marry into the aristocracy during the 'Gilded Age' of massive commercial fortunes. These young women were not only immensely rich; they tended also to be more forthright, more ebullient and more amusing than their comparatively passive English counterparts. They included Jennie's friend Consuelo Vanderbilt, whose marriage to the 9th Duke of Marlborough, in November 1896, brought a huge financial settlement to the Marlboroughs.

From the time of her own marriage at the age of 20, Jennie captured the affection of English society. Strikingly attractive, she had immense vivacity and personal charisma, and this gained her a number of very devoted admirers. Encouraged by her father to be outgoing and assertive, she had developed the masculine skill of horsemanship as well as the more feminine accomplishment of playing the piano. She was also a respectably proficient painter.

Jennie possessed all the social abilities necessary for the wife of an important and ambitious politician: wide interests and patience with small-talk, a sense of humour, tact and circumspection. In elections she campaigned vigorously for her husband and was able to deal confidently with hecklers and opponents. She befriended artists, musicians and writers, and her son's lifelong feeling for poetry and literature will have derived from her (in the 1890s she was to found, with Winston's help, a literary journal, the *Anglo-Saxon Review*). Her gift for friendship is affirmed in numerous memoirs, and in some cases her relationships went beyond this. Her marriage to Lord Randolph became a formality and her romantic conquests included the Prince of Wales, with whom, because he appreciated her intelligence as well as her discretion, she remained a close friend and confidante after their affair was over. It was because of this association that the Prince maintained a friendly interest in her son's career, both in the army and in Parliament.

Other men with whom she became involved provided Winston with vital influence when he was making his way in the world. While his father was often preoccupied, or absent, his mother's friend Count Kinsky showed an avuncular interest in him that made a deep impression. Kinsky, a wealthy Austrian diplomat who won the Grand National in 1883 on his own horse, Zoedone, provided an example of sophistication and elegance. He took the schoolboy Winston to an event at Crystal Palace where they saw Kaiser William II. This was Winston's first glimpse of Britain's future Great War opponent, whom he was next to see while a guest in 1906 at German army manoeuvres.

Of vastly greater significance was Jennie's friendship with Bourke Cockran, an American politician. Cockran was an Irish-born New Yorker who had worked his way through night school to a law degree and, as a successful attorney, gone into politics, serving three terms as a congressman. Though largely forgotten today, he was seen in the United States as one of the most compelling and accomplished orators of his generation, as well as being among the most interesting conversationalists. Jennie had met him in Paris just after her husband's death, and they had instantly become friends. They were united by a passion for horses, politics and literature, and again their relationship continued to flourish after its physical aspect had ended. Cockran saw her son's potential and took immense trouble to help him, particularly on Winston's early American visits, when he enabled him to meet both President McKinley and Theodore Roosevelt. The younger man, in turn, memorized several of Cockran's speeches and emulated a number of his oratorical tricks and gestures. He would, all his life, acknowledge Cockran's role in shaping his political outlook and performance.

Thus lovers, admirers and acquaintances helped her son's career. These included Colonel John Brabazon, the commanding officer of the 4th Hussars, through whom Winston's transfer into the regiment was made easier than it might otherwise have been. Sir Bindon Blood, commander of the Malakand Field Force, had met Winston through his mother and promised him an appointment with the expedition.

Jennie made up for any past neglect of which she was guilty by working tirelessly to further her son's interests, and he came to depend on her to clear a path for him. He had always turned on her the full force of his affectionate nature, and now their relationship blossomed into one of mutual adult regard as well as shrewd pragmatism. He was later to write of her:

> My mother was always on hand to help and advise. She became my ardent ally, furthering my plans and guarding my interests with all her influence and boundless energy. We worked together on even terms, more like brother and sister than mother and son. And so it continued to the end.

It was Lady Randolph who created the Winston Churchill of 1940, because it was from her that he inherited a streak of boundless determination, and learned the value of perseverance and refusal to accept defeat. Added to his own entrenched stubbornness, this was to make him a formidable opponent indeed.

Once he was in the army, she energetically lobbied her influential friends on his behalf, finding and arranging newspaper contracts and acting as a sort of literary agent. She did this so efficiently that, when in 1897 war broke out between Greece and Turkey and he sought to cover the conflict for a newspaper, he was able to send her from India a long list of his requirements and end his message: 'These arrangements I leave to you and I hope when I arrive in Brindisi to find the whole thing cut and dried.'

Though she would quibble at the prospect of his going to Cuba, she seems to have had few concerns regarding the danger in which his other adventures landed him, remaining sanguine when he went off to fight Pathan tribesmen or Sudanese dervishes. But then she herself had something of the same restless energy and desire to be involved in great events. During his final colonial campaign, against the Boers, Jennie even went to South Africa with a hospital ship that she had organized, and in World War I she founded an American military hospital in London. She married, altogether, three times (her second husband was the same age as Winston) and died in 1921, tragically after toppling down some stairs while wearing fashionably high-heeled shoes.

HOME AND SCHOOL

Members of Parliament of Lord Randolph's era received no salary, and Lady Randolph's father, whose fortunes waxed and waned, was not always able to help. On their return from Ireland, the Churchills therefore spent long periods staying at Blenheim, or lived in a succession of homes in London. One of them (now bearing a commemorative plaque) was in Connaught Place near the top of Park Lane, on the unfashionable north side of Hyde Park. A solid, white-stuccoed house, the rear windows of which look out on the Bayswater Road, this was to be Winston's home throughout his youth, though much of the time he was naturally away at school. It proved too expensive to maintain and Lord Randolph decided to move his family, as an economy measure, a mile or so to his mother's home on a corner of Grosvenor Square.

Economy was clearly not a consideration in choosing Winston's preparatory school: St George's, at Ascot in Berkshire, was, at £55 a term, decidedly not cheap. His experience with a governess had been unhappy, but his encounter with the full panoply of education – masters, classrooms, examinations and punishments – was to be deeply traumatic. Winston was at the school for two years and they were without question the unhappiest of his life. His reports made clear that he could not be induced to learn subjects that did not interest him. He was beaten for this by the headmaster. He was also beaten for using foul language that he may have picked up in the stables at Blenheim. The punishing of boys in Victorian schools in this way was commonplace, but here it appears to have been so savage that Winston hated the school for the rest of his life, and never forgave the headmaster. It may well have been the marks of these punishments, seen on Winston during one holidays by his devoted nanny Mrs Everest and brought to the notice of his mother, that caused him to be removed from St George's. Even without this, his lack of progress would have been reason enough.

At school he terribly missed his playthings. He recalled that in the nursery at home he had:

> . . . such wonderful toys: a real steam-engine, a magic lantern, and a collection of soldiers nearly a thousand strong . . . I counted the days and hours to the end of every term, when I should return home from this hateful servitude and range my soldiers in line of battle on the nursery floor.

Winston's toy soldiers – the first army he ever commanded – are, justifiably, part of the legend of his youth. They ultimately numbered 1,500, but they have not survived, as has so much else from his early years. The soldiers that could be bought in his childhood will have been well made and authentic, though the heyday of the toy soldier came somewhat later. His toys would not have been made by the famous Britain's Ltd, for that firm did not begin trading until 1893. They are likely to have come from Germany (as so many of the best toys did), perhaps from the firm of Heinrichson, though they will have been dressed as British soldiers.

They were probably flat tin figures, each about an inch high. Three-dimensional toy soldiers were beginning to appear, but they were so costly that even a child of a wealthy family would be unlikely to have had over a thousand of them. Winston's infantry would have been bought in boxes of 20 for sixpence, cavalry will have come in boxes of ten and the larger items necessary for an army – cannon, gun-limbers and other vehicles (also flat) – will have cost several shillings. One can easily imagine the birthdays, Christmases and visits to the nursery by friends of his parents that will have built up this collection. It became a splendid spectacle, but the troops had a great deal to endure. His cousin Clare Frewen remembered:

> Winston was a large school boy when I was still in the nursery. His playroom contained from one end to the other a plank table on trestles, upon which were thousands of lead soldiers arranged for battle. He organized wars. The lead battalions were manoeuvred into action, peas and pebbles committed great casualties, forts were stormed, cavalry charged, bridges were destroyed – real water tanks engulfed the advancing foe. Altogether it was a most impressive show, and played with an interest that was no ordinary child game.

During these fights, Winston's long-suffering brother Jack was never allowed to command the British forces, or to have the use of artillery. Despite this puerile possessiveness, Winston's model army gave significant evidence of a precocious understanding of military matters. It was intelligently set out and accurately reflected the deployment of real soldiers. He was later to recall that the troops 'were all of one size, all British, and organized as an infantry division with a cavalry brigade'. He also remembered: 'Sir John Willoughby was one of my oldest friends. In fact it was he who had first shown me how to arrange my toy cavalry soldiers in the proper formation of an advanced guard.'

Another important aspect of a modern army was pointed out to him by a visiting adult:

> All the services were complete – except one. It is what every army is always short of – transport. My father's old friend, Sir Henry Drummond Wolff, admiring my array, noticed this deficiency and provided a fund from which it was to some extent supplied.

Winston recalled that his father, on an infrequent visit to the nursery, had inspected the miniature warriors and then asked him if he would like to go into the army. The boy's affirmative reply settled the issue for both of them. He mentioned ruefully that he thought Lord Randolph had detected signs of aptitude, but later discovered he had merely felt Winston did not have the brains for a career at the Bar.

In truth, might Lord Randolph not genuinely have been impressed by his son's detailed technical knowledge and enthusiasm? It is not unlikely that Winston's obvious leanings toward the military profession made this a sensible, positive choice rather than a last resort. Churchill was in the habit of disparaging his younger self and the notion of his father as an unrelenting critic is probably an exaggeration. Though Lord Randolph was often brutally unsympathetic towards Winston's shortcomings, there seem also to have been moments when he was genuinely impressed. Although he did not credit his son with any potential as a politician, he does seem to have recognized in him some latent but powerful ability, whether military or otherwise. It was at about this time that he said, when introducing Winston to Bram Stoker, the author of *Dracula*, 'He's not much yet, but he's a good 'un.'

Winston would have been an able lawyer, and while at Harrow he briefly considered a career in the Church. In both professions his power of oratory would have served him well, though his lifelong lack of any but the most nominal Christian faith might have been a drawback in one of them. Had he opted for either of these fields he would probably still have volunteered for military service in the Boer War, and used the resulting experience and achievements to write books and to stand for Parliament. His life thereafter might thus have followed much the pattern that it did in any case.

But this is to anticipate. His militaristic tendencies meanwhile found another youthful outlet, as Clare Frewen elaborated:

> One summer the Churchills rented a small house in the country for the holidays. It was called Banstead. Winston and Jack, his brother, built a log house with the help of the gardener's children and dug a ditch around it which they contrived to fill with water, and made a drawbridge that really could pull up and down.
> Here again war proceeded. The fort was stormed. I was hurriedly removed from the scene of action as mud and stones began to fly with effect. But the incident impressed me and Winston became a very important person in my estimation.

Another cousin, Shane Leslie, also remembered Winston's dictatorial manner during these sieges:

> In his army there were only two rules but they were strictly enforced on the cousins: firstly, Winston was always General, and secondly there was no promotion. Our chief occupation was digging out the moated 'Den', which Winston had designed. There in the damp straw we were told to await the enemies of

England. Our artillery consisted of an immense catapult which
discharged unripe apples and once struck an inoffensive cow.

For all this energy and aggression, the young Churchill's constitution was
not robust and he was never to achieve the level of physical fitness that armies
think desirable. His fragility was underlined when, in March 1886, he caught
pneumonia and hovered for several days between life and death, constantly
watched by the family physician. He recovered, slowly but fully, but his
health continued to be a cause for concern and the appellation 'delicate' was
to follow him even through his noisy, energetic years at Harrow.

Before going there he had to finish prep school. From St George's he had
been sent to an establishment run by two sisters, the Misses Thomson, in
the genteel seaside resort of Hove, next to Brighton. The sea air, the kindlier
regime and the presence in the town of his family doctor combined to
make this a less arduous experience. He also found learning there more
enjoyable. He loved sea-bathing, riding, cricket and learning poetry, and he
also took part in plays. With his excellent memory and outgoing, confident
personality it would have been surprising if, his speech impediment
notwithstanding, he had not had a good deal of acting ability. Despite
this, and despite his American mother with her artistic leanings, his nature
responded most directly to romantic notions of patriotism and military
adventure, so that a great man of letters, HG Wells, was later to say, 'Empire
and Anglo-Saxon and Boy-Scout and sleuth are the stuff in your mind,' and
to lament that his school had 'be-Kiplinged' him.

HARROW

Winston sat the entrance exams for Harrow, one of the eminent English
public schools, in the spring of 1888. Set on a hill some 12 miles north-
west of central London, the school clusters around the village church, the
thousand-year-old St Mary's, whose slender steeple soars above the trees
and dominates the skyline. To the distant observer, the school's buildings
are a pleasant jumble of rooftops and spires and cupolas. Closer to, they
become an assembly of structures in a multitude of styles, shapes and
periods. Among them are the venerable Old Schools, whose stepped gables
and mullioned windows look down on the school yard; Speech Room, the
semi-circular theatre that is the scene of recitations and prize-givings; the
stone-and-flint chapel; the equally ecclesiastical-looking Vaughan Library;
the red-brick 17th-century Headmaster's House, in which Winston was a
boarder; and beyond these, on the flanks of the hill, are the spreading acres
of football and cricket fields.

The school had been founded in 1571. Though less ancient than Eton and Winchester, it had long since caught up with them in terms of prestige and had been fashionable (largely with Tory families, while Whigs patronized Eton) throughout the 18th and 19th centuries. Past pupils included Lord Byron, Lord Shaftesbury and Sir Robert Peel, one of five prime ministers the school had already produced (Stanley Baldwin and Churchill were to be the sixth and seventh). The Churchills had been educated at Eton since 1722, though Winston was so little aware of the details of his father's life that he wrote to him, at age 12, 'Did you go to Harrow or Eton? I should like to know.' Lord Randolph had been at Eton, but because of Winston's pneumonia the damp of the Thames valley was deemed to be too dangerous to his health. Harrow, on its hilltop, was considered safer.

His arrival was to coincide almost exactly with the loss of Harrow's isolation. One of his contemporaries, JWS Tomlin, recalled that during this period of the 1880s:

> Harrow was still in the country. You could look from the windows of the Headmaster's House and see nothing but green fields; from the churchyard you had an uninterrupted view of English landscape as far as Windsor, which was visible on a clear day. The Metropolitan railway was stretching out its tentacles to Pinner and Rickmansworth . . .

In the wake of the railway came an advancing tide of bricks and mortar, as developers built the myriad houses that closed the gap between Harrow and London and turned it into a suburb. Winston was among the last to enjoy the comparative tranquillity of the fast-disappearing countryside.

Legend insists that Winston was unhappy at the school, but he was certainly not put off by the thought of attending it, having said, after a preliminary visit, 'I am longing to go to Harrow.' To do so, he had to pass the entrance examination. He recalled this experience in his memoir *My Early Life*, and it is among the most well-known stories about him. He tells how, when faced with the Latin questions, he was unable to answer a single one of them. Having written his name at the top of the page, he wrote the Roman numeral 'I', and then put it in brackets. By the end of the exam this had been joined by an ink blot, but the paper was otherwise blank. On the strength of this, it is implied, he was admitted to the school.

The late Harrow historian Jim Golland has pointed out that, however bad his performance may have been in Latin, this was only one paper out of several, and that his answers in the others were good enough for him to pass the overall exam; indeed in one subject, mathematics, he gained the highest marks of all the candidates. He was, admittedly, put into the lowest form, but in maths he was taught with more advanced pupils, and even in Latin he had risen to a respectable position within a year or so. Though he was several times punished while at the school, it was his character and conduct that brought this about, and never a lack of ability.

In photographs of the time Winston looks proud enough, dressed in the uniform appropriate to his size and his modest position in the community: an Eton collar, a short black jacket colloquially known as a 'bum-freezer' because it does not reach the seat of the trousers, and the type of shallow-crowned, wide-brimmed straw hat, unique to the School, that is still worn by Harrovians.

Despite his years at one of England's most traditional public schools, Churchill did not match the stereotypes of behaviour associated with these places. Impatient with authority and disrespectful of his elders, uninspired by team games, emotional, opinionated and everlastingly talkative, he was not destined to fit effortlessly into a hierarchical society or to be widely popular. Sebastian Haffner, a German writer who spent the Nazi years in exile in Britain, perceptively observed:

> His expensive school was wasted on him. He came away untamed and unmoulded as well as uneducated. Among Englishmen of his class – indeed among Englishmen in general – it rendered him something of a lifelong outsider. Despite his years at Harrow, he never became a genuine product of the English public school system: not a man of understatement and arrogant self-effacement, not a cricketer, not a polished 'English gentleman', but rather a character from Shakespeare's England, where public schools were still unknown. And, in spite of his zealous autodidactic endeavours in later years and his own vast achievements in the fields of literature and historiography, he always lacked a solid, conventional education.

Be that as it may, the school was an immensely important interlude in Churchill's life and had a marked influence on his military as well as his general development. Here he first handled weapons and took part in manoeuvres. More significantly it was here that he learned to love – and to write – military history.

AW Siddons, a master who came to the school after Winston left but who later studied his Harrow career, said of him:

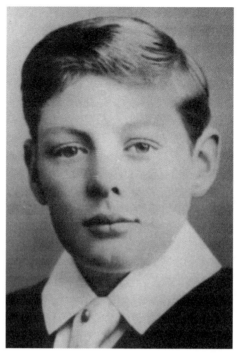

Winston's Harrow 'leaver' – a portrait photograph taken for distribution among his friends when he was about to depart from the school in 1892. He had red-gold hair, blue eyes, a snub nose and slightly crooked mouth. The famous 'bulldog features' were already noticeable.

> Churchill was no ordinary schoolboy . . . he did not distinguish himself in work or play. But he was a marked boy; people talked about him, and his great ability was recognized by at least some masters. Shyness and conventionality were not characteristics of his. It is said that at breakfast on the day after his arrival he said to his housemaster, 'Please, sir, what is your opinion about so and so?' the so and so being one of the big political topics of the day.

He was already, by that age (he was 14), in the habit of studying the press every day. Through this, as well as the political discussion that flourished in his home environment, he was extremely well-informed about current affairs. For the same reasons he also had a precocious confidence and ease in talking to adults that made a striking impression on others.

As a new boy Winston attracted notice in part because of his famous father. Attending 'Bill' (a daily roll-call) in the school yard, he was aware of being pointed out to tourists. The boys, in single file, passed a master and raised their hats as their names were read out. He often heard someone say, 'Why, he's the last of all.' This was due not to academic ranking but to the fact that his name in the school list was 'Spencer-Churchill' and he was alphabetically last in his form.

His father's prominence in public affairs made him equally interesting to those within the school. One young man, JEB Seely (later a major general and Lord Mottistone), described his first encounter:

> I vividly remember the first time I set eyes on Winston. It was a hot July morning and we were all enjoying ourselves swimming and diving in Ducker, Harrow's big open-air bathing pool. One of our amusements was to try and scramble on to smooth logs of wood about 3 feet long and 8 inches in diameter; a tough variation on the modern inflated horse. I stood on the little bridge spanning the narrow end with two sixth-form boys, while we all three munched buns in accordance with custom. One of my companions said; 'You see that little red-haired fellow having a row with the log – that's Churchill.' I was greatly interested, for my father and grandfather were members of the House of Commons and had many stories to tell of Lord Randolph, who was then at the height of his Parliamentary fame.
>
> At the moment when I saw Winston first, he was trying to push a heavy log on to the bank. 'Hi, Churchill,' called my companion, 'bet you two buns to one you don't get it out.'
>
> The little boy turned and rested his arms on the log, for he was out of his depth. After looking up at his questioner, he bent his head down and appeared to be thinking deeply, just as he does now in the House of Commons. He said 'No, I won't bet, because I have been told never to bet if I am likely to lose.' We ran down and pulled the log out for him, which did not interest him much, but we bought him a bun, which he appreciated greatly.
>
> He was a happy little boy that day, but I do not think on the whole he really enjoyed his young life at Harrow, and this although he had a naturally happy disposition. He really hated much of the school curriculum; it seemed to him such a shocking waste to spend so much time on dead languages and so little on his native tongue. I remember the Headmaster, Welldon, told me that it was an extraordinary thing to see in a boy of fourteen; I think his exact words were, 'such a love and veneration for the English language'.

While other people, and even masters who were teaching him literature, could remember a line or two of a Shakespearian play, young Winston could quote whole scenes straight off; nor was he slow to take advantage of his remarkable gift of memory. If a master, however imposing, quoted a passage wrongly, Winston would instantly correct him. He was a most intrepid pupil . . .

Another senior boy also met Churchill in the surroundings of the school bathing-pool. This, like the story of his Latin paper, became one of the most often recounted tales of his youth. Leo Amery was to become a distinguished cabinet minister, serving as Secretary of State for India and as a wartime colleague of Churchill. He recalled the circumstances of their first encounter:

My first impression of Winston Churchill was characteristically forceful. Standing on the edge of Ducker I suddenly felt myself propelled into the water by a foot in the small of my back, while unseen hands reft me of my towel. I emerged spluttering to see which of my friends had done this, only to meet the gleeful grin of a small, freckled, red-haired boy whom I had never seen before. Glee turned to alarm when I gave chase, and, being in those days both swifter and stronger, caught and duly ducked him. Next day at Bill, Winston came up to me and with the same ingenuous frankness that has so often disarmed an angry opposition in the House, explained that he had not realised that I was in the Sixth Form, but only that I was small enough to be the most suitable victim to hand, adding: 'My father, too, is small and he is also a great man.'

Amery had further dealings with this spirited and impertinent boy, who several times wrote articles under a pseudonym for the *Harrovian*, the school magazine. Looking back in 1941 he remembered that:

As schoolboy editor of the *Harrovian* it fell to me to be the Prime Minister's first editor and press censor. He submitted a trilogy of articles on Ducker, Gym and the school workshop, breezy, entertaining and frankly critical of all these departments. I can still see the look of misery on his face as, in spite of his impassioned protests, I blue pencilled out some of his best jibes. However, even my pedantic zeal for the Victorian respectability of the *Harrovian* did not altogether save the unexpurgated text from criticism by the authorities concerned. Mr Welldon summoned the young author to his study and thus addressed him: 'My boy, I have observed certain articles which have recently appeared in the *Harrovian*, of a character not calculated to increase the respect of the boys for the constituted authorities of the school. As the *Harrovian* is anonymous I shall not dream of enquiring who wrote those articles, but if any more of the same sort appear, it might be my painful duty to swish (cane) you!'

There is little indication in these accounts of the disdain with which senior boys traditionally regard those at the bottom of a school. If lack of ability in classics or games made Churchill unpopular, there is less evidence of this than of a sort of amused indulgence. One has the impression of a community that, from the Headmaster downwards, tolerated individualism and respected ability, no matter how unconventionally expressed. An anonymous correspondent later told one of the masters that:

As a boy I formed the highest opinion of his abilities and never ceased to wonder why he did not rise higher in the School. But he hated the Classics, and in his time that kept him down. The Headmaster also encouraged him to be a free lance . . .

And JWS Tomlin, who went on to become an Anglican canon, recalled:

Although he never shone at school on the scholastic side, and never rose to a high position during his school days, he was a boy who from the very first could not be ignored. He apparently hated Latin; it became a hurdle that he could not or would not jump. In those classical days to shy at Latin was a serious obstacle to success. He was in consequence a late starter, and he has described himself as 'just a pack-horse that had to crop what herbage he could find by the roadside in the halts of long marches, a bit here and a bit there'.

None who can remember that vital spark of humanity that was the boy Churchill could ever think of him as a dunce. The one vivid memory that I have of him, corroborated independently by two of my Harrow friends, is of this small red-haired snub-nosed jolly-faced youngster darting up during a house debate, against all the rules, to refute one of his seniors and carrying all before him in a magnificent speech.

Mr JF Moore, manager of the school book shop, remembered that:

> . . . in his schooldays [he] already showed evidences of his unusual command of words. He would argue in the shop on any subject, and, as a result of this he was, I am afraid, often left in sole possession of the floor . . .

JW Wright-Cooper, a near neighbour who was proprietor of a 'tuck shop' that sold snacks in the High Street, also had no difficulty in recalling him, and remarked that he was:

> . . . an extraordinarily good boy. He was honest and generous in a day when robust appetites were not always accompanied by well-lined pockets. My family lived over the shop, and when Churchill was downstairs we all knew it. Boys always crowded round his table. He talked loudly and usually led the conversation. He knew, too, what he was talking about, and nothing came amiss to him. He was witty and critical and kept the other boys in roars of laughter. He was exceedingly popular and even the seniors sought his company. He was well behaved and had the ear of everyone. When his father or his mother came to see him, he used to book a table in the tuck shop, and that was a great occasion for him. He was extremely happy at Harrow and full of high spirits.

This image of him may have been exaggerated (his letters home suggest that he was perennially too short of money to be quite so generous, and he was unlikely to be fully happy in any circumstances that prohibited him from doing as he wanted) and some of these recollections smack too much of hindsight. Nevertheless, observers several times remark on his cheerfulness and sense of fun. One of them was Emma Prue, who grew up near the school:

> Our house was a large old house and behind it was a derelict brewery. He and other boys always used to be rambling about the buildings. In the garden was a mulberry tree, and Mr Churchill used to collect the leaves for silkworms which he kept. He was bright and happy, full of mischief, and wandered where he would.

He had a set of carpenter's tools, and one day I found a chisel
which he had left behind after he had been doing something in
the old house. I picked it up and put it away and have kept it to
this day.

AW Siddons discovered another of his interests:

At one time he kept two dogs in West Street, which was, of
course, quite contrary to School Rules; he used to take them out
for walks with a friend of his who was the local detective.

However cheerful and happy he may have been in the memories of
these contemporaries, Winston's schooldays undoubtedly contained some
unpleasant incidents, and he was frequently the author of his own
misfortune. A leitmotif that ran through his schooldays was a fixation with
his destiny, and this must have seemed risible to others, for all around him
were examples of more accomplished and promising young men. When
caned for insolence by Nugent Hicks, a senior boy who went on to become
Bishop of Lincoln, he blurted, 'I shall be a greater man than you,' and was
given two more strokes. When 'ragged' by some schoolmates he angrily
shouted that 'one day he would be a great man when they were nobodies
and he would stamp and crush them'.

His personality reflected a robust – and probably not untypical – sense of
anarchy. Winston promised, in a letter to his mother, that 'I will leave off
smoking at any rate for 6 months'. On another occasion he informed her
that 'I have paid my debts and relinquished betting'. He was taken to task
by the Headmaster for using bad language and, as one of several found
guilty of smashing the windows in an abandoned building, was 'swished'
(flogged with a birch-rod). Despite an outburst in one of Winston's letters:
'– Welldon, he is the cause of all my misfortunes,' they had a mutual regard
that outlasted his schooldays; it was his old Headmaster who conducted
the service at his wedding.

Legend dictates that his parents, intent on their own pleasures, ignored
him at Harrow and that this left him feeling abandoned and unhappy. His
letters to them contain a number of plaintive, and vain, requests that they
come to see him. To a large extent this notion is justified, for both had a
multitude of social commitments and they undoubtedly disappointed him
by failing to attend Speech Days and other significant events. What must
be remembered, however, is that he was an exceptionally demanding and
self-centred child, who hated not to be the constant focus of his parents'

attention and who, not unnaturally, wanted their presence at his various moments of glory. In fact he was not as neglected as his recollections suggest. One or other of his parents visited the school on several occasions. His father, after inspecting the room he shared with Jack, reported to Lady Randolph in tones that do not suggest indifference:

> I went down to Harrow Friday afternoon and saw the boys. They seemed vy happy & comfortable & have an excellent room which was trim & tidy. Welldon told me that Winston was sure to pass the next examination if only he worked steadily. It will be his own fault if he don't [*sic*] pass. I bought a small hamper of things for them at Fortnum & Mason's . . .

Similarly, when Winston was required to improve his French by staying in France one holidays (a prospect he abhorred), his father indulgently suggested a less onerous means of doing this by employing a French-speaking servant, as Winston himself recorded:

> I told Papa when he came down that I ought (in Mr. W's opinion) to go, and he said 'Utter nonsense. If you like I'll get a servant scullerymaid for [their house at] Banstead.'

His mother wrote to him constantly during these years. Significantly, she gave him a push towards his eventual career by arranging for Edward Carson, the immensely able lawyer and MP, to visit him at the school and discuss his future as well as inviting him to attend a Commons debate. She was present for at least one of the Rifle Corps field days (mock battles) in which he took part. In addition, he became a protégé of a family friend – Laura, Lady Wilton. Discerning that he needed more attention than he was receiving from his parents, and styling herself 'your Deputy Mother', she wrote him letters filled with affectionate advice and sent him money. The tone of their relationship was informal and bantering, as suggested when she wrote: 'So you are coming to France to study the "lingo". Well – I think you ought to study it here! Under my maternal wing! What do you say?'

Though he remained in the Lower School for the whole of his Harrow career, Winston's scholastic record was certainly not poor. He made better progress through the School than some of his contemporaries, and won an impressive number of honours: he was awarded the form prize in history in his first two terms, and while still in his first year won a school prize for recitation by memorizing, and declaiming, 1,200 lines from Macaulay's

Lays of Ancient Rome. He also won a house prize for composing a 12-verse poem on the subject of influenza (there was at the time a worldwide epidemic), and when competing for the School Shakespeare Prize he was placed a respectable fourth. Though he was not a natural sportsman and did not, as a Harrow song puts it, 'rise by feats athletic / to the shining ranks of power', here too his achievements were better than average. Though small of stature and usually unfit, he must have tried hard. He was clearly no stranger to the gymnasium (one of his *Harrovian* articles urged his schoolmates to make better use of it). He was a member of his House swimming team, which in his final year was the best in the school. He also won a rifle-shooting competition, sending his mother a diagram showing where his shots had struck the target. He decided to take up fencing and badgered Lady Randolph to write to the school granting her permission:

> I want to learn fencing. I go to the Gymnasium a great deal and I think it would be so much better for me to learn something which would be useful to me in the army, as well as affording me exercise and amusement. I'm sure, since I have been working well, you will not hesitate to sign the enclosed order and return it by post.

In this sport he succeeded so well that he beat all rivals at Harrow before going on to become Public Schools Fencing Champion in 1892, as the school magazine recorded:

> Our representatives at Aldershot this year were fairly successful – at least they have brought back two medals, which is as good as has been done for the last few years.
>   In the fencing, Churchill beat Johnson, of Bradfield College, and Ticehurst, of Tonbridge School, thus winning the silver medal. His success was chiefly due to his quick and dashing attack, which quite took his opponents by surprise. This is the second time Harrow has won the fencing, Openshaw having won it the year before last . . .

This was a notable accomplishment. He also won a cup, and lost no time in celebrating by ordering copies of a photograph showing himself with it, dressed in fencing gear. Lord Randolph, to whom he had conveyed the news of his victory, sent a present of £2 – for his instructor.

In his work, he had already developed a writing style that was recognizably 'Churchillian'. An essay written by him at the age of 14 on the subject of

'Palestine in the Time of John the Baptist' contains phrases that would not have been out of place in one of his speeches more than 60 years later:

> The River Jordan which passes through the Lake of Genessareth & the Dead Sea; so shall they be till hoary Time be merged in boundless Eternity . . . In the N. & N.W. were a class of people always willing to risk their lives, their houses, their all for their country's freedom. Rebellion after rebellion broke out, but the stern and splendidly organized legions of Rome crushed and stamped these outbreaks into nothing . . . and of the Pharisees. Their faults were many – Whose faults are few? For let him, with all the advantages of Christianity avouch that they are more [uncivilized].

Another essay he composed was a work of fiction, dealing with a war caused by a Russian invasion of Afghanistan (this was a dangerous possibility in 1889, with Anglo-Russian rivalry on the North-West Frontier, and was finally to happen in 1979). It describes an attack on the Ukraine. A British force becomes surrounded at Kharkov (ironically the scene of bitter fighting during the Second World War), and a column attempting to relieve it is ambushed. The British troops, from county regiments, Guards and cavalry units, manage to defeat the attackers. With further irony, the distant future in which he set his story was 25 years hence: 1914. The title page describes:

> The Engagement of 'La Marais', July 7th, 1914, by an Aidecamp of Gen. C—, Officer Commanding H.M. Troops in R—

The style is brisk, owing much to the then-fashionable adventure stories of the GA Henty novels that he loved, but the observation of topography, organization and military detail are superb (several pages of maps accompany the text). The essay demonstrates an adult, specialist understanding of tactics, of the exact wording of orders and how they were carried out, and of the problems of manoeuvring large bodies of troops for attack, defence or pursuit. The first-hand description, by a colonel who witnessed the action, is very vivid:

> The 17th Lancers & the 10th & 11th Hussars . . . These 3 splendid Cavalry Regiments charged the horde of 'Cossaques', who, performing the usual Russian Cavalry mistake, received

the charge at the halt. (Cf. Charge of Heavy & Light Cavalry
at Balaklava) The British Cavalry struck the mass, pierced it &
bursting through it charged the infantry behind.

The Cavalry . . . bursting through struck the infantry behind . . .
the Odessa and Dnieper regiments . . . formed 'in line' disdaining
'double column' and aided by a Battery of Artillery poured in so
awful a volley the remnants of the cavalry were glad to turn and
ride back.

This anticipates the books he was shortly to write on his own experiences
of war. He already had the ability – to be demonstrated later in his histories
of the World Wars – to present scenes he had imagined or heard about with
a clarity and colour that suggest he was there. All the signs of his mature
style are evident: fast narrative pace, vivid description of places and events,
attention to detail and an impressive grasp of terminology. Despite the
uncomplicated patriotism of his outlook, he is already on the verge of
adult credibility as an author.

His narrator survives capture and several near-fatal incidents, and the
Russians, defeated, retire across the Volga. The story ends:

The enemy retreated slowly & deliberately at first, but at the
Volga they became broken & our Cavalry, Light & Heavy executed
a most Brilliant charge which completed the confusion. And thus
the 63000 Russians fled across the Volga in disorder pursued By
6000 cavalry & 40000 infantry.

Curious as this may seem it re[al]ly illustrates the power of
'morale' over troops, and the superiority of John Bull over the
Russian Bear. This victory is acknowledged by all military critics
to be General C—['s] masterpiece . . .

How did a 14-year-old schoolboy acquire this depth of knowledge? It was
partly from his own recent experience: he had taken part in a Rifle Corps
field day in which the attacking of a convoy had been practised. Largely,
however, he based his story on the military history that he was studying.
Lectures were given by two masters, LM Moriarty and EE Bowen, who were
considerable authorities on recent wars, and he was fortunate that their
passionate enthusiasm was available at precisely the moment at which
he could benefit from it. Under their influence, which he later fulsomely
acknowledged, his ideas matured. The Crimean War, from which he derived
the Russian setting and the type of fighting described in his essay, had been

less than 40 years earlier, and a friend of his parents, Sir George Womwell, had ridden in the Charge of the Light Brigade in 1854. The American Civil War had been just over 30 years previously (the father of some boys at the school was a veteran of Gettysburg) and the Franco-Prussian War less than 20. These were brought to life in illustrated lectures with lively, penetrating discourse by men who had, in some cases, walked the battlefields and talked to survivors.

Winston's photographic memory enabled him to absorb the knowledge of others and thus give the impression of wide reading or extensive study that he did not yet possess. When staying in France during one holidays he met some French officers who were discussing a particular battle. They confessed to knowing little about it, so he at once described it in detail. It transpired that he had heard a talk on it by Mr Moriarty some months earlier, and was able to recite this almost verbatim.

JOINING THE CORPS

For putting theoretical knowledge into 'practice' there was the Harrow Rifle Corps. This, like many British militia units, had been founded in 1859 when fear of a French invasion had led to a need for troops. Since this threat had receded, the Corps was not especially popular, with only about 100 members (a large school like Harrow should have had twice that number). By the time Winston arrived there were repeated pleas for members, as can be seen in the pages of the *Harrovian*:

> The Rifle Corps is in great need of recruits this Term, as many have left. All who will be seventeen years old between November 1st, 1888 and October 31st 1889, should, if possible, enrol in the 9th Middlesex, thus earning, if efficient, 35 shillings a year for the Corps.

The editors elaborated on the benefits of service:

> The attractions of the Corps this term are great and varied. There are Field Days talked about to Hatfield and to Althorp Park . . . there is the Brigade Drill in Hyde Park; there is a Guard of Honour for HRH Princess Louise [a daughter of Queen Victoria]. But we would rather not refer to such things; let us put duty first, plum pudding afterwards. What is certain is that the school is not so numerously represented as it should be by the Rifle Corps; there must be more recruits.

Winston was very keen to join, but even had he been old enough there was no uniform small enough to fit him. He somehow nevertheless managed to become involved in a number of their activities, including a field day.

These could be elaborate affairs, staged across the gentle landscapes of commons or country house parks. They involved the transporting of the two sides to some mutually convenient Armageddon, the battle often preceded by a picnic and concluding with tea. They tested, on a small scale, the discipline, cohesion and determination of the participants. Here is a typical occasion, as seen by the *Harrovian*:

> On Friday, the 27th May, was the Corps whole holiday, and a field-day was arranged in Hatfield Park. Haileybury, and a detachment of the Cambridge Corps, also took part in the engagement. On arriving at Hatfield the Corps first marched through the Park to a place where lunch had been provided under some trees. Actual hostilities did not commence till after two. The military operations were divided into two battles, in the first of which the Harrow Corps retreated before the attack of the combined forces of Haileybury and Cambridge, who were marching on London. The defence and retreat were very well carried out, and the volleys were sometimes quite excellent. The enemy advanced somewhat rashly in face of a strong and well-directed fire, and would in all probability have had considerable losses before getting possession of the Park.
>
> In the next battle the Harrow and Cambridge Corps attacked Haileybury. The advance was careful and steady, with the exception perhaps of some of the Cambridge Cyclists, who were too ready to risk their lives, Haileybury made one mistake in their retreat, which exposd a whole company to a sharp cross-fire from Harrow and Cambridge, and would certainly have cost them dear in actual warfare. After the conclusion of the second battle the Corps marched off to Hatfield Station, and arrived there in plenty of time to allow the men to disperse and look round the place, instead of having to rush wildly for the train as the year before. The Field-day was a great success, as the weather was splendid, without being oppressively hot. Both engagements were very exciting, and there was plenty of firing for all the companies. The supper in the Public Hall after the Field-day was no less successful. The speeches of Captain Kemp and Captain

The Harrow Rifle Corps forming square – a manoeuvre unchanged since Waterloo. Inspired by lectures on military history, Winston was impatient to join, and he delighted in their mock battles and shooting practice. He is believed to be somewhere in this photograph.

Bailey were vigorously applauded, and so were the songs . . .

Winston wrote to Lady Randolph:

> My own Mummy . . . I have some news. I joined the Corps as you know and attended my drills punctually. On Saturday I went with the Corps & we fought Haileybury it was very exciting.
> As I had not got a uniform I only carried cartridges I carried 100 rounds to give away in the thick of the fight consequently my business enabled me to get a good view of the field it was most exciting you could see through the smoke the enemy getting nearer and nearer. We were beaten and forced to retire.

He also took part in another of the promised highlights, about which he told Lord Randolph:

> My Dear Papa,
> . . . I would also have written yesterday but I was part of a Guard of Honour all the afternoon, for the Princess Louise . . .

At least one of his contemporaries, JWS Tomlin, regarded this training as entirely without value:

> Churchill was a member of the school rifle corps, but I doubt

whether in spite of his military instincts he derived much benefit from that quarter. The Rifle Corps in my time was not in great favour. Sergeant Grisdale, a fine specimen of the old army, used to drill a small squad every morning in the school yard, but very few kept their drills, and the field days, though jolly picnics, were often ludicrous from a military point of view.

I remember on one occasion during a sham fight in Cassiobury Park, Watford, a master, who was captain of the corps, tying a white handkerchief on the point of his sword, and going out in front of his company shouting to the enemy, who were in close formation about 50 yards off: 'Gentlemen, I maintain that you are all dead men'.

Winston enjoyed acquiring the basic martial skills that the Corps could provide. However dismissive some boys may have been about the realism of these exercises, they did introduce the young riflemen to modern weapons, including cannon and machine-guns. He wrote to his mother after yet another fight with Haileybury: 'It was great fun. The noise was tremendous. There were 4 Batteries of Guns on the Field & a Maxim, & several Nordenfeldts.' He added, 'I have bought a Book on Drill as I intend going in for the Corporal Examinations next term. I went down to the Range on Tuesday & fired away 20 rounds.'

In a unit as lethargic as the Harrow Rifle Corps, this sort of energy and keenness would have made Winston stand out. A master, quoted by AW Siddons, remembered: 'One field day he came and asked me to let him act as my aide-de-camp, and his alertness and zeal for action were amazing.'

Winston wrote to Lady Randolph: 'You will be glad to hear that I have passed in Recruit Drill, my Manual Drill and in Shooting – I made 22 out of a possible 25.' He was also promoted to lance-corporal.

AIMING FOR THE ARMY

For his chosen career the most important aspect of his life at Harrow was the Army Class. The purpose of this specialist course was to give boys intensive coaching in the specific subjects they needed to master in order to be accepted for officer training in the army. The class had only recently been established, in an attempt to prevent senior boys from leaving the school to attend military 'crammers'. It gave tuition in mathematics, drawing (both freehand and geometrical), Latin, French, chemistry and history. It was run by Mr Moriarty but his, and Winston's, feeling for military history had little scope; it was considered necessary for officers to know only the important themes of English history, not to debate the tactics, motives or personalities of the great commanders. Attendance at this class was a major commitment that prevented members from having time to devote to other academic activities. As a result Winston, like most of his fellows, did not rise higher in the school.

The procedure for entering the army was complex. An obstacle course of examinations had to be negotiated to gain admission to one of Britain's two military schools: the Royal Military Academy at Woolwich and the Royal Military College, Sandhurst. The former, founded in 1741 and known as 'The Shop' because a number of armourers' workshops had been attached to its original buildings, trained officers for the artillery and engineers, and therefore demanded greater academic and technical ability. The latter, at which Winston aimed, had begun in 1802 schooling infantry and cavalry cadets (the two establishments were to merge on the outbreak of war in 1939). Though Sandhurst was less academically demanding, it could still afford to reject the majority of its applicants; competition was fierce and the exams a significant ordeal. Many candidates sought the help of private tutors to get them through. The Sandhurst historian Alan Shepperd examined the process as it was a few years before Churchill's time:

> The first hurdle for the aspiring cadet was a preliminary examination taken at school at the age of about fifteen or sixteen. Some public schools had Army classes to prepare boys for the 'further' Army Entrance Examination set by the Civil Service Commissioners. Even where there was an army class, many boys left school to attend a crammer which specialized in preparing them for the Army Entrance Examination, but only those who passed at the top of the list gained places. Between 1876 and 1882 there were over 2,740 candidates for entry to Woolwich, but only 715 gained places. For Sandhurst over the same period the chances were even more slender; out of 6,000 who took the examination, less than one in four passed high enough to be accepted.

Michael Yardley, author of another book on Sandhurst, explained that:

> Deficiencies could be made up for at specialist crammers, the most famous of which was Captain James' ('Jimmies')

in [London's] Cromwell Road. Fifty per cent or more of all candidates would attend such establishments.

This was the route that Winston followed. He later told the story of how lucky guesswork had smoothed his path through the preliminary exam. Candidates were required to draw an accurate map of a particular country. The night before, he wrote on slips of paper the names of the world's countries, put them into a hat, and pulled out New Zealand. He studied this thoroughly, and the next day found it on the question paper. While this no doubt happened, his good fortune did not open the gates to a military career, for though he passed this exam he failed the next, gaining 5,100 marks but needing at least 6,457. He in fact twice failed the 'further' exam, and left Harrow in December 1892 to attend Captain James' crammer, from which he passed at the next attempt.

Winston was to recall his defeats in these exams with unnecessary self-deprecation, suggesting that he was dull-witted and that going to James' was a final act of desperation. In truth, because the standard was extremely high even repeated failure was no disgrace. It is also worth emphasizing that being sent to a crammer was not a last refuge for the hopeless but a sensible means of improving one's chances; many boys *wanted* to go to one. He had written to Lord Randolph at length on this matter before taking the first exam.

> Here I shall never get through my 'further'. 1 per cent of those boys who go up pass their 'further' from Harrow. The Army class takes me away from all the interesting work of my form and altogether spoils my term. Still I am bound to pass my preliminary from here but more than that is not in the bounds of possibility.
>
> 9/10 of the boys in the Army class will go to a Crammer before their exam. They all dislike the army class because it makes them come out low in their forms . . . Mr Welldon . . . cannot deny that a boy who gives 2 hours a day to the Army class work has not so good a chance as a boy who gives 6 hours.
>
> Harrow is all right for a Preliminary exam but 6 months [at] James or any other crammer is more to a chap than 2 years at Harrow.

He did go to Captain James', though his time there was interrupted by misfortune. In January 1893 he had suffered a serious injury while jumping 30 feet from a bridge during a game with his relatives, and spent many months convalescing (as he put it: 'For a year I looked at life round a corner') but he continued with his work, and made the characteristic impression on those who taught him. Lord Randolph received an exasperated letter from 'Jimmy' himself, Captain Walter James:

> I think the boy means well but he is distinctly inclined
> to be inattentive and to think too much of his abilities. He
> has been rather too much inclined up to the present to teach
> his instructors instead of endeavouring to learn from them.
> I may give as an instance that he suggested to me that his
> knowledge of history was such that he did not want any more
> teaching in it!

Indeed when he passed the 'further' at this third attempt his marks for history were much better than those of any other candidate. His overall performance was still disappointing, in that he had not been placed highly enough to be gazetted to an infantry regiment. He had come 95th out of 389 candidates, and missed the infantry by 18 marks . . .

It must be explained that, in the army of Victorian Britain (and most European armies were much the same), the majority of young men had had their careers arranged before they even began their training. All appointments of officers to regiments had to be approved by the Commander-in-Chief, Field Marshal His Royal Highness the Duke of Cambridge. In the case of fashionable units – the Guards, the cavalry, the light infantry – it would be necessary to make use of whatever private influence a boy's family could muster and this, together with the willingness of the regiment's officers to have him as a comrade, would influence the Duke's decision. At the same time, the cavalry was more expensive because officers had to pay for their own horses, as well as having to support the lavish social life that this branch of service involved. Less wealthy candidates, and their parents, preferred the infantry. This meant that, in the Sandhurst entrance exams, competition for the infantry was greater and places were given to those higher up the academic ladder. Churchill was, it seemed, destined for the cavalry, and his father was furious.

Lord Randolph was not wealthy by the standards of his class and he had to make economies wherever possible. He had used his influence with the Duke to have his son assigned to a crack light infantry regiment, the 60th Rifles. The Duke had agreed, the formalities had been settled, and the matter was considered closed. Now the whole process would have to be gone through again. Not only that, but the purchase of chargers and horse-furniture would cost Lord Randolph, he estimated, an additional £200 a year. Winston himself was ecstatic, writing that:

> I was delighted at having passed the examination and even more at the prospect of soldiering on horseback. I had already formed a definite opinion upon the relative advantages of riding and walking. Also the uniforms of the cavalry were far more magnificent than those of the Foot.

But the bubble of euphoria was quickly burst when he received from his father a stinging rebuke that has been much quoted by biographers:

> I am rather surprised at your tone of exultation over your appearance in the Sandhurst list. There are two ways of winning in an examination, one creditable and the other the reverse. You have unfortunately chosen the latter method, and appear to be much pleased with your success.
>
> The first extremely discreditable failure of your performance was missing the infantry, for in that failure is demonstrated beyond refutation your slovenly happy-go-lucky harum scarum style of work for which you have always been distinguished . . .
>
> With all the advantages you had, with all the abilities which you foolishly think yourself to possess & which some of your relatives claim for you, with all the efforts that have been made to make your life easy & agreeable & your work neither oppressive or distasteful, this is the grand result that you come up among the 2nd and 3rd rate who are good only for commissions in a cavalry regiment.
>
> You may find some consolation that you have failed to get into the 60th Rifles one of the finest regiments in the army . . . not that I shall allow you to remain in the Cavalry. As soon as possible I shall arrange for your exchange into an infantry regiment of the line. If your conduct at Sandhurst is similar to what it has been in the other establishments, my responsibility for you is over . . . if you cannot prevent yourself leading the idle useless and unprofitable life you have had during your schooldays, you will become a mere social wastrel, and you will degenerate into a shabby unhappy and futile existence . . .

Shabby, futile and unhappy might have been adequate terms to describe

Lord Randolph's own life. His political career in ruins, he was increasingly in the grip of a brain disease that was to kill him prematurely. It is possible that some of his anger was caused by a sense of frustration at his own decline. Nevertheless his letter must have been a staggering blow to his son, whose self-confidence was otherwise notoriously unshakeable.

Regarding the cavalry, he was worrying needlessly. By the time Winston arrived at Sandhurst enough of those above him in the list had moved up themselves (many had got into Woolwich) to create an infantry vacancy after all. Informed of this, Lord Randolph was appropriately pleased and, a degree of good humour restored, guaranteed his son an allowance of £10 a month during his time at the college.

THE SANDHURST CADET

Churchill entered Sandhurst as a gentleman cadet in September 1893. Anyone with his sense of history and love of the military profession could not have failed to respond to the college and its environs. The Royal Military College (after merging with Woolwich it was to change its name to 'Academy') was situated outside Camberley in Surrey. It might have carried echoes of his ancestral home, for within its severe, neo-classical buildings – naturally more Spartan than Blenheim – it bristled with similar trophies, flags, weapons and portraits. Bordering its parade ground were captured Napoleonic cannon, and below this was a lake dug by French prisoners of war. Churchill and those of his fellow cadets who had come from great schools were no strangers to illustrious surroundings, yet Sandhurst evoked in him, as Harrow had not, a feeling that he was where he belonged. With a pleasure in dressing up and in uniforms that went back to the sailor-suits of his childhood, he will have loved wearing the cadets' dark blue service dress and their dress uniform with its scarlet tunic and blue, brass-spiked helmet. He was now entered on his chosen profession, and the serious business of life could begin.

Sandhurst was not, however, a truly important milestone in his life. The special ingredients of his character had already become evident at school, and his career at the college did not add significantly to them. Sandhurst was not, then or later, equivalent to the great military academies of West Point and St Cyr, in which the course of instruction lasts for several years. The British Army has always preferred to give its officer cadets a short grounding in basic skills and professional knowledge before sending them on to their designated units. There their military education would begin in earnest under the control of senior officers and NCOs, who would mould them according to the character and traditions of their particular regiment.

Sandhurst was thus a way-station, and it never tended to attract the degree of loyalty and nostalgia that an American officer might feel for West Point. Many of the qualities taught in other nations' military academies – social graces, ease in exercising responsibility, accountability to those above – would already be thoroughly familiar to boys from public schools, and time would not have to be spent on teaching them. The college did not, as much military training does, begin by treating every participant as a 'blank page'. Gentleman cadets were expected already to be gentlemen and, through involvement in a unit like the Harrow Rifle Corps, to be on their way to military proficiency. Major General JFC Fuller, who passed through it shortly after Winston, remembered:

> When I went to Sandhurst we were not taught to behave like gentlemen, because it never occurred to anyone that we could behave otherwise. We were taught a lot of obsolete tactics, as in every army of that day; did a tremendous lot of useless drill; but never heard a word about 'responsibility', 'loyalty', 'guts' etc. because – so I suppose – these were held to be necessary prerequisites of gentlemen.

Ernest Craig-Brown, who entered the college at the same time, clearly recalled his first sight of Winston: 'I remember him arriving at Sandhurst, looking like a dandy – sort of cloak on, dingle-dangles on his watch-chain, and a walking-stick with a tassel on it.'

Before Churchill's time, the course had lasted only three terms, but it had just been extended to 18 months to allow for more emphasis on the study of fortification, musketry and riding.

As for the academic side of things, the approach remained rather simplistic, as Michael Yardley explains:

> Sub-Lieutenants were taught six basic subjects which did not change significantly to the end of the century: Queen's Regulations, regimental economy, military accounts and correspondence, military law, tactics and field and permanent fortifications . . . however impressive they might sound, [the courses] consisted of little but sitting in a classroom reading a book.

And General Fuller remembered the classes in Military Law as something of a waste of time:

Once a week for two hours at a stretch we sat in a classroom and read the Manual, and when we had exhausted those sections dealing with murder, rape, and indecency, we either destroyed Her Majesty's property with our penknives or twiddled our thumbs. Fortunately our instructor was as deaf as a post, for this enabled us to keep up a running conversation, broken on occasion by a wild Irishman, named Meldon, banging on his desk to make our teacher look up. Then Meldon would solemnly say: 'Please, sir, may I come and kick your bottom?' and our unsuspecting master, not having heard a word, would invariably reply: 'Come to me afterwards, boy, come to me afterwards.'

The number of cadets was so small that they would all have known each other, at least by sight. Their crowded syllabus allowed time to supplement their riding instruction with foxhunting, a sport highly popular with officers and one in which, despite the evident reluctance of the authorities to sanction it for cadets, they were actively encouraged to participate. For Winston's generation of soldiers, hunting developed riding skills and 'a good eye for country', enabling them to read a landscape, gain exercise and experience in the saddle, and practise risk-taking by jumping their horses over obstacles.

After Churchill's death, the Royal Military Academy's magazine published an account by Alan Shepperd. It described in detail the college of which Winston had been a part and the type of officers who were his instructors:

Sandhurst at the end of the last century was a good deal smaller than it is now and, in 1893 and 94 there were only 315 Gentlemen Cadets . . .

The Governor and Commandant was Lieut.-General E. H. Clive . . . General Clive was commissioned into the Grenadier Guards in 1854 and, after service in the Crimean War, was later appointed Lieut.-General commanding his Regiment and, before becoming Governor of the Royal Military College, was Commandant of the Staff College.

At the end of 1893, Major-General C.J. East, C.B.E., succeeded General Clive. General Sir C.J. East, as he subsequently became, had been commissioned into the 82nd Foot in 1854 and, after service in the Crimean War and the Indian Mutiny (where he was seriously wounded), played a prominent part in the Lushai

Expedition. He later served through the Zulu War of 1877 and the Burma War of 1886–87, where he commanded a Brigade with some distinction.

The Assistant Commandant was Lieut.-Colonel M. Wynward of the 50th Foot. Soon after commissioning, Wynward served in New Zealand (in 1866) and was Adjutant of the Regiment in the Egyptian Campaign of 1882 until being invalided from Kassassin. While he was Assistant Commandant at the R.M.C. he was also Secretary to the Collegiate Board.

The Riding Master was Major D. Hodgkins and the Chaplain the Rev. C.H. Murphy, M.A. In addition to a Medical Officer, there were only three other officers on the establishment of the Headquarters, namely the three professors in Fortification, Military Topography, Tactics and Military Administration and Law, and these were all serving officers. There were twenty-one other instructors.

Discipline within the college was based on its organization as a battalion of six companies, lettered A to F. Churchill was in E Company:

> The Company Commander was Major O.J.H. Ball of the Welch Regiment [who signed the leave book for Churchill on an occasion when he saw the latter in Aldershot without permission (an event recounted in Churchill's memoirs)]. Major Ball later commanded the 1st battalion of his Regiment in South Africa from 1902–04.
>
> In those days the Company Commanders had overall responsibility for the discipline and administration of about fifty to sixty Gentlemen Cadets, but it is evident that the system of discipline was very largely maintained by the Cadets themselves through the Under Officers and Corporals. In each Company there was one Under Officer, two Senior Corporals and four Corporals. The Under Officers had the power of awarding one day's restriction and two extra drills; Corporals could award one extra drill.
>
> The College buildings consisted of the Old Building, the Gymnasium (which is now the Central Library), and the Chapel, which was only a third of its present size. The officers were quartered in the Square and the Terrace with the Governor, of course, occupying Government House. The other buildings

consisted merely of stables, riding schools, a small hospital, a few Other Ranks Married Quarters and the R.E. Yard.

When Churchill joined the college in 1893, a number of changes were taking place in the curriculum and these resulted in a far wider and more practical military syllabus than previously:

> In 1893 the course was extended by an extra term and now lasted eighteen months instead of a year. The subjects studied were tactics, fortification, topography, i.e. map reading, military law and military administration and that this 'formed the whole curriculum. In addition were drill, gymnastics and riding.' The result of the extension of the course was to make extra time available for the study of fortification and to increase generally the practical work that was carried out in this subject. In addition the number of hours daily devoted to riding was increased as far as the means were available.
>
> We find that, in the following year of 1894, the eight hours work a day carried out on the syllabus was divided between five hours' study which included practical work and languages, and three hours daily devoted to drill, riding or gymnastics.
>
> Many of the improvements to the curriculum resulted from a report of the War Office Board of Visitors which took place in the summer of 1893, which had recommended certain new studies such as military history and geography and the methods of reconnaissance on horseback and that an extra hour a day should be devoted to study.
>
> They had also recommended that Cadets should continue with the study of some of the subjects that they had taken for the Entrance Examination and strongly recommended the study of French and German.

Gentleman Cadet Churchill proved to be an excellent student in those areas of the curriculum that particularly interested him:

> It is interesting to note that, while the Board was recommending the study of military history (which was not, in fact, on the syllabus until 1897), young Churchill had already taken steps to form his own military library. This, which he recalled 'invested the regular instruction with some sort of background', included

Maine's work on the 'American Civil, Franco-German and Russo-Turkish Wars,' as well as Hamley's 'Operations of War' and Prince Kraft's 'Letters on Infantry, Cavalry and Artillery.'

As regards theoretical studies, Sir Winston's marks in tactics and the study of Fortifications were very high and in Equitation his marks were exceptional.

It is evident that, in Churchill's time, riding instruction was carried out by companies, although a report by the Riding Master shows that the system was about to be changed to a division by 'Rides' where the instruction would be graded according to the capabilities of the individual cadet. Hunting was permitted, and Churchill is believed to have kept horses stabled near the present Harcourt Hotel on the Frimley Road. A movement in 1894 by Horseguards (e.g. army headquarters) to stop Gentlemen Cadets hunting was strongly resisted by the cadets, whose views were supported by the Governor. The Horseguards' argument was that the extension of the syllabus left too little time for such outdoor pursuits. In the end permission was given for hunting leave to be allowed as before.

Though happy at the college and obviously proficient in several of the subjects taught there, Churchill was not an all-round cadet. He had little talent for drill, no doubt resenting the long hours of 'square-bashing', and for several months needed remedial instruction as part of the 'Awkward Squad'. Not yet having seen the importance of sartorial smartness, he was not especially well turned out (in a well-known formal photograph of him with two other cadets, one of his tunic buttons is undone!). He also retained the cocksure attitude to authority that had characterized him since infancy. Ernest Craig-Brown remembered: 'He was very unpopular amongst the Instructors – he asked them difficult questions which he knew jolly well they couldn't answer.'

The College syllabus was organized to allow the five hours' theoretical instruction to be largely dealt with in the morning and the practical subjects to occupy the afternoon and early evening. Reveille was sounded at 6.30 am. There was an hour of lessons ('First Study') from seven until eight, then breakfast and 'sick parade'. Between nine and ten there was parade or riding instruction. Second, Third and Fourth Study filled the rest of the morning until lunch at 2 pm. After this there was riding until three o'clock, when drill was taught. At four the cadets received instruction in gymnastics and the hour from six until seven in the evening was spent in sword exercises. 'Mess,' or dinner, was at eight, and Lights Out was at eleven – a tiring but not exhausting regimen. Nevertheless the army does not seem to have insisted then, as it does today, that recruits should get themselves thoroughly fit before beginning training. Winston visibly suffered on route marches and sometimes had to be assisted (he might have found service in the infantry beyond his stamina), and wrote: 'I am cursed with so feeble a body that I can hardly support the fatigues of the day.'

As at all British institutions, the food was unimaginative. General Sir Ian Hamilton was a cadet of a previous generation who was to meet Winston in several wars. He recalled how the college was fed in the 1870s. Even if subsequent changes in administration had improved matters, there was probably much in this description that would have been recognizable to his counterparts in the 1890s:

> Breakfast – a pint of milk for each cadet and bread and butter ad lib. For dinner, a shoulder of mutton weighing ten pounds on each table of ten cadets, and ten pounds of what the authorities called plum-pudding – the cadets, 'stick-jaw'. The large lumps of suet found in it were known as 'Bagshot diamonds'. The beer, otherwise 'swipes', was said to be the water in which the brewers' aprons had been washed – but this is probably an exaggeration. The cadets at each table of ten had to drink it out of one pewter pot which was passed round; there was rarely anything left but a faint odour of malt for the last two. The cadets were allowed to make tea in their own rooms at their own expense but these were the only two meals supplied by the State.

Whatever charm the kitchen may have lacked, Churchill thoroughly enjoyed the work. The creator of the 'Den' at Banstead was delighted to study proper fortifications and to practise digging trenches or building breastworks. The owner of a toy army was already well versed in the movement of bodies of troops, the posting of picquets and the sending out of reconnaissance patrols, but now it could be simulated with real soldiers. His practical mind was enthralled with the mechanics of how to demolish bridges or sever railway lines using explosives, and how to cross streams with pontoon bridges. With a rudimentary gift for drawing (as witnessed in the scribbles and maps with which he had illustrated his letters since childhood), he enjoyed map-making and field-sketching.

He also learned something about the army's loose and informal code of honour. Cadets going out of college bounds had to sign their names in a leave book. One day Churchill set off to drive to Aldershot in a small carriage and, through his own admission, was too 'lazy or careless' to do this. Before he had gone far he met his company officer, Major Ball, returning to the college. Churchill greeted him, but then realized the trouble he would be in if the Major saw that he had broken the rules. He returned early from his visit and rushed to sign the book, but discovered he was too late. The Major's initials were already entered at the bottom of the page:

> He had seen me and had seen that my name was not in the book. Then I looked again, and there to my astonishment was my own name written in the Major's hand-writing and duly approved by his initials.
>
> This opened my eyes to the kind of life which existed in the old British army and how the very strictest discipline could be maintained among officers without the slightest departure from the standards of a courteous and easy society. Naturally after such a rebuke I was never so neglectful again.

Horses were Winston's greatest pleasure. Though hunting was not officially encouraged, cadets were able to rent horses at local livery stables and to ride in cross-country races – steeplechases or 'point-to-points'. Churchill was one of these enthusiasts, and he spent much of his free time in the saddle, as he put it, 'bucket[ing] about the countryside'. Recalling this time, he later made the oft-quoted remark: 'No hour of life is wasted that is spent in the saddle'.

A NEW LIFE

Winston found, to his great joy, that he now had status in the eyes of his father. Lord Randolph took him to social and sporting events and showed him off to his friends. This was still not the companionship for which he had longed, but he felt they were entering a happier phase in their relationship.

Unfortunately this was not to be. Lord Randolph, visiting his London watchmaker, was shown Winston's gold 'hunter' which had been left for repair. A highly expensive timepiece, engraved and enamelled with the family's coat of arms and only recently given to him, it had been dropped in a pool and was badly damaged. Lord Randolph saw in this accident all the feckless slovenliness of which he had found his son guilty throughout his life, and wrote him a blistering lecture on the subject of irresponsibility.

Winston replied in detail, describing the efforts he had made to retrieve his watch from the water. After diving several times (it had fallen from his tunic pocket into a six-foot-deep pool), he had had the entire pool drained, at a cost of £3 in labour, before finding it. It has been convincingly argued that this shows considerable persistence and organizational ability, but Lord Randolph was not mollified. Winston was given a cheap replacement while the 'heirloom' went to his brother Jack. A generation later it was stolen from one of the family and has never been found – a relic that still waits rediscovery.

This was Winston's last altercation with his father, for Lord Randolph was soon too ill to display more than a sketchy awareness of his son's progress, and he died several months before Winston passed out of Sandhurst. In his final examinations, his marks were outstanding and showed how much he had improved since his arrival. From the Awkward Squad he had managed to rise to a score of 95 out of 100 in drill; his 'feeble body' had gained 85 out of 100 in gymnastics; he earned 227 out of 300 in Military Law, 263 out of 300 in Tactics, 532 out of 600 in Fortification, 232 of 300 in Military Administration, 471 of 600 in Military Topography and 290 of a possible 300 in Riding. He passed out 20th of 130 cadets. The fact that his father did not live to see this was one of the great tragedies of Churchill's life, for it was at precisely this moment that he emerged from the troubled, doubtful years of adolescence into what he might later call a 'sunlit upland'. For the first time, he had displayed unambiguous ability. From now on he would begin his steady ascent to fame and, within an astonishingly short time, reality would match the grand self-assessment of his schoolboy boasts. He was to retain a lifelong interest in Sandhurst, though his memories of it were never to have the same resonance as those he had of Harrow. The academy remembers him with a lecture theatre named in his honour, and in the chapel is a stained-glass window bearing his coat of arms.

Rites of passage passed, he was now on his way. His short career as a regular army officer was to condense a respectable lifetime's soldiering into half a decade, and to give him opportunities for experience, recognition and wealth that he could not possibly have attained in any other profession, and which must have been unimaginable when he began his service. Only a kindly Fate could have opened so many doors at once, or offered him his heart's desire so swiftly.

It remained to sort out his regiment. He was still intent on joining the 4th Hussars. As a cadet he had dined several times with the officers and had been seduced by the opulence of their mess – the glitter of candlelight on regimental silver, the orchestral music provided by the regimental band, the splendour of the blue-and-gold uniforms, the talk of horses. The commanding officer was willing to accept him and the other officers were eager to welcome him into their ranks. He could be extremely charming when he wanted, and they discerned none of the obnoxious qualities that had struck so many others. He continued to lobby his mother relentlessly to pull strings for him and she had no difficulty in doing so. She sought the advice of the commanding officer, Colonel John Brabazon, who replied that no time was to be lost:

> You must write to the Duke & at once . . . What I should say was that the boy had always been anxious to go into the Cavalry, but for certain reasons Randolph put his name down for Infantry. That latterly he completely came round to Winston & your wishes & was anxious he should join my regiment. You can say there is now a vacancy in the 4th hussars, that you are very anxious he should not be idling about in London & that I personally knew the boy, liked him, & was very anxious to have him. I should add – which is the case – that Winston passed very much higher than any of the candidates for Cavalry & hope that the Duke will allow him to be appointed to the 4th hussars, and thus fulfil one of Randolph's last wishes.
>
> There are more men passed for Cavalry than there are vacancies, and that's the hitch, but I feel certain that if you write to the Duke, he will make a personal matter of it and that all will be arranged.

Lady Randolph immediately appealed to the Duke, and he replied with equal swiftness: 'I will write at once to the Military Secretary, and if it can be arranged, it shall be carried out.'

3
THE 4TH HUSSARS

MILITARY DEVELOPMENTS IN THE AGE OF EMPIRES

Churchill was entering a world that had experienced bewildering changes during the previous few decades. Rapid advances in technology were transforming the art of war both on land and at sea. The process would continue, through the period of Churchill's first campaigns, up to 1914 and beyond into the era of aircraft, tanks and atomic weaponry.

It has been said that Churchill's military career spanned the Victorian age and the nuclear age, the cavalry charge and the atom bomb. While this is true, it is an oversimplification, for in history there are few clear-cut beginnings and endings. By the time he became a soldier, a series of important developments had already transformed the art of war, and the era of modern conflict had unmistakably arrived. On the other hand a number of anachronistic practices continued well into his lifetime.

For instance, he was to serve in the cavalry at a time when it was still a vital element in military operations (though it was largely employed in reconnaissance, a function that today would be fulfilled by armoured cars or helicopters). The importance of horses did not come to an end with the 19th century and they did not disappear suddenly from the battlefields of the world. Cavalry continued to see extensive action in the Boer War and the 1914–18 conflict. It was used, bravely but disastrously, by the Polish Army in 1939 and with success by Soviet forces right through to the fall of Berlin – in the same year that atomic weapons were introduced. The age of the horse and the age of the bomb all but overlapped.

Churchill was born into the Pax Britannica created by the defeat of Napoleon. Nelson's victory at Trafalgar had swept from the seas any plausible rival to the Royal Navy and left Britain to dominate the world's oceans for almost a century: only towards the end of that period would the navies of two other powers – the United States and Germany – challenge this pre-eminence. But British ascendancy was not a foregone conclusion, for the advent of new weapons redefined the character and experience of warfare.

On the oceans, steam had replaced sail. Fleets no longer needed to depend on wind and tide. Warships became bigger, better protected and better armed, their guns able to swivel and thus to fire ahead or astern, so that ships no longer had to fight side-to-side. Another crucial innovation was the torpedo, . Most significantly, though it did not see action until World War I, the submarine revolutionized sea warfare. Sailors were accustomed to detecting an enemy's approach by seeing distant sails or far-off columns of smoke. Now they could be attacked without the slightest warning.

The use of coal to power ships meant that maritime nations had to establish 'coaling stations' throughout the world for refuelling. These coastal pinpricks often developed into permanent settlements and colonies. The race to establish colonies merged with the race to build larger fleets and this rivalry became acute between Britain and Germany from 1898 onward. The commissioning of the first 'dreadnought' type of ship in 1906 made all existing battleships obsolete and so the race had to begin all over again. Fleets at this time began to convert from coal to oil power, and the importance of the Middle East as a source of raw materials dates from that time.

Following the equally decisive victory at Waterloo in 1815, Britain was not to be involved in fighting in western Europe for another 99 years, and her only conflict with a European power was the Crimean War (1853–56). In this Russian territory, British forces, in alliance with France and Turkey, thwarted the Tsar's designs on Constantinople.

Land warfare, however, underwent momentous changes. Most significant was the coming of the railway. An efficient rail network meant that huge forces could be mobilized with unprecedented speed. While previously armies had had to march all the way to a battlefront, they could now be rushed to the front and arrive fresh, while supplies of food and armaments could be sent with equal dispatch. The equipment used by soldiers improved steadily. The introduction of the long shell – the pointed shape we know today, as opposed to the cannon ball of the Crimea or the Civil War – was brought about by the development of the 'rifled' gun-barrel (grooved inside so that a projectile would spin as it was fired, greatly increasing its speed and accuracy). The bolt-action rifle could be fired quickly using bullets in a 'clip' or magazine, saving the complicated procedure of loading before each shot. The advent of smokeless powder meant that rifles no longer gave away a shooter's position – a considerable advantage to snipers. The Gatling gun and the Maxim, the first machine-guns, were large and cumbersome but highly effective. The latter were used at Omdurman and caused a great deal of the destruction among the Khalifa's troops.

Europe was not at peace during the 19th century. The first half of the century saw an explosion of nationalism that culminated in the revolutions of 1848. In the second half, two significant new nations came into being. The struggle to unite the Italian peninsula ended in 1870 with the establishment of the kingdom of Italy. Prussia, the largest and most powerful of the German states, expanded its territory through a series of short, successful wars against Denmark (1863), Austria (1866) and France (1870–71). Having decisively defeated the latter – which had been considered virtually invincible – Prussia, guided by its able Chancellor, Otto von Bismarck, created a German Empire ('Reich') with its king as the first German Kaiser, or Emperor. Germany was now a powerful modern state, an industrial giant, well armed, and ambitious to move up from the status of European power to world power. In the 1880s she began to acquire overseas colonies and to build a navy to protect them. She demanded the respect of her neighbours, and a role in the world commensurate with her might.

This rise to eminence was not without cost, for Germany had sown the seeds of hatred and envy that were to poison Europe in the future. For France, defeat in 1871 was a major humiliation that was to fester for more than 40 years. Germany had annexed two French provinces, Alsace and Lorraine, and their recovery became a national obsession. France's government, army and people expected another war to win them back, a fact of which Germany was fully aware.

A future clash between the two countries was considered inevitable and in 1894 France made an alliance with Russia to ensure that, when it came, Germany would be caught between two hostile nations and would have to dissipate her resources fighting them both at once. When Britain too joined this alliance in 1907, Germany saw herself as 'encircled'. The sense that she was surrounded by enemies intent on her destruction, and that a pre-emptive strike against them might be necessary, was to contribute greatly to Germany's pugnacious mood in the years before 1914. The solution to encirclement formulated by the German General Staff was the Schlieffen Plan. This dictated that, because Russia's cumbersome armies would take six weeks to mobilize, the Kaiser's forces could all be thrown into an attack in the west. Cutting through Belgium to outflank the French armies, they would seize Paris, knock France out of the war and then, carried by train, rush to their country's eastern frontier to face the Russians. Failure to keep up with this timetable would mean having to fight simultaneously on two fronts. Encirclement indeed.

Elsewhere in the world there had been only one significant conflict. The American Civil War (1861–65), which solved the decades-old question of slavery, was the first 'modern' war, fought by large citizen armies and using industrial technology created by the industrial revolution: the railway, the telegraph, the steamship. Despite some brilliant commanders and dedicated, valiant soldiers, the Confederates were unable to compensate for the greater manpower and resources of the northern states. The struggle had shown the direction that warfare was taking and the campaigns were closely observed at the time, or studied afterwards, by military authorities throughout the world. (As a young and ambitious writer, Churchill had intended to produce a history of the war at the end of the 1890s, but the rush of events – and the chance to take part in other wars – denied him the time to do so.)

In 1870 the Franco-Prussian conflict brought this same industrial warfare to Europe. It demonstrated the awesome efficiency of Prussian weaponry, planning and organization, as well as the woeful lack of these things on the part of the French. The Emperor Napoleon's forces were routed in a matter of weeks. He surrendered and his regime was overthrown. The population, now a republic, fought on and the people of Paris therefore suffered a long siege that added agony to defeat.

The next important conflagration took place in Asia over Russian demands for a sphere of influence in China. The Russo-Japanese War (1904–05) introduced a new power to the world stage and demonstrated again that a perceived military colossus could have feet of clay. Russia was decisively beaten at sea and was unable to make headway on land. Her humiliation was so complete that unrest at home – the 1905 Revolution – almost overthrew her government.

The 19th century was also an era of small wars, involving the military forces of major powers in conflict abroad. France fought to extend military control over her possessions in north and west Africa, Britain to protect or to further her political and commercial interests throughout the world. While her European neighbours practised conscription and therefore fielded armies numbering millions, Britain had a small, professional army that was designed to garrison her overseas colonies, but her soldiers made up in skill and experience for what they lacked in numbers. The Empire, particularly Africa and the North-West Frontier of India, gave British (and Indian Army) troops almost continuous and highly useful experience of warfare. Not all colonial campaigns were successful but the lessons learned in this type of campaign sharpened their skills and, when war came in August 1914, gave them a significant initial advantage over their still-unblooded German opponents.

In 1899 Britain's most important, and expensive, conflict since the Crimea had been fought against the South African Boer republics of Transvaal and Orange Free State. Her professional army had expected a swift victory over the irregular Boer farmers, but had instead become drawn into a three-year campaign that involved several humiliating defeats. International opinion sided overwhelmingly with the Boers and Britain was seen as a bully who had got what she deserved.

Lacking sufficient troops to conduct the fighting, the War Office made use of two significant factors: soldiers were brought from other British colonies and dominions to serve alongside those from the mother country, and the army made use of temporary volunteers. For the first time, civilians with some skill in riding or shooting were able to enlist for the duration of hostilities, and whole units of these men were assembled under the designation 'Imperial Yeomanry'. Both of these concepts were to characterize the wars of the 20th century.

The era in which Churchill grew up was unique in that, for a few decades, war was regarded – in Britain at least – as a wholesome adventure. It had been hideous in the Crimea, and it would be hideous again in Flanders and Gallipoli. It was deeply unpleasant in the Sudan and the Transvaal, yet it enjoyed a spurious glamour. The British had lost any sense of warfare as a desperate matter of survival. For them, campaigns were far away and usually successful, fought by a professional army. The latter years of Victoria's reign brought a sense of triumphant fulfilment, a pride in being the world's richest nation and in having the largest overseas empire, that included for the first time a wide and growing public interest in the army. In the years during which Churchill was at school, at Sandhurst and in the 4th Hussars, this new attitude became noticeable in 'the media'. Reports of distant battles, telegraphed straight from the scene, could be seen shortly afterwards in the newspapers. Generals were popular celebrities; music-hall songs celebrated the sterling qualities of the soldier. Regiments, recently given names instead of numbers, engendered local pride. Churchill, who had seen the awful effects of war and had lost friends in battle, nevertheless retained throughout his life a sense of excitement at the prospect of armed conflict that was born in this era of Victorian confidence.

RIDING OUT WITH THE REGIMENT

In February 1895 Churchill, aged 20, reported to the regiment at East Cavalry Barracks in Aldershot. As a garrison town it was only 40 years old, but had already become established as 'The Home of the British Army'. In a history of the town, Colonel Wilfrid Jelf describes it as Churchill would have seen it at that time:

They were good days those in the early nineties in Aldershot
. . . There was a glamour which is gone, a romance of dash
and colour, which was part of the everyday life . . . in the
daily walks across the old Canal, over the Queen's Parade
and into the North Camp Gardens we were kept alive to the
identity of every regiment in the station by the gay uniforms
which were met with everywhere and were recognizable half a
mile away, on mounted orderlies busily trotting around with
leather dispatch bags, parties at drill and soldiers 'walking out'
. . . it was soldiers, soldiers everywhere . . . The weekly routine
included attendance at Church Parades in the little tin church
by the canal bridge, route marches in marching order, sham
fights and field days in the Fox Hills, Reviews and Queen's
Birthday Parades in all the full dress glories of Ceremonial
and on Laffan's Plain. And there was colour, colour, colour
all the way.

Because of the British Army's system of providing much of an officer's
education once he had gone to his unit, Churchill was obliged to
undergo the same basic training as every newly enlisted trooper. The
horses were bigger than he was used to and the stiffness caused by
long hours in the saddle had to be cured with massage and hot baths.
The drills were often agony because of a torn muscle in his hand, but
he could not complain, much less opt out of any training, for fear of
losing face.

There was another daily routine to learn, but though intensive it was not
a protracted syllabus: woken at 7.30 am with breakfast in bed (he was to
make this a lifelong habit); riding practice for two hours at 8.45; bath and
massage at 10.45; followed by carbine exercises and a noon inspection of
the stables to make sure that the mounts of his 30 men were groomed, fed
and watered. After that, his own lunch, then drill for one-and-a-half hours,
another bath and miscellaneous administrative duties until the evening.

He was as talkative, and inquisitive, as ever. Lance-Corporal S Hallaway
recalled meeting him shortly after his arrival:

When Mr. Churchill joined I was in charge of the 3rd Troop of
'C' Squadron, and as Captain Kincaid-Smith and Mr. Churchill
walked over the squadron parade ground towards my stable I
thought how odd he looked, his hair and his gold lace forage
cap the same colour. Captain Kincaid-Smith introduced me

to him. I had to tell him all I knew about my troops, men and horses and stable management. He kept me very busy asking questions.

The men spent long hours practising the technicalities of climbing on and off their horses and of manoeuvring them in formation according to the precise instructions in the drill manual. A glimpse at this gives some indication of the concentration that was required:

SECTION 6, MOUNTING

Prepare to Mount. – Turn to the right on the left heel, placing the right foot opposite the stirrup parallel to the side of the horse, heels 6 inches apart, take up the bridoon reins at the end with the right hand, and place the left hand between them, the near or left rein passing outside the left hand, and the off or right rein between the first and second finger; the left hand resting on the neck of the horse about 12 inches from the saddle.

With the right hand draw the reins up until an even and gentle feeling of both reins on the horse's mouth is obtained, and throw the end of the reins over to the off side. Twist a lock of the mane round the thumb of the left hand, which closes firmly on the mane and reins. Place the left foot in the stirrup as far as the ball of the foot, and the left knee against the saddle, the right hand on the cantle of the saddle.

The bridoon reins will be held as detailed above, and the bit reins will be brought up inside them, the near or left bit rein between the second and third finger.

Mount. – Spring off the right foot, rise to the stirrup, and shifting the right hand from the cantle to the pommel of the saddle, bring the right leg over the saddle clear of the horse and drop gently into the saddle, placing the right foot in the stirrup without help of hand or eye: quit the mane with the left hand, the pommel with the right hand.

This, of course, was one of the simpler movements. Churchill also had to learn to mount and dismount from a moving horse that had no saddle, and to jump his mount, again bareback, over a bar with his hands on his head or behind his back.

Perseverance was worthwhile, for he was soon able to enjoy the sensation of riding out with the regiment, as he himself recorded:

> There is a thrill and charm in the glittering jingle of a cavalry
> squadron manoeuvring at the trot; and this deepens into joyous
> excitement when the same evolutions are performed at a gallop.
> The stir of the horses, the clank of their equipment, the thrill of
> motion, the tossing plumes, the sense of incorporation in a living
> machine, the suave dignity of the uniform – all combine to make
> cavalry drill a fine thing in itself.

The 4th Hussars had been raised in July 1685. They were originally known, according to the old custom of naming a regiment after its colonel, as Berkeley's Dragoons, but officially they were named (an intriguing connection for a Churchill) Princess Anne of Denmark's Regiment, after the future Queen Anne. They were later designated a Hussar regiment, a term that entered the vocabulary of European armies in the 18th century from Hungary. The word 'Huszar' meant a freebooter, but was applied to a type of light cavalry soldier.

The regiment fought in Scotland against the troops of 'Bonnie Dundee'. They then went on to take part in a number of historic engagements. As the battle honours on the their colours testify, they were at Steenkirk, Namur, Dettingen, Talavera, Albuhera and Salamanca, the Alma and Balaklava. In this latter engagement, during the Crimean War against Russia, they were part of the Light Brigade and took part in the famous charge, one of their troopers winning the Victoria Cross for rescuing an unhorsed officer.

This splendid record of service was matched by an equally splendid uniform, which would not have looked out of place in a Viennese operetta, and which typified a sense of dash and colour that can still be found in the British Army. Shortly after being commissioned, on 20 February 1895, Churchill had photographs taken of himself, in different poses, in this uniform, which was made to measure; skilful tailoring had made Second Lieutenant Churchill look both taller and slimmer than he really was.

The tight-fitting tunic and 'overalls' or trousers are dark blue. The elaborate frogging is gold, as are the lace-entwined cuffs and collar and the stripe on the trousers. Gold lanyards or 'cap-lines' swoop across the chest and a gold bandolier, worn from the left shoulder, carries a despatch case. There are patent leather, knee-high boots, swan-necked spurs and a 'busby' – the drum-shaped black sealskin hat that is worn by some mounted regiments – with its busby bag hanging to the right, and its red and white feather plume. In Churchill's case, this was bought on account from a London military tailor. The uniform, spare clothes and

Ambitious, intellectually enquiring and – as always – impatient with authority, Churchill was no more suited to the world of an officers' mess than he had been to life at school, but skill at polo helped gain him acceptance among his comrades.

accessories so far exceeded his means that he finished paying for them only six years later, by which time he had long since left the regiment.

Even in Churchill's day this dress uniform was worn only on ceremonial occasions. The British Army had not gone to war in such kit since the Crimea, and even the scarlet tunic of infantrymen had not been worn in action since the Egypt expedition of 1882. Nevertheless, the flamboyant dress of Churchill's regiment symbolized the power of tradition and the swagger that mounted troops have always manifested. Whatever his father Lord Randolph may have thought of them, cavalrymen looked down from a very great height on all other soldiers. The caption to a famous cartoon in Punch, in which an examiner puts to a debonair young officer the question: 'What is the role of cavalry in modern war?' and receives the languid response, 'I suppose to add tone to what otherwise would be a mere vulgar brawl', delighted no one so much as the cavalry themselves and it became virtually their unofficial motto. They could not know that within a few decades they would have vanished from British orders of battle, and that their replacement – the tank – would be created by one of their own.

As a fashionable regiment, stationed near London, the 4th Hussars were often visited by distinguished persons for whom a glittering spectacle had to be contrived. The meticulous work that was put into these occasions is illustrated by this account of an inspection by the Prince of Wales in the year before Churchill joined. He himself would have taken part in similar occasions during the following years:

> The Prince was met at the railway station by Colonel Brabazon, and driven to the barracks in the regimental drag – a four-in-hand – accompanied by a travelling escort. At the barracks Colonel Brabazon conducted the Prince of Wales through all the stables, where great preparations had been made. The stables were lavishly decorated with straw plaits, and with bows in the squadron colours on the stable posts. The feed buckets were meticulously placed in rows behind the horses, and the walls were decorated with the Prince of Wales' feathers in chalk. Everything was immaculate.
>
> The Prince dined with the officers and spent the night with the regiment. The next morning he inspected the regiment in review order in the presence of a large crowd of spectators. He rode down the ranks and minutely inspected the general turn-out. Then the regiment marched past by squadrons, ranked past by sections at the trot, trotted past by wings, and, finally, reversing the front, galloped past by squadrons.
>
> After that there was a demonstration of sword exercises, pursuing practice at the gallop, and a variety of field exercises. When it was all over the regiment paraded and the Prince of Wales called Colonel Brabazon and the officers to the front, and congratulated them on faultless turn-out and drill. The Prince of Wales lunched with the officers and was driven back to the railway station in the regimental drag.

An even greater compliment was paid a few years later:

> One of the nicest of the many good reports the regiment received in those days was made by the Inspector-General of Cavalry in 1896. The inspection was held on Hounslow Heath, and afterwards the General said: 'Colonel Brabazon, you ought to be proud to

command such a smart and well-drilled regiment, for in the whole of my military experience I have never inspected a smarter, cleaner and [more] well-drilled corps as I have done this day: in fact, it is the smartest cavalry regiment in the British service.'

By that time Brabazon was about to relinquish command and the regiment was due to sail for India to undertake garrison duty. His replacement was Lieutenant Colonel WA Ramsay, a member of a distinguished military family. Ramsay's son, Bertram, was to grow up with vivid memories of Aldershot and of the carrot-haired subaltern whom he often saw on the barrack square. In another era their paths would cross again. The boy went into the Royal Navy, and in 1940, he organized the entire Dunkirk evacuation. Four years after that, as Admiral Sir Bertram Ramsay, he was in charge of Operation Neptune – the ferrying of Allied forces across the Channel on D-Day.

TROUBLED TIMES

Between arriving at Aldershot and departing for India (a period of about 18 months) he found himself involved in two unpleasant scandals, one of which was caused by regimental 'tone'. He was accused of misconduct not as an individual but as one of a group, though his family's social prominence made him the most conspicuous and his was the name most bandied about.

Shortly after he joined the regiment there was a steeplechase called the 4th Hussars Subalterns' Challenge Cup. This was no mere lark. It was organized according to the rules of Britain's governing body for this sport, the National Hunt Committee. One of the horses had been Surefoot, and many months afterwards information surfaced to the effect that several officers had swapped a better horse for Surefoot and then bet heavily on the result. Churchill, who had perhaps promised his mother that he would not ride in steeplechases but who had done so under the transparent pseudonym 'Mr Spencer', was one of those implicated. The Committee set up an investigation and was sufficiently concerned by its findings to declare the race result void and to ban any horse that had taken part in it from competing in future events held under their auspices.

The second instance was more serious and more unpleasant, for it resulted in legal action. Churchill was accused of 'gross immorality'. The trial of Oscar Wilde for a homosexual liaison had recently taken place, and the nature of this immorality was alleged to be the same.

Alan Bruce had passed out of Sandhurst and wanted to join the regiment. He was invited to dinner at a London club by a group of the officers whose purpose was not to welcome him but to tell him he was not wanted. He was considered unsuitable, not least because with an allowance of only £500 he could not afford the social life. He was further informed that the officers had got rid of his predecessor, for similar reasons, by hauling him out of bed and half drowning him in a horse-trough. After this had happened twice he resigned. The spokesman for these officers was said to have been Winston Churchill.

Bruce had persisted in joining, but within a short time he was accused of misconduct and obliged to resign. Some months later his father Alan Cameron Bruce, a barrister, wrote to the officer who had replaced him. Referring to his son, he said:

> His real offence was that he was at Sandhurst with Mr. Churchill and that they had been rivals in shooting, fencing and riding throughout his career and incidentally that he knew too much about Mr. Churchill.
>
> There was for instance one man whose initial is C, flogged publicly by a subaltern court-martial for acts of gross immorality of the Oscar Wilde type with Mr. Churchill.
>
> I have not as yet ascertained what was done by E Company to Mr. Churchill, but as soon as I do I shall lay the statement before the War Office.

This and the racing irregularities were made public by Henry Labouchere, MP for Northampton and editor of the investigative magazine *Truth*. Winston and his mother quickly issued a writ, which is preserved in the Churchill Archives:

> The Defendant meant and was understood to mean that the Plaintiff was a person of vile and disreputable character unworthy of associating with the officers of his regiment or any honourable men and unfit to hold Her Majesty's commission. That he had been guilty of gross indecency . . .
>
> By reason of the premises the Plaintiff has been grievously injured in his credit and reputation and in his said profession and in his position as officer in Her Majesty's Army and has been held up to hatred and contempt.

They asked for an astronomical £20,000 in damages. Not a shred of proof could be found to support the allegation and it seems to have been no more than an attempt at revenge. Bruce was forced to sign a formal letter of apology and Churchill settled for damages of £500. The Member for Northampton, who had kept both cases in front of the public through his magazine, eventually let both matters drop, though he informed his readers that pressure had been exerted on him:

> The public must bear in mind that the young officer who assumed the part of ringleader in the conspiracy to eject Mr. Bruce from the 4th Hussars belongs to an influential family, and that all the influence at his back has been used to prevent a reopening of the case, as I can testify from my own experience.

Deeply unpleasant though this affair clearly was, it is necessary to see it in context. Such kangaroo courts within a regiment were commonplace both before and since. As mentioned earlier, it was important that a potential officer should be acceptable to those with whom he would live and work. In such a close-knit world everyone needed to share the same background, tastes, pastimes, outlook and even vocabulary. This would create a harmonious community in which everyone could work well with his comrades. In Churchill's era, money was an important part of this. Officially, the Army's rationale for preferring wealthy officers was that if they had private means they could go to war without the distraction and worry of financial troubles. In practice, no fashionable regiment wanted the embarrassment or nuisance of an officer who could not keep up with its social obligations: hunting, racing, polo and smart restaurants.

What is in question, in the case of Lieutenant Bruce, is that if he failed to meet the social requirements of the 4th Hussars, why had he been allowed to join in the first place? Since no officer could hope to keep up with the social requirements of his rank on the salary he was paid, he was expected to have private means (usually in the form of a parental allowance) three or four or five times greater than this, and anyone who could not command such funds would be rejected. In addition, all potential officers would be 'screened' by the Colonel, and perhaps by the Regimental Sergeant Major, to ensure their suitability. Churchill's own visits to the regiment from Sandhurst were part of this process, the ease with which he mingled being proof that he met requirements. One can only wonder how candidates had managed to slip through this system and join a unit in which they were so clearly unwelcome. The army, having investigated the matter, concluded that Bruce had indeed not been 4th Hussars material, and Churchill received letters of congratulation on the success of his legal action, one of them from the Commanding Officer whose mistake, presumably, had led to the unpleasantness in the first place. From few incidents in his life does Churchill emerge with so little credit, and his behaviour is made worse by the knowledge that Bruce's allowance (£500) was the same as his own.

Fortunately, distraction from scandal at home was about to appear in the shape of service abroad.

CUBA

In the last weeks of 1895 there might have been war between Britain and the United States. The cause was a boundary dispute between British Guiana and the Republic of Venezuela, in which America had economic interests. Washington supported the Venezuelan claim to territory within the British colony; London refused to be browbeaten. In the event, the crisis was defused. Had it not been, Churchill's first experience of war might have been fighting against his mother's people in a South American jungle.

As it was, he did spend some weeks, during that winter, involved in fighting in the Western Hemisphere, in a war that was later to involve American troops. The Spanish island of Cuba was in a state of insurrection, seeking independence from Madrid, and fighting rumbled continuously through its forests, mountains and cane fields. There were no heroic battles, just a continuing guerrilla war of small raids and skirmishes and harassment. As he surveyed the world, this was the nearest thing Churchill could find to a proper war and he decided to have a look at it. If he could gain permission to visit the Spanish Army in the field he could experience war at first hand – something none of his contemporaries had done. He would not be allowed to do any fighting, and could therefore win no glory, but it would be better than nothing.

The key to this adventure was Sir Henry Drummond Wolff, once a political ally of his father and now British Ambassador in Madrid. Wolff was to prove as useful in helping Churchill to see action as he had been in supplying his toy army with transport. Churchill fired off a letter asking that he obtain the necessary passes and letters of introduction, and these were arranged through the Minister of Foreign Affairs, the Duke of Tetuan. They were forthcoming remarkably quickly. No matter how much it was pointed out that Churchill was merely, as it were, a schoolboy on holiday, the Spanish Government insisted on seeing the presence of a famous English politician's son as a gesture of at least quasi-official endorsement. International opinion strongly sided with the rebels, and Spain was glad of all the support it could get.

He did not need to fear that he would be missed by his own army. In the spacious years of Victoria's reign, officers like Churchill were entitled to spend five months out of every 12 on leave, and 10 weeks of that amount could be taken consecutively. This was because many of them were posted thousands of miles from home on tours of duty that could last for over a decade, and with slow sea travel it was only worthwhile going home once a year. Even those stationed in Aldershot, an hour's journey from London, were allowed to make themselves scarce. No officer, or his skills and knowledge, was irreplaceable, and these young men were able to spend long stretches of each winter in visiting Continental health resorts or pursuing foxes across the English shires.

The Cuban rebellion was a source of interest to the public, and if Churchill could arrange to write reports on the fighting for a newspaper, he could perhaps recoup the cost of his ticket. In the end it was Lady Randolph who paid for the tickets – and there were two of them, because he persuaded his fellow subaltern Reginald Barnes to go with him. Churchill made preparations and costed the enterprise before telling his mother of his plans. She accepted matters with good grace and, since they were stopping in New York on their way, arranged for Bourke Cockran to look after them there. Churchill obtained consent from Brabazon, but felt he had better gain clearance higher up the chain of command. With characteristic impudence he wrote to the army's new Commander-in-Chief, Sir Garnet Wolseley. He also consulted Military Intelligence, receiving maps and information as well as a request to observe Spanish weapons, and their effects, with a view to debriefing on his return.

They sailed from Liverpool at the beginning of November. Churchill's first sea voyage put him a foul mood, but this evaporated as soon as the ship docked in New York. He loved the city, and the United States. He was intrigued by the elevated railroad, impressed by a visit to a warship, fascinated by a court case, and appreciative of all the attention he received. No one with Churchill's drive and energy could fail to feel at home among Americans. He wrote to Jack:

> Picture to yourself the American people as a great lusty youth
> – who treads on your sensibilities, perpetrates every possible
> horror of ill manners – whom neither age nor just tradition
> inspire with reverence – but who moves about his affairs with
> a good hearted freshness which may well be the envy of older
> nations of the earth. Of course there are here charming people
> who are just as refined and cultured as the best in any country

in the world – but I believe my impressions of the nation are broadly speaking correct.

One thing that did not impress him was the United States Military Academy. Situated 50 miles up the Hudson river from New York, West Point was a place of obvious interest to army officers. An apoplectic account of his visit there, again written to his brother, suggests that Gentleman Cadet Churchill would not have had the qualities necessary to graduate from that institution:

> You will be horrified by some of the Regulations . . . The cadets enter from 19–22 and stay 4 years. This means that they are most of them 24 years of age. They are not allowed to smoke or have any money in their possession nor are they given any leave except two months after the first two years. In fact they have far less liberty than any private school boys (e.g. prep school pupils aged 8–13) in our country. I think such a state of things is positively disgraceful and young men of 24 or 25 who would resign their personal liberty to such an extent can never make good citizens or fine soldiers. A child who rebels against that sort of control should be whipped – so should a man who does not rebel.

One is tempted to wonder if he ever shared these views with General Eisenhower – of the class of 1915!

After a week in New York, the two young officers went by train to Key West and caught a steamer for Havana. On 20 November they saw their destination with its sea wall, its ancient grey fortifications and its white buildings framed by lush greenery. Given his characteristic thoroughness, Churchill will have made himself familiar with the island's troubled history.

Sugar and tobacco had made Cuba, the 'Pearl of the Caribbean', the richest of Spain's remaining colonial possessions. It had long been of interest to the United States, where Southern politicians viewed this tobacco-producing island as a sort of annexe, and many sought to add it to their country to bolster the slave-holding element in Congress. In 1848 President James Polk had sought to buy the island, for its commercial and strategic value, for a hundred million dollars, only to be told that Spain would rather see it 'sunk in the ocean'.

America supported Cuban independence by giving shelter to exiled insurgents. Sometimes they requested more concrete assistance: in 1849

Jefferson Davis, later President of the Confederate States, was asked to take command of an expedition to liberate the island. He declined, as did Robert E Lee. The venture was tried with Cuban leadership, but failed. In a second attempt the following year the rebels were again defeated. Those who survived the rout were put to death and their leader, Narciso Lopez, was publicly strangled. This provoked outrage in the US, and over the following decades public anger was kept at perpetual boiling-point by the press, which gave publicity to every atrocity story that came to its attention.

In 1868 there was another rebellion. This one lasted a decade and became known as the Ten Years' War, or the First War of Independence. The island adopted a constitution and elected a president, but division among the rebels led to failure and the Spanish once again took reprisals. Spain was not a benign colonial master, but together with these draconian measures there were promises of political reform and of Cuban representation in the Cortes, or Spanish Parliament – the same combination of stick and carrot that was to be used by Britain during its own colonial troubles.

These promises were largely forgotten and rebellion therefore smouldered once again. The economic depression of the 1890s, and the consequent fall in sugar prices, lit the spark. In the middle of the decade three rebel leaders – Maximo Gomez, Antonio Maceo and José Marti – landed in Cuba and were killed almost at once, but the insurrection went on.

By the end of the 19th century the Spanish Army was immensely skilled at dealing with indigenous rebellions for the same reason that Britain was to gain a similar reputation in the 20th, namely the break-up of the country's overseas empire. Spain had been involved in wars of independence since the days of Simon Bolivar, and by 1895 had little left to learn about counter-insurgency. Spanish troops, whether Peninsular (from Spain) or Provincials (locally recruited militia), were courageous, well equipped (they wore practical and comfortable lightweight cotton uniforms) and well armed with modern Mauser rifles. They operated in battalion-sized units, but each battalion had attached to it a company of 'guerrillas' – troops with local knowledge who performed specific tasks such as capturing known rebels. They were an ancestor of the special forces unit that was to become so characteristic of 20th-century warfare, and the Cuban insurrection was to provide Churchill with a glimpse of a type of conflict – the long-lasting, seemingly unwinnable 'police action' – that would fall to Britain's lot during his last years.

Spain fielded 150,000 troops. The number of their opponents is unknown. The rebels were badly armed and led, and had no stomach for pitched battle against professional soldiers. They had a wide following in the countryside and were able to carry out innumerable nuisance acts of petty sabotage, such as derailing trains or sniping at convoys. They also destroyed sugar crops and prevented mills from grinding the cane, thus wrecking the economy and bringing trade to a halt (America was infuriated by this measure) as well as gaining international publicity for their cause, a tactic that modern terrorists have not been slow to emulate.

Madrid's response was to seize tight control of the island's cities and to create protected routes through the countryside, turning Cuba into a fortress. An American journalist, Richard Harding Davis, who was not unsympathetic to the Spaniards, described the measures taken and their effect on movement around the island:

> These forts now stretch all over the island, some in straight lines, some in circles, and some zig-zagging from hill-top to hill-top, some within a quarter of a mile of the next, and others so near that the sentries can toss a cartridge from one to the other.
>
> The island is divided into two great military camps, one situated within the forts, and the other scattered over the fields and mountains outside of them. The Spaniards have absolute control over everything within the fortified places; that is, in all cities, towns, seaports, and along the lines of the railroad; the insurgents are in possession of all the rest. They are not in fixed possession, but they have control much as a mad bull may be said to have control of a ten-acre lot when he goes on the rampage. Some farmer may hold a legal right to the ten-acre lot, through title deeds or in the shape of a mortgage, and the bull may occupy but one part of it at a time, but he has possession, which is better than the law.
>
> It is difficult to imagine a line drawn so closely, not about one city or town, but around every city and town in Cuba, that no one can pass the line from either the outside or the inside. The Spaniards, however, have succeeded in effecting and maintaining a blockade of that kind. They have placed forts next to the rows of houses or huts on the outskirts of each town, within a hundred yards of one another, and outside of this circle is another circle, and beyond that, on every high piece of ground, are still more of these little square forts, which are not much larger than the signal stations along the lines of our railroads and not unlike them in appearance. No one can cross the line

of the forts without a pass, nor enter from the country beyond them without an order showing from what place he comes, at what time he left that place, and that he had permission from the commandante to leave it. A stranger in any city in Cuba to-day is virtually in a prison, and is as isolated from the rest of the world as though he were on a desert island or a floating ship of war.

It was not just within the cities that Spanish control of a stranger's movements was so thorough:

When he wishes to depart he is free to do so, but he cannot leave on foot nor on horseback. He must make his departure on a railroad train, of which seldom more than two leave any town in twenty-four hours, one going east and the other west. From Havana a number of trains depart daily in different directions, but once outside of Havana, there is only one train back to it again. When on the cars you are still in the presence and under the care of Spanish soldiers, and the progress of the train is closely guarded. A pilot engine precedes it at a distance of one hundred yards to test the rails and pick up dynamite bombs, and in front of it is a car covered with armor plate, with slits in the sides like those in a letter box, through which the soldiers may fire. There are generally from twenty to fifty soldiers in each armored car. Back of the armored car is a flat car loaded with ties [sleepers], girders and rails, which are used to repair bridges or those portions of the track that may have been blown up by the insurgents. Wherever a track crosses a bridge there are two forts, one at each end of the bridge, and also at almost every cross-road. When the train passes one of these forts, two soldiers appear in the door and stand at salute to show, probably, that they are awake, and at every station there are two or more forts, while the stations themselves are usually protected by ramparts of ties and steel rails. There is no situation where it is so distinctly evident that those who are not with you are against you, for you are either inside of one circle of forts or passing under guard by rail to another circle, or you are with the insurgents. There is no alternative. If you walk fifty yards away from the circle you are, in the eyes of the Spaniards, as much in 'the field' as though you were two hundred miles away on the mountains.

However efficient the blockade system might seem, Davis could see its weaknesses:

> The lines are so closely drawn that when you consider the tremendous amount of time and labor expended in keeping up this blockade, you must admire the Spaniards for doing it so well, but you would admire them more, if, instead of stopping content with that they went further and invaded the field. The forts are an excellent precaution; they prevent sympathizers from joining the insurgents and from sending them food, arms, medicine or messages. But the next step, after blockading the cities, would appear to be to follow the insurgents into the field and give them battle. This the Spaniards do not seem to consider important, nor wish to do. Flying columns of regular troops and guerrillas are sent out daily, but they always return each evening within the circle of forts. If they meet a band of insurgents they give battle readily enough, but they never pursue the enemy, and, instead of camping on the ground and following him up the next morning, they retreat as soon as the battle is over, to the town where they are stationed. When occasionally objection is made to this by a superior officer, they give as an explanation that they were afraid of being led into an ambush, and that as an officer's first consideration must be for his men, they decided that it was wiser not to follow the enemy into what might prove a death-trap; or the officers say they could not abandon their wounded while they pursued the rebels. Sometimes a force of one thousand men will return with three men wounded, and will offer their condition as an excuse for having failed to follow the enemy.

The day after their arrival, Churchill and Barnes set out for the headquarters of Marshal Martinez Campos, the Commander-in-Chief. It was a long journey, naturally undertaken by train. Winston described it in one of his letters to the *Daily Graphic*:

> As far as Colon the journey is safe, but thenceforward the country is much disturbed. The insurgents have given notice that they will wreck any train carrying troops and have several times succeeded in so doing. Every station from Colon to Santa Clara is a small fort. Sometimes it is a stockade of logs, sometimes a loop-holed house or other defensive work.

> At Santa Domingo a pilot engine is added to the train, as
> the rebels often indulge in target practice – from a respectful
> distance. In the car rides the escort, the passengers being
> permitted the privilege of using the ordinary compartments . . .

They were warmly received by the genial Campos, but found they had missed the last military column. To catch up with it they were obliged to make another – and roundabout – journey by rail and steamer, but arrived at the rendezvous, Sancti Spiritus, before General Valdez and his men.

The column was protecting supplies for an isolated post, but on hearing that a rebel force was camped in woods nearby it took on the additional duty of hunting this down. There were 1,700 soldiers – cavalry, infantry and artillery – against 4,000 rebels. These retreated into the landscape of forest and fields of long grass, leaving a trail of evidence that Valdez and his soldiers followed.

On 30 November, Churchill's 21st birthday, the column set out before dawn. The mist and darkness created ideal conditions for an ambush and the rebels duly struck. There was a sudden explosion of firing from nearby trees, but no one was hit and the soldiers did not even return fire. When the soldiers stopped for lunch in a forest clearing there was another outburst of firing, this time hitting a horse. At the end of the day's march a halt was made on a riverbank, and Churchill went bathing with some others. They had just climbed out when a crackling volley of shots flew over their heads. He described the reaction of nearby troops:

> . . . in this war no soldier ever goes a yard without his weapon
> . . . and these men doubled up in high delight and gave the
> rebels a volley from their Mausers which checked the enemy's
> advance. There was a regular skirmish going on half a mile away,
> and the bullets were falling over the camp. The rebels, who use
> Remingtons, fired independently, and the deep notes of their
> pieces contrasted strangely with the shrill rattle of the magazine
> rifles of the Spaniards. After about half an hour the insurgents
> had enough, and went off carrying their wounded and dead away
> with them.

That night, more bullets pierced Churchill's hut and wounded a nearby orderly. He had celebrated his coming of age by coming several times under fire.

Churchill greatly admired the toughness and professionalism of the

Churchill's visit to Cuba was a dress-rehearsal for the colonial wars, in which he was to participate, and successfully launched him in the role of soldier-correspondent. His first experience of warfare was gained while accompanying a column of Spanish troops like these.

soldiers, who could march enormous distances, fight bravely and show contempt for the rebel sharpshooters. The next day he recorded that 'the enemy's bullets whizzed over our heads or cut into the soft ground underfoot. The soldiers grinned and mimicked the sound of the passing projectiles.'

Emerging from woods into open ground, the column fanned out. Rebels were firing from behind a ridge and the two sides engaged. General Valdez made no effort to be inconspicuous, riding up and down behind his troops' positions. His white-and-gold uniform, and grey horse, drew considerable enemy fire and Churchill – like the others on the General Staff – was thus in some danger. Once again there were no casualties, however, and the rebels, finding the cannon and rifle fire too hot, melted into the forest where they could not be pursued. Churchill was surprised by what followed:

> The Government troops had taken a week's hard marching to
> find the enemy, and, having found them, had attacked them

promptly and driven them from their position. The natural course was to have kept in touch at all costs, and to have bucketed them until they were forced to either disperse or fight. No pursuit was . . . attempted. Honour was satisfied, and the column adjourned to breakfast. It seems a strange and unaccountable thing that a force, after making such vigorous marches, showing such energy in finding the enemy, and displaying such steadiness in attacking them, should deliberately sacrifice all that these efforts had gained . . .

Whatever the quality of its troops, the Spanish Army would never subdue the rebellion with this lack of will, but this was no longer Churchill's concern. He sympathized with the rebels but deplored the rebellion which would, he realized, drag the island into even greater ruin and misery if it succeeded. In the meantime, with leave running out, he must return to England, and within a few days of the action he and Barnes were on their way to New York. Both in America and in Britain he was to be interviewed by the press, and in both countries he was criticized for associating with the unpopular side in a quarrel that was none of Britain's concern. He had to point out at length that he had not carried a weapon or taken part in fighting.

Nevertheless, he received a medal. General Valdez had recommended both officers for the Spanish Order of Military Merit, a distinguished-looking enamelled cross with a red and white ribbon. No doubt it proved a very welcome 21st birthday present for Churchill, but he was forbidden to wear it on his uniform. Another souvenir he took with him was a bullet that had killed a nearby Spanish soldier.

In fact, he brought back from Cuba something more worthwhile. He had got his military and political views into print and shown immense promise as a commentator on these subjects. He had written colourful, amusing and enlightening descriptions of the places he had visited and the events he had witnessed. He had analysed the background, the nature and the conduct of the rebellion, and offered intelligent speculation about the island's future. He had also established himself in the role that he was to expand during the next few years – that of both participant and witness, actor and audience.

As for Cuba, the war dragged on and American indignation finally reached a crescendo. On 15 February 1898 the battleship USS *Maine* exploded, in mysterious circumstances, in Havana harbour with the loss of 268 crew, and shortly afterwards Spain and the United States were at war. The conflict was brief, ending with the complete surrender of Spanish forces on 18 July. Spain's empire in the Western Hemisphere was gone.

Though America took over Spain's other colonies – Puerto Rico and the Philippines – Cuba was eventually given the independence it had sought. In 1902, US control ended and a presidential democracy was established, but this did not flourish. By 1909 the island was in the grip of dictatorship, as it has been ever since. Only in Churchill's last years would it once again, fleetingly, come near to being a source of conflict.

4
INDIA, 1897

The 4th Hussars were in the last few months of their duty at Hounslow Barracks and were preparing to leave for India. There they would join the garrison at Bangalore. With little to do, they would live in a Kiplingesque world of polo and servants and drinks on club verandas. Many officers looked forward to this prospect. To Churchill it seemed a prison sentence.

He had by now decided to leave the army and enter politics. The thought of long years stranded thousands of miles from the seat of government filled him with horror. His frustration was the more acute because, since his return from Havana, he had been able to make a number of useful contacts in social and political circles. Should a parliamentary seat become available, he could offer himself as a candidate. He knew that his father's name would guarantee him some reflected lustre. Years hence, when he returned from the Bangalore posting, the memory evoked by that name would have faded, he himself would be forgotten, and he would have to start laboriously cultivating contacts all over again. He could not afford this lengthy exile.

Since he had no university background to lend credibility to his political aspirations, he needed to win renown as a soldier. A few medals, a reputation for courage – any fragment of kudos would help. While he was in the army he would have to see some fighting and do something noteworthy, and this was not necessarily easy. For 40 years the British Army had fought only in small wars. As a result many soldiers, including his Commanding Officer, Colonel Ramsay, and his Sandhurst Company Officer, Major Ball, had never seen action. He could not risk the same fate. Should he succeed in getting to a battlefield, and should some moment of glory arrive, he could not rely on others to trumpet his achievements in the press, which is why he was so anxious to write the descriptions of campaigns himself.

The 4th Hussars had no prospect of action. Bangalore was peaceful and the only place in India that offered excitement – the North-West Frontier – was over 2,000 miles away. The regiment's posting was for eight or nine years (they were to remain in India until 1905, missing the Boer War completely). As his departure drew nearer, he therefore pestered Lady

Randolph to arrange his transfer to another unit with more acceptable prospects. He wrote to her:

> I daresay you have read in the papers that the 9th Lancers are to go to Durban. If they are to be sent straight to Rhodesia they will have to take two or three extra subaltern officers – who will be attached from cavalry regiments. I have applied to their Colonel to take me should such a contingency arise. A few months in South Africa would earn me the S. A. Medal . . . Thence hot-foot to Egypt – to return with two more decorations in a year or two – and beat my sword into an iron dispatch box . . .

As this letter explains, regiments were often short of their complement of officers, and members of other units – if they had the requisite training and skills – could apply to the colonel for temporary secondment. If his regiment were likely to see action, a commanding officer could receive numerous requests, with several candidates for every vacancy. The War Office, and senior officers, might also have a say in such appointments, and Churchill's extensive network of influence could no doubt easily have come into play had Lady Randolph been willing to exert herself. She was not. She disliked her son's lack of patience, consistency and staying power. She let him go to India.

He arrived at Bombay, aboard the SS *Britannia*, at the beginning of October 1896. Unwilling to wait to disembark, he and some others hired a small boat to ferry them ashore. As this vessel came alongside the quay, rising and falling in the swell, Churchill reached out to grab an iron ring at precisely the moment the boat plunged downwards. He dislocated his right shoulder, and was to suffer from this injury for the rest of his life. (Ever afterwards, when playing polo, he had to strap his right arm to his body, swinging the mallet only from the elbow. Since he was similarly unable to swing a cavalry sabre, he adopted a Mauser pistol instead. He attributed his survival at the Battle of Omdurman to this circumstance.)

POLO IN BANGALORE

Bangalore was a popular posting. A soldier who was there some years later described it in a letter home:

> This place is known as the garden of India and is accepted as being one of the healthiest places in this country and suitable to British troops as the climate resembles a decent 'Blighty' [British]

summer and vegetation grows abundantly. Bangalore is divided into two parts: the Cantonment and the City. The former is composed mainly of camps for British troops, shops, municipal buildings and English residents. There are lovely walks, and the parks are just like England . . .

In Bangalore Churchill was, as he had expected, quickly bored. He and Barnes shared with another officer a 'chummery' (bachelor quarters), a pink stucco villa with an extensive rose garden, and had a small army of native butlers, valets and grooms.

An officer in another regiment, who was soon to begin a lifelong friendship with Churchill, viewed a similar posting with a less jaundiced eye. Hastings Ismay recalled that in his own cavalry regiment:

Sometimes there was a little office work to be done; sometimes we had a rifle inspection or a kit inspection or an inspection of saddlery; sometimes either a British or Indian officer gave a short lecture on a variety of topics, such as horse management or musketry. By lunch-time the day's work was over. Soldiering was not then the highly technical profession that it has become, and the afternoons were nearly always free to do whatever we wished. Most of us played polo three days a week, and schooled ponies on the other afternoons. In addition there were occasional race meetings at neighbouring stations, and rough shooting for all who wanted it. I could never help thinking, as I drew my admittedly meagre salary at the end of each month, that it was very odd that I should be paid anything at all for doing what I loved doing above all else.

This was probably the prevailing view among Churchill's colleagues, but he could not be content with such inactivity. He briefly took up butterfly collecting (there were beautiful specimens everywhere) but a rat ate his collection. He studied the newspapers, but their coverage of British politics was vague and inaccurate. He threw himself into regimental polo and began to take it very seriously.

In India the sheer lack of alternative amusements made polo a passion, and the 4th were determined to excel. They bought the entire stud of another regiment, the Poona Light Horse, and they played not two or three times a week but every day. They gained a trophy within a month of arriving in Bangalore, and conceived the ambition, regarded as absurd for such an inexperienced team, of winning within a few years the All-India Regimental Polo Tournament. Churchill trained hard and played well enough to be placed in the team, in spite of his injury.

With his regimental duties finished by noon and polo practice not until five o'clock, there was a good deal of spare time to fill every day. The afternoon was deliberately left clear so that troops would not have to work or parade during the hottest part of the day, and his comrades spent this time in sleeping, drinking or card-playing. Churchill used it to educate himself. He had brought to India a number of serious books and he was soon inundating his mother with requests for additions to this collection. It is well known that he studied Gibbon and Macaulay, modelling his own writing style on theirs, but he also read Henry Hallam's *Constitutional History of England*, Plato's *Republic* and Adam Smith's *Wealth of Nations*. To gain a solid grounding in recent British politics he asked for copies of the *Annual Register*, a yearly review of governmental business, covering the years from 1870 onwards (Lady Randolph complained that they cost 14 shillings each). These enabled him to familiarize himself not only with the political issues of the previous generation but with his father's ministerial career. When studying parliamentary debates, he formed his own opinions and reached his own conclusions before reading the outcome. His volumes were quickly filled with notes. A later prime minister, Sir Harold Wilson, paid tribute to the painstaking attention to detail involved in the course of study at Churchill's 'university of one':

> When he was twenty-one, he annotated a report on Stafford
> Northcote's 1876 Budget with a detailed fiscal commentary
> of his own, even urging taxation on unearned income. In 1897,
> from Bangalore, he sent his mother a comprehensive personal
> political manifesto covering electoral reform, India, imperialism,
> Europe – isolation for Britain on defence, the colonies;
> including significant extension of compulsory education
> and the franchise.

This was impressive, especially since his views on some of these issues obviously differed from those typical of his social class. However, he still lacked the guidance of tutors that university undergraduates would have had. More importantly, he had no opportunity to test his ideas through debate.

Sergeant Major Hallaway, who had earlier met Churchill as a newly joined Subaltern at Aldershot, remembered his studious nature while in India:

The great thing about him was the way he worked. He was busier than all the others put together. I never saw him without pencils sticking out all over him. Once, when I went to his bungalow, I could scarcely get in, what with books and papers and foolscap all over the place . . .

His fellow officers must have found his behaviour odd, as well as antisocial – a cardinal sin in that environment. It was reported that on one occasion during horseplay in the mess they had tried to squash him under a large sofa, but that he had struggled free and told them they would never succeed in keeping him down. Only his skill at polo must have earned their indulgence of his pronounced eccentricity.

Mr Churchill was easygoing and always ready for a joke. Not at all like some of the other officers. He hated to see chaps punished. The officers used to inspect the stables every day, and we never knew when they were coming. But Mr Churchill would whisper to me, ''leven-thirty, Sergeant Major'.

The drill manual explains the importance of this ritual inspection:

. . . the men will 'Fall in' in fatigue dress, by troops, with their grooming articles, and answer their names. The non-commissioned officers of troops report to the squadron sergeant major, who will report to the senior officer, when the command will be 'Right Turn – File in.' During stable hours no man is to stop grooming to clean his saddlery until his horse is passed as sufficiently groomed; at the 'Turn in' to morning stables all men are to help clean out stables or horse lines before commencing grooming. Officers are to watch the men grooming, and see that time is not wasted. To test the condition of a horse's coat, both as to cleanliness and health, it should be felt with the bare hand. Mane and tail should also be examined.

IN SEARCH OF A WAR: MALAKAND

This was not enough to keep Churchill in Bangalore. Restlessly he looked around for another war. There was one in progress between Greece and Turkey that would suit him because it was on his way home from India. He ordered his mother to make all necessary arrangements so that a newspaper commission would be waiting when he arrived, but he also made some enquiries himself. In response to his offer to cover the conflict, the *News Chronicle* showed some enthusiasm. They would not pay his expenses, but stated that:

> If you should visit the points of the island which are now attracting attention, and should find the material for, say, five letters of about a column and a half each, we should be willing to pay you for such correspondence at the rate of ten guineas a letter.

The war ended before anything came of this, but he had almost doubled his rate of pay since Cuba.

In fact, his next adventure was already on the horizon. On leave in England in the spring of 1897, he discovered while at Goodwood races that a punitive expedition was going to the North-West Frontier to quell unrest among the Pathan tribesmen. It would be commanded by Major General Sir Bindon Blood, whom Churchill had not only met but who had promised him a post with any such expedition. Churchill at once cut short his leave and returned to India to remind the General of his promise. He was too late. Vacancies in the Malakand Field Force were already filled. The

Expeditions to subdue recalcitrant tribesmen on India's lawless North-West Frontier were a frequent occurrence. To the danger from a skilled and savage enemy was added the difficulty of moving men and equipment long distances through inhospitable terrain.

General kindly suggested, however, that if Churchill could arrange a job as a correspondent, he would be welcome. After having his mother set the usual wheels in motion, and doing his best to arrange a commission with an Indian paper, he managed to gain a month's leave from his endlessly-patient colonel. He set off by train without knowing if he was employed.

Lady Randolph, having failed with *The Times*, had been luckier with the *Daily Telegraph*. They took him on, though at rates that he considered 'a fraud', and his own efforts had gained him a commission from the *Allahabad Pioneer*. He knew that being on the spot was what mattered. If any officer was killed or wounded, he would at once be able to replace them.

Commanders traditionally disliked civilian correspondents ('drunken swabs', as Kitchener called them), but at that time there was no major objection by the army to officers working as war correspondents – an attitude that would soon be altered by the hostility Churchill himself aroused. Some great writers on travel and conflict had simultaneously been serving as soldiers, most notably one of Churchill's boyhood heroes, Fred Burnaby, who, as well as being a politician and balloonist, had written entertaining travel books while commanding officer of the Royal Horse Guards. From an editor's point of view there were solid advantages in employing officers: they understood the technicalities of warfare; as part of the army they did not need to be fed or transported at the newspaper's expense; and if anything happened to them the government was responsible.

The North-West Frontier was a source of continual irritation to the British authorities in India. A remote and mountainous region bordering Afghanistan (it is now part of Pakistan), its fiercely independent tribesmen lived in fortified villages from which they could raid each others' cattle and defy government officials. A handbook written for young officers by Sir Andrew Skeen, a general experienced in frontier fighting, described the terrain and its inhabitants:

> What is the North-West Frontier like? The country and its
> fighting men? Not easy to answer. You can never find ground
> of the same nature for twenty miles on end. First, miles of cliff
> and stony slopes giving way to open fans of cultivation backed
> by steeps and sheer cliffs, narrow river gorges opening out of fir-
> covered mountains, which drop to swelling bush-covered hills or
> bare grazing grounds with patches of forest. Then open plains
> flanked by low, bare hills, and scored by deep ravines, after which
> you come to great bare hills . . .

The people differ less than the parts they live in. All are men to reckon with. All are apt in war, and taken all in all are probably the finest individual fighters in the east, really formidable, to despise whom means sure trouble. They have a great reputation for cunning, which really is based on great mobility on cliffs and steep slopes, marked ability, which their warring life fosters, to make use of ground, to hide their movements, and to protect them when not moving. Great patience, and intimate knowledge of the ground.

Mobility is a weak word for the tribesman's power of movement. In pursuit, where everything holds out promise of success, these fellows are wonderful. They come down hillsides like falling boulders, not running but bounding, and in crags they literally drop from foothold to foothold. To deal with such mobility on their own lines is impossible. These men are hard as nails; they live on little, carry nothing but a rifle and a few cartridges, a knife and a bit of food, and they are shod for quick and sure movement. Their power of moving concealed is astounding, not only in moving from cover to cover, but in slipping from light to shadow, and background to background. It has to be seen to be believed. And their stillness in cover is really striking.

And that brings me to the tribesman's patience. These folk have nothing to do but to watch for an opportunity. If it doesn't come one day, it is bound to come the next . . . And if, when it comes, it looks like being too costly, they are perfectly ready to put it off till a better chance comes. Remember, they have no work to do, no camp to get to, they have range upon range of hill to screen them for as long as they choose, and night has no terrors for them. They will return to the job day after day without anyone having an inkling of their presence, and then when the real chance comes they seize it like lightning. You can never train your men to the same pitch, but you can do a great deal . . .

Because this unrest was continuous, the army's punitive expeditions were frequent. There were no fewer than 34 of them between 1858 and 1897. Sometimes there would be one in two or three years, on other occasions two or three in one year. An alternative to these punishments was that tribes would receive 'subsidies' (i.e. bribes) to encourage good conduct, but they simply could not be tamed. The region was guarded by a network of forts and blockhouses, but these were easily attacked. The British response to any act of defiance was to enter the valleys in force, burn villages and have the tribesmen's fortifications – especially the stone towers they favoured – blown up by military engineers. The exercise always carried a high risk because troops were constantly exposed to hidden sharpshooters (Churchill informed his readers that they were called 'snipers' in the Anglo-Indian Army) higher up the slope. The tribesmen could often surround a British force and take a ghastly toll of the men as they retreated. Casualties tended to be high. General Skeen gave advice on the method of retreat:

> If the enemy have taken a good knock, the return will probably be quiet, but I should take all precautions and I advise you to. The commander has two great responsibilities. The first is to make his decision to withdraw as early as he can. Anything may hold the move up. The second is to direct the main lines of the withdrawal and not leave the troops to find their own way.
>
> The moment you learn the orders, fill up pouches if not already done, and send all animals back except those needed for actual fighting loads. Then dispose for covering fire in the withdrawal, if this has not been provided for by other troops, and if the enemy is close push him back.
>
> Train your men to move fast and to glance behind them from time to time – to see if a comrade is hit – and to see if the enemy swordsmen are rushing behind.

The crisis that brought about the Malakand expedition is described in an anonymous history of the 11th Sikh Regiment:

> On 26th July, 1897, a large force of tribesmen of Swat and Utman Khel, estimated at 1,000, suddenly attacked the fort of Chakdara. The garrison, consisting of two companies of the Regiment and forty sabres of the 11th Bengal Lancers, was closely besieged for seven days, during which time the enemy made repeated vigorous attacks on the walls of the fort, even using ladders to scale the walls, but were always defeated with great slaughter. On the first night of the siege the enemy had cut the telegraph communication with Malakand and the only means of signalling was from a spur on the hill near [the] signal tower outside the fort. Repeatedly during the first three days the signallers with great gallantry had run out, regardless of the murderous fire, and had endeavoured to send a message for help. Each time they had been forced back with casualties. On the third day Prem Singh

ran out alone, set up his helio and signalled the words 'Help us' before his helio was smashed by a bullet, and he succeeded in returning to the tower unhurt. At 10.30 p.m. the Fort at Malakand was also suddenly attacked by a thousand tribesmen . . .

The fighting lasted a week. Whatever the danger in which the Chakdara garrison had found themselves, the Indian Army suffered only five dead and ten wounded, while their opponents lost between two and four thousand.

Sir Bindon Blood, describing the outbreak of the rebellion, explained other reasons for the savagery of the tribesmen:

The Malakand position is at the top of the Malakand Pass and consists of a strong central castle, built by the Graeco-Buddhists, perhaps over 2,000 years ago, modernized by us, and proof against attack without artillery. Secondly there was in 1897 a considerable outside area of sepoys' 'lines', commissariat stores, bazaar, engineer park, political agents' headquarters, etc. etc. very inefficiently protected, especially against a surprise attack by night . . .

The garrison of the Lower Swat area, in which these poorly fortified positions were situated, consisted of a Brigade of all arms, comprising three battalions, one company of sappers, one squadron of Guides Cavalry, one Mountain Battery and one company of Sappers (military engineers), all of the native army.

All the tribesmen of the districts near the Malakand were very fanatical and very hostile to the British at all times; while in July 1897 they were unfavourably affected by the disturbances elsewhere on the Frontier; and consequently there was need for exceptional military vigilance and precaution in Lower Swat.

Moreover it was notorious that in July 1897, several holy men were doing their best to stir up trouble in various places near the Malakand, especially one fakir known as the 'Mad Mullah', who according to reports received by the Political Agent at the Malakand, had established himself in Upper Swat about twelve miles off, before the 26th July, and on that day was advancing into Lower Swat.

Now the 26th of July was a polo day at the Malakand, and on that evening the usual game was played on ground near the village of Khar in the Swat Valley, three miles or so from the Fort.

It was noticed that quite an unusual crowd of spectators came to look on at the game. As a matter of fact these were the 'Mad Mullah's' advance fighting men, passing the time until it was dark and they could begin an attack on the Malakand position! They behaved as spectators in the most perfect manner and did not interfere with anyone . . .

All remained calm until 9.45 p.m., when a telegram came from Chakdara reporting that large bodies of tribesmen were moving down the valley evidently to attack the British positions. A few minutes later the Chakdara wire was cut, but further news came in that the 'Mad Mullah' was at Khar, three miles off, and that his men were swarming up the hill to the attack of the Malakand. Of course the garrison was turned out at once, but most of the more or less open areas in the position were penetrated in the attacks; these began immediately and were kept up in a determined manner till daylight next morning, the 27th, when the enemy drew off, but kept up a desultory fire all day. They repeated this arrangement of determined night attacks and day withdrawals regularly until the 31st.

Sir Bindon led his troops into the Mahmund country during September, and described the impression that was made by Churchill on the members of the Force:

When I returned from Upper Swat at the end of August, I had found my young friend (in his early twenties then) Winston Churchill, of the 4th Queen's Own Hussars, who joined me as an extra A.D.C. – and a right good one he was!

I sent for Churchill and suggested his joining General Jeffreys in order to see a little fighting. He was all for it, so I sent him over at once and he saw more fighting than I expected, and very hard fighting too! He was personally engaged in some very serious work in a retirement, and did excellent service with a party of Sikhs to which he carried an order, using a rifle which he borrowed from a severely wounded man.

The Colonel of the Sikh regiment asked for him to be attached in place of one of his officers who had been invalided, and he was useful for several weeks, though he knew only a few words of the language. The Sikhs took to him at once, recognizing immediately that his heart was in the right place.

Not everyone was so impressed. The correspondent Lionel James remembered that:

He was a rather tempestuous youth with a ready tongue that was much given to laying down the law. Soldiers smiled at him, and said that he had been spoiled by the Colonel of his regiment, who had given him more rope than was good for a subaltern.

Churchill's adventures could still sound something of a holiday lark, but this encounter was horrifying. The Pathans were without mercy, and the scramble to rescue wounded from tribesmen who were only feet away will have been one of the most dangerous of his life. He wrote to his mother:

When the retirement began I remained till the last and here I was perhaps very near my end. This retirement was an awful rout in which the wounded were left to be cut up horribly by these wild beasts. I was close to both officers when they were hit and fired my revolver at a man at 31 yards who tried to cut up poor Hughes' body. He dropped but came on again. A subaltern and I carried a wounded sepoy for some distance and might perhaps, if there had been any gallery, have received some notice. We also remained until the enemy came within 40 yards firing our revolvers. They actually threw stones at us. It was a horrible business. I felt no excitement and very little fear. All the excitement went out when things became really deadly. Later on I used a rifle which a wounded man had dropped and fired 40 rounds with some effect at close quarters. I cannot be sure, but I think I hit 4 men . . .

Sir Bindon has made me his orderly officer, so I shall get a medal and perhaps a couple of clasps . . .

Churchill was later to describe this fighting not only in his history of the campaign but also in his later memoir, *My Early Life*. A copy of this, held by the Imperial War Museum, was read in 1946 by General Sir Hubert Gough, who witnessed the campaign. Gough has left a number of pertinent observations in the form of comments pencilled in the book's margins, and these suggest that the fighting was not as savage, or as exciting, as the young author had claimed.

Where the attack on the Chakdara fort is described, Churchill says: 'The tribesmen broke through the walls, or clambered through the roofs, firing and stabbing . . . A third of the sappers and gunners were casualties, and nearly all the mules were streaming with blood . . .' Gough's marginal remark is: 'This is a hell of a story but I never heard it before and I was in India at the time. I wonder how much is journalistic exaggeration?'

And where Churchill writes about a withdrawal under heavy fire 'Hundreds of soldiers and thousands of animals were shot [in] the retreat . . . It looked more like a rout than the victorious withdrawal of a punitive force.' Gough snorts: 'Bunk. Pure fabrication. I was there with the transport animals. There was the capture of Dargai and one or two picquet fights but otherwise little fighting and few casualties.'

The campaign continued into October, but before it had ended a second expedition – the Tirah Field Force – set out to deal with further tribal unrest. Wasting no time, Churchill did his utmost to be attached to this too. Sir Ian Hamilton, who served in the Force, remembered that:

> In 1897 Winston got leave from his Regiment and had managed to take part in the Malakand Campaign where he did very well. When the operations of that Force came to an end, he hoped to join the Expeditionary Force for Tirah; but his Commanding Officer thought otherwise and ordered him to return.
>
> Characteristically, Winston had set his heart on sampling this, the most dangerous, disagreeable and thankless task in the whole military box of tricks. Sir William Lockhart was still with the bulk of the Force but under pressure from Simla (e.g. the Viceroy), who were sick of the expense of the whole business, he had patched up a peace with the Maliks or heads of the Afridi tribe. Under the terms they had surrendered some thousands of their rifles, most of them captured or stolen from us, and were being given umpteen heavy bags of silver to induce them to go on pretending they had been defeated. Then it was that Winston, who with his brother officers of the 4th Hussars had fitted themselves out with a splendid team of ponies and had been working like fiends to win the all-India polo tournament, wired me from Meerut, 600 miles away, begging me to fix him an interview with Sir William Lockhart. Sir William agreed and Winston managed to persuade him to take him on as an extra aide-de-camp. Hardly had he done so when Sir William was recalled to Simla to take up his duties as Commander-in-Chief. And there was Winston! Really it was enough to make a cat laugh.

The outbreak of peace and the promotion of the expedition's commanding officer had deprived Churchill of another medal. There was nothing for it but to return to polo and garrison duties. However, this time his dispatches could be used as the basis for a book, and he quickly got to work. *The Story of the Malakand Field Force* was written in the space of five weeks. It was sent to England to be published (the arrangements were left to a brother-in-law of Lady Randolph) and it appeared in March 1898 as a volume of 300 pages. He was horrified to find that it had not been proof-read and that the text was therefore riddled with errors. In spite of this, it had considerable success, and he received enthusiastic letters from the Prince of Wales and the Prime Minister, Lord Salisbury. As if this was not enough, he was able to publish in the book the 'Mention in Dispatches' – the permanent record of praise by a commanding officer that ranks just below a medal:

> Brigadier-General Jeffreys . . . has praised the courage and resolution of Lieutenant W.L.S. Churchill, 4th Hussars, the correspondent of the *Pioneer* newspaper with the Force, who made himself useful at a critical moment.

Professor Manfred Weidhorn accurately describes some of the emerging characteristics of Churchill's style:

> In a sense Churchill the author was born, like Athena, fully mature. We find already in his early works many of the ideas and structural devices, as well as the sophistication of style, humour and imagery, that were to mark his writing through the decades. His conversion of the dispatches, for instance, into a consecutive narrative . . . was to become in most of his works a systematic compilation of original documents for the sake of authenticity.
>
> The result is that peculiar blend of journalism and memoir that was [later] to characterize his world war books . . . Incidents are recorded because they occur to Churchill, whose career and experiences are, he thinks, the most interesting in the world and will remain at, or be imposed upon, the centre of his many books.

At the same moment that he began participating in war, he began to describe it. His ability to do this ensured that his own role in events and his own interpretation of them would shape public perception of him.

5
OMDURMAN, 1898

Churchill had already seen more action than any of his contemporaries in the 4th Hussars, but for him the old saying 'ambition knows no repose' was literally true. He was not seeking military glory or promotion, as his comrades would have done, so much as the basis of a national reputation to launch him in public life in England. To do this he needed to serve not in a frontier expedition but in a major campaign that would attract wide public interest at home. Of all the operations involving the British Army in the last years of the 19th century, none promised greater opportunities than the Anglo-Egyptian force that would descend on the Sudan under the command of Lord Kitchener.

This would be a bigger and more significant operation than the previous year's fighting in India, and it also held enormous patriotic, political and emotional potential. The completion of Kitchener's re-conquest of the Sudan would settle an old score, for it would avenge the death of General Gordon more than a decade earlier and eliminate a continuing threat to Britain's security in the Middle East. This promised to be a moment of national vindication. To be 'in at the kill' would be a valuable and interesting military experience and, no matter how events fell out, would provide material for another book, or at least a series of articles.

Similar books on other campaigns had proved popular. Public interest in the expedition and its climax – the final showdown with an army of vicious and fearsome religious fanatics – was guaranteed. Churchill was already known to a wide readership as an author gifted in describing topography and military operations. If he could reach the theatre of conflict, as reporter or soldier or both, he could produce a vivid narrative that would generate further fame and income.

THE CAMPAIGN
The Sudan, a huge, empty and barren desert region south of Egypt, had come to be regarded by Whitehall as a major nuisance. It was under the control of Egypt, which was itself a fiefdom of the Ottoman Empire though

nominally ruled by a local viceroy, the Khedive. In practical terms, Egypt was run by France and Britain, the two powers that controlled the Suez Canal, and the latter had by far the greatest financial, administrative and military influence. If the Sudan was volatile, the stability of Egypt and the security of the canal were under threat, for it controlled the headwaters of the Nile.

The region had had a number of incompetent or rapacious governors. It was administered by corrupt officials and oppressed by tax collectors. Its people were vulnerable to kidnap by roaming slave traders. When in 1881 a Moslem teacher named Mohammed Ahmed Ibn al-Seyyid Abdullah proclaimed himself the Mahdi, or Messiah, and preached violent rebellion against the Egyptian authorities, local desperation and anger produced many recruits. More significantly, he won the allegiance of a number of warlike Sudanese tribes – seasoned, aggressive fighters whose skill and cohesion made his army a formidable military force. He created a body of militant Islamic fundamentalists of a type well known to the 21st century. His disciples, called 'dervishes' (poor men, or mendicants) inflicted several crushing defeats on Egyptian and Anglo-Egyptian forces. Each triumph brought more followers, more captured weaponry and more renown. Two British commanders, 'Hicks Pasha' and Valentine Baker, were killed in battle against Mahdist troops, which by 1884 had made the southern Sudan ungovernable.

As an enemy, the dervishes were terrifying. The sight of one of their formations, strung out across a wide front, advancing at a trot amid a storm of yelling and a thicket of bright banners, with the sun glinting menacingly on their spear points, must have won the reluctant awe of the most hardened European soldier. For half-trained Egyptians, it was often enough to cause fatal panic. The dervishes' wild, long hair, which flowed behind them or stuck upward in greased, outlandish coifs, gave them an appearance of implacable savagery. They were courageous warriors, and this courage was buttressed by the belief that the coloured patches on their white jibbahs (loose cotton tunics) had the power to ward off bullets; despite copious evidence to the contrary, they continued in this conviction until their final battle. They were well disciplined, controlled and directed by mounted officers. Their principal weapons were swords, often of medieval design, and spears with broad, leaf-shaped points. They also made wide use of captured firearms and even had artillery. They were thorough and effective in close-quarter fighting, spearing, slashing and chopping until their opponents were wiped out, and they hacked victims into unrecognizable gore. Expecting no mercy when defeated, they gave none when victorious. They routinely massacred women and children, non-combatants and the wounded. Though their leaders sometimes observed civilized practices (they might allow a truce party to enter their camp, or keep a European prisoner without putting him to death) they were not a foe with whom there could be negotiation.

Britain's Liberal Prime Minister, William Gladstone, was averse to any imperial adventure and did not want to spend British funds or lives in defending the Sudan. His government decided to abandon the region to the rebels by evacuating the Egyptian garrisons and foreign residents. Gordon, who had already served as governor general, was persuaded to return to the capital, Khartoum, in February 1884 and resume his former position, without any military support. His task was to supervise the withdrawal while providing whatever stability his name and prestige could command. Instead he made preparations for the defence of the city, strengthening walls and recruiting a local military force. He also tried to buy off the Mahdi by granting him the title of Sultan and proclaiming the territories he occupied independent of Egypt and the Ottomans.

It didn't work, and when northern tribes joined the revolt and cut the telegraph wires, Khartoum was isolated and besieged. Though the inhabitants held out, the plight of Gordon created a steadily mounting sense of alarm in Britain. Gladstone, whose instructions to withdraw had been ignored by Gordon, came under increasing attack as press and public demanded the sending of an expedition to rescue him. In the event, it was nearly six months before a force of 6,000 was assembled and dispatched. Even after arriving in Egypt, their progress was agonizingly slow. Instead of travelling via the Red Sea, the army journeyed 1,250 miles up the Nile in whale boats. They had to be rowed against the current, as well as manhandled over the cataracts.

Khartoum held out for 317 days, but this was not enough. By the time the first British vessels appeared offshore on 28 January 1885, it was two days since the city had been put to the sword. Somewhere among the burned-out ruins and piled corpses was Gordon, whose head had been carried off as a trophy.

Winston Churchill was 11 when these events occurred, but he will never have forgotten the tide of shame and fury that swept the country in the wake of Gordon's death. Nor, as the son of a prominent Tory, will he have had any doubt as to the culpability of the Liberals. Odium was heaped on the Prime Minister by all sections of the public; Queen Victoria wrote in her diary: 'The Government alone is to blame' and told Gladstone that 'to think all this might have been prevented and many precious lives saved by earlier action is too frightful'. This was a national insult that could not be left unpunished, and the Conservatives reaped the benefit of the country's belligerent mood; within a matter of months Lord Salisbury had ousted Gladstone's Liberals at the polls.

Although it was to be more than a decade before a full-scale military operation was launched to crush the dervishes, the war, in fact, 'never went away'. The Mahdi, like Gordon, had died in 1885 but a disciple, or 'Khalifa', took his place as leader and maintained the fanaticism and aggression of the Mahdist warriors. During those years they fought seven battles against Anglo-Egyptian forces, losing all of them. The Egyptian Army, led by Herbert Kitchener (who was appointed 'Sirdar', or commander-in-chief of the Khedive's troops), was recreated as a more efficient body. Its Sudanese units fought well under British command, their discipline balancing the ferocity of their opponents. Kitchener also had a military railway built into the Sudan so that troops and supplies did not need to depend for movement on the lengthy meanderings of the Nile or the measured, unhurried tread of camel trains.

By the end of 1896 they had occupied the Sudanese province of Dongola. The force was clearly in no hurry to strike the knockout blow at the rebels. They travelled south, slowly and methodically, laying railway tracks, consolidating positions, destroying or driving off opposition when it appeared. This process continued through the whole of 1897 and the first half of the following year, but by that time the end was in sight. In April 1898 they decisively beat a dervish force at Atbara. From there the way was open to their next objective, the city of Omdurman. This lay across the Nile from the ruins of Khartoum. It was the site of the Mahdi's elaborate mausoleum, which made it holy to the dervishes. There, if not before, the biggest and probably the last battle would take place against the largest force the Khalifa could muster. Kitchener's plans had long been made. The Royal Navy would bring gunboats up river to add firepower to an army of over 25,000 British and Egyptian troops. The War Office in London had been asked for the reinforcements necessary to make up this number.

This was the situation when Lieutenant Churchill came home from India for three months' leave, and he lost no time in mobilizing his mother's formidable social and political network. He had been trying for two years to get in on the Sudan expedition, in order to see action and win medals instead of languishing on garrison duty. He knew that, even with all the help his connections would afford him, his chances of acceptance were slim. The Sirdar required a division of infantry and a brigade of artillery, but only a single regiment of cavalry. Kitchener, who emphatically disliked Churchill, had absolute control over which officers went with the expedition. Nor was there the option of travelling with the army as a journalist: well aware of the news potential of the campaign, the national papers had long since assigned correspondents.

Nevertheless, he did not give up. Writing to Lord Salisbury, who had once made him a general offer of assistance, Churchill was disarmingly frank about his motives:

> I am vy anxious to go to Egypt and to proceed to Khartoum with the expedition. It is not my intention, under any circumstances to stay in the army long. I want to go, first, because the recapture of Khartoum will be a historic event: second, because I can, I anticipate, write a book about it which will from a monetary, as well as from other points of view, . . . be useful to me.

Not even the Prime Minister was able to help him, but in the event it was his social connections that bore fruit. It transpired that while Kitchener's will was unchallengeable within the Egyptian Army, he did not have absolute say regarding officers sent out from Britain. His high-handedness was resented by the Adjutant General, Sir Evelyn Wood, and Churchill's appointment owed much to this. The death of an officer created a vacancy with the 21st Lancers and energetic lobbying gained this for Churchill, though it was made clear to him that, attached as a supernumerary lieutenant, he would travel entirely at his own expense and that the regiment would not take care of him if he were wounded.

Once in Egypt he tried to avoid the Sirdar, but Kitchener was soon aware of his presence and a comment was reported back to him that showed how well his nature and motives were understood:

> Kitchener said he had known I was not going to stay in the army – was only making a convenience of it; that he disapproved of my coming in place of others whose professions were at stake.

It appears that Kitchener was not the only one to dislike the expedition's new member. Churchill had been foisted on the 21st Lancers, and it is likely that his manner irritated them as much as it did everyone else. This may be why he sought the company of writers more than soldiers. Lionel James, a *Times* correspondent, remembered:

> During the stay at Atbara the [journalists'] Mess never dined less than eight. One of the most frequent guests was Winston

By the time he arrived in Egypt in the summer of 1898, Churchill had decided to leave the army for politics, and expected this to be his last campaign. He felt that this large-scale expedition would prove a suitably glorious climax to his career as a soldier and correspondent.

Churchill who, though attached to the 21st Lancers, seemed to prefer the Correspondents' corner to his own bivouac.

The same observer went on to say:

I made several marches in company with Winston Churchill. The 21st Lancers had a down on this ambitious young subaltern, who had been attached to them for the campaign. In order to mark this displeasure some one in authority was small-minded enough to put the future Minister in charge of the Officers' Mess caravan, which consisted of an overladen mule and two donkeys. Far from being chagrined at this duty Churchill was amused. 'These are little people,' he said of his superiors as he urged the mess servants to keep the cortège moving, 'I can afford to laugh at them. They will live to see the mistake they have made!'

On 1 September, Kitchener's gunboats and artillery were close enough to shell the town of Omdurman. Before nightfall, the Anglo-Egyptian troops had deployed in a wide arc, facing outwards, with its two ends on the riverbank covered by gunboats, and a 'zariba' had been built (a high protective barricade of thorn bushes) to shelter the army and its equipment from sudden attack. Lieutenant Ronald Meiklejohn describes the events of the afternoon:

> We heard the guns in the distance and everybody cheered
> up promptly. Our cavalry sighted some 400 horsemen and
> 1,000 infantry about 8 miles ahead of us. We were just getting
> some lunch when we saw a gunboat returning at full speed. It
> brought news that the whole dervish army was massing outside
> Omdurman, and meant to attack. We hastily bolted a little food,
> packed up and fell in by 2 p.m. Then the whole army marched
> out, and took up position in a huge semi-circle, and sat down
> and waited. The two British Brigades held the left, or south,
> side of the semi-circle, the 2nd Brigade being on our left and
> extending to the river bank, since it was anticipated that the main
> attack would come from there.
>   . . . The 21st Lancers reported some 60,000 or more of the
> enemy were halted just outside Omdurman, and apparently
> drilling. The Lancers had picquets on a hill south of us, whence
> they could see Omdurman . . .

Churchill was one of those watching from the hilltop. Across the spreading plain he saw the moving dark mass of the Khalifa's forces, approaching rapidly and in perfectly ordered lines across the arid, buff-coloured landscape. He reported to Kitchener that the enemy could arrive within an hour and that the battle might therefore begin very shortly.

The dervishes did not strike that day, however, and as darkness fell the army made ready in case of a night attack. There was some opportunity for relaxation and Meiklejohn spent the evening with several of those who would make the famous charge the next day. His account continues:

> The 21st Lancers withdrew from Signal Hill at dusk to inside
> the zariba. Captain Caldecott, Grenfell and Etches came and we
> all had a chat. The two former declared that we should not have
> a fight at all, but a naval officer from one of the gunboats, who
> joined us, said: 'If you fellows had seen what I saw this afternoon

you'd think differently'. Caldecott laughed and remarked that the [enemy] would all bolt during the night, to which the reply was, 'Well, if you are alive this time tomorrow you will have a different opinion of these dervishes'. Both Caldecott and Grenfell were killed, and Etches wounded . . .

Then Winston Churchill, who was attached to the 21st, strolled up and we had a long talk. He was far less argumentative and self-assertive than usual. He said the enemy had a huge force, and if they attacked during the night it would be 'touch and go' about the result. A massed attack against the Gyppies or Soudanese would probably break through, with highly unpleasant results . . .

In fact, the dervishes encamped for the night. Churchill and one of his comrades went for a walk along the riverbank and were hailed by a naval officer aboard a gunboat offshore. The young man threw them a bottle of champagne, which Churchill retrieved from the shallow water. This was his first meeting with David Beatty, who was to win fame as an admiral in the Great War.

THE BATTLE

Before daylight the next morning – exactly a year since he had come under fire in India – Churchill was back on patrol, viewing the Mahdist army from the same hilltop where he had sat the previous afternoon. They were once again advancing, at the familiar jog-trot, the sound of their voices reduced by distance to an angry hum. There had been no formal start to the battle; it would begin as soon as they were in range of Kitchener's guns. One of the enemy's own scouting parties came within 400 yards of his patrol and opened fire. He and his men were hastily ordered inside the zariba. As the momentum built up, George Teigh, a private in the Lincolnshire Regiment, described the scene:

We are now formed up waiting for them. It is about 6 a.m. There has been firing going on since daybreak. The Dervishes are advancing and have been in sight for about half an hour; the shells started bursting. The artillery started first, and then we started about 7 a.m. and the whole force are now engaged . . .

Another witness, Ronald Meiklejohn, recalled the bravado that mingled with tension when the clash was only minutes away:

We had finished off our work, and were chatting, when suddenly a subdued, but general, exclamation of surprise made us look up. We saw a really wonderful sight. All along the crests of the high ground to our right . . . a solid black multitude of men began to appear for over two miles all along the crest line, in considerable depth, while we heard distant shouts and war-cries. Soon after another mass appeared over Signal Hill ridge, and along the British front . . . Caldecott exclaimed: 'That's the best sight I've ever seen!' I remarked that it looked like being a big fight, and he said he did not suppose all of us would get through it.

General Gatacre came riding round and remarked, 'You look very fierce, Captain Caldecott.' He then pointed to a huge black flag (the Khalifa's personal standard) in the middle of the dervish line and said, 'I mean to have that flag before long.'

Meanwhile the enemy forces were moving forward fairly quickly. Then suddenly slowed down, made a really very orderly 'right wheel', then deployed into one huge and nearly uninterrupted line, and came straight at us.

Earle, our Adjutant, came galloping up and shouted, 'Get into your places please, Gentlemen, the show is starting!,' and we took up our stations . . .

War correspondent GW Steevens, who had met the dervishes before, described the moment when it became clear that the storm was about to burst:

A shiver of expectancy ran through our army, and then a sigh of content. They were coming on. Allah help them! They were coming on.

After all the years of preparation and the months of marching and waiting, the moment had come.

Kitchener was astonished that they should make a frontal attack on a well-equipped army in a strong defensive position. Their determination to do so put their annihilation beyond doubt; the matter could now be settled quickly, and with minimal casualties to the Sirdar's troops. Lieutenant Meiklejohn continued:

When the enemy were about 3,000 yards from us we were almost startled as our artillery opened fire. The first shell burst a little short, but the second fell amongst them. Then the gunboats joined in, and white puffs of shrapnel showed up all over the enemy mass . . .

Suddenly they seemed to halt for a moment or two. A cloud of smoke came from them and an enormous rattle of musketry. I personally, and I think most of us, held my breath for a moment, expecting to hear a hail of bullets, but nearly all fell short, causing dust-spurts well in front of the zariba, or passing over very high. They were now coming on fairly fast, firing every description of weapon, and I saw one man of the Seaforths go down, then another.

Now the Sirdar's army opened fire and the dervishes, carried on by fanaticism and their own momentum, ran straight into a blistering fusillade that cut to shreds their well-ordered ranks. GW Steevens described how:

They came very fast, and they came very straight; and then presently they came no farther. With a crash the bullets leapt out of the British rifles. It began with the Guards and Warwicks – section volleys at 2,000 yards; then, as the Dervishes edged rightward, it ran along to the Highlanders, the Lincolns, and to Maxwell's Brigade. The British stood up in double rank behind their zariba; the [Sudanese troops] lay down in their shelter-trench; both poured out death as fast as they could load and press trigger. Shrapnel whistled and Maxims growled savagely. From all the line came perpetual fire, fire, fire, and shrieked forth in great gusts of destruction.

And the enemy? No white troops would have faced that torrent of death for five minutes, but the blacks came on. The torrent swept into them and hurled them down in whole companies. The line was yet unbroken, but it was quite still. But other lines gathered up again, again, and yet again; they went down, and yet others rushed on. Sometimes they came near enough to see single features quite plainly. One old man with a white flag started with five comrades; all dropped, but he alone came bounding on within 200 yards of the 14th Sudanese. Then he folded his arms across his face, and his limbs loosened, and he dropped sprawling to earth beside his flag.

It was the last day of Mahdism, and the greatest. They could never get near, and they refused to hold back. By now the ground was all white with dead men's drapery. Rifles grew red-hot; the soldiers seized them by the slings and dragged them back to the reserve to change for cool ones. It was not a battle, but an execution.

In the middle of it all you were surprised to find that we were losing men. The crash of our own fire was so prodigious that we could not hear their bullets whistle; yet they came and swooped down and found victims . . . so that while you might have thought you were at a shoot of rabbits, you suddenly heard the sharp cry, 'Bearer Party there, quick', and a man was being borne rearward. Few went down, but there was a steady trickle to hospital.

The losses on his own side were inconsiderable in comparison with the 'awful slaughter' of the dervishes:

If they still came on our men needed only time and ammunition and strength to point a rifle to kill them off to the very last man. Only by now – small wonder – they were not coming on. They were not driven back, they were all killed in coming on. One section of fire after another hushed, and at eight o'clock the plain [was] still again. The last shell had burst over the last visible group of Dervishes; now there was nothing but the unbending, grimly expectant line before Agaiga (the riverbank village inside the zariba) and the still carpet of white in front.

We waited half an hour or so, and then the sudden bugle called us to our feet. 'Advance', it cried, 'to Omdurman!' added we.

Movement was slow. We passed over a corner of the field of fire, and saw for certain what awful slaughter we had done. The bodies were not in heaps – bodies hardly ever are; but they spread evenly over acres and acres. And . . . you hardly saw a black; nearly all the dead had the high forehead and taper cheeks of the Arab. Some lay composedly, with their slippers placed under their heads for a last pillow; some knelt, cut short in the middle of a last prayer. Others were torn to pieces, vermilion blood already drying on brown skin, killed instantly beyond doubt. Others again, seemingly as dead as these, sprang up as we approached, and rushed savagely, hurling spears at the nearest enemy. They were bayoneted or shot.

Even in defeat there was no end to their proud defiance. Steevens described them as:

> . . . death-enamoured desperadoes, strolling one by one towards the rifles, pausing to shake a spear, turning aside to recognise a corpse, then, caught by a sudden jet of fury, bounding forward, checking, sinking, limply to the ground. Now under the black flag in a ring of bodies stood only three men, facing the three thousand of the Third Brigade. They folded their arms about the staff and gazed steadily forward. Two fell. The last Dervish stood up and filled his chest; he shouted the name of his God and hurled his spear. Then he stood quite still, waiting. It took him full; he quivered, gave at the knees, and toppled with his head on his arms and his face towards the legions of his conquerors . . .

Cavalry had had no role in the battle, which the Lancers had watched from behind the British positions. Now that it was over, it seemed unlikely they would see any action other than in helping to clear up. Churchill had seen the 'historic event' he had sought, and had a number of graphic images to record. He would doubtless write another book, and would qualify for another campaign medal.

THE CHARGE

But it was not quite over. The dervish survivors were streaming back towards the city and Kitchener did not want them to reach it. At 8.30 he sent a signal to the 21st: 'Annoy them as far as possible on their flank & head them off if possible from Omdurman.' They set out to perform this task (it is not difficult for fresh men and horses to control exhausted troops on foot) with no expectation that it would be other than routine. Bennet Burleigh, another war correspondent, told what happened:

> . . . the 21st Lancers trotted out towards Jebel Surgham to make sure there were no large bodies of the enemy in hiding. Keeping close to the river, and avoiding the main field of battle, they passed to the east of the hill. Part of their duty was to check, if possible, any attempt of the enemy to fall back into Omdurman, or at least delay such an operation.
>
> Great numbers of scattered dervishes were seen, some of whom fired at the troopers. Keeping on until about half a mile or more south of Surgham, a small party of dervish cavalry, about thirty,

and what was thought to be a few footmen, were seen hiding in a depression or khor. Colonel Martin determined to push the party back and interpose his regiment between them and Omdurman. A few spattering shots came from the khor, as the four squadrons formed in line to charge.

'A' squadron, under Major Finn, was on the right, next it was 'B' squadron, commanded by Major Fowle. On the left of 'B' was 'D', or the made-up squadron, led by Captain Eadon, and 'C' squadron, under Captain Doyne, was on the extreme left.

Churchill was in 'A' Squadron. One of his men, Private Wade Rix, had a clear recollection of events:

We had taken no active part in the battle and so far had no idea if we would or no. At about 8.30 a.m. there was a lull in the battle. Then we noticed that there was some activity amongst our officers and we soon learned that General Kitchener had given orders that we were to move out and make for Omdurman to prevent the dervishes from occupying the town. We tightened the girth on our horses, looked to our arms, mounted and were away within minutes.

Two patrols scouted ahead to make sure that our path, which passed between the hill ebel Surgham and the river, was clear of the enemy. We had barely covered a couple of miles when the patrols came galloping back to report, enemy ahead. The regiment continued at a walk when suddenly we came under sporadic fire. It came from a line of kneeling dervishes, I should say they numbered about 100, then the bullets began to fly and several men and horses were hit. The Colonel had to make a quick decision, ignore this enemy group and push on to Omdurman or dispose of this group first. He took the latter course and the trumpet call 'right wheel into line' gave the answer.

As we completed the movement the trumpet sounded 'trot'. Now here are 400 cavalry men, facing an enemy shooting to kill, there is nothing that will stop them from digging their spurs in and urging the horses into a gallop. The die is cast and down go the lances into the 'engage infantry' position. The galloping horses, beating hooves and the flying bullets produced an increased awareness of the action, a mixture of excitement and

fear as we raced on towards the enemy. But what is this, 100
yards to go and before us an alarming sight presents itself. A dry
stream bed is crammed with hundreds of dervishes who were
hidden and waiting for the kill. Too late, it's a trap, nothing for it
now, must go on, and on we go.

As my horse leapt the deep depression my lance entered the
left eye of a white robed figure who had raised his double-edged
sword to strike. The enormous impact and the weight of the
man's body shattered the lance and I cast the broken pieces from
me. I quickly drew my sword just in time as another man pointed
his flintlock. I struck him down and blood splattered his white
robe. Then it was parry and thrust as I spurred my horse on
through the melee. Luck was with us, the horse bravely scrambled
up the opposite bank of the stream bed and we were through
without a scratch.

Bennet Burleigh also saw what happened, though his account was
assembled after the event:

Leading the regiment forward at a gallop from a point 300 yards
away, the Lancers dashed at the enemy, who at once opened a
sharp musketry fire upon our troopers.

A few casualties occurred before the dervishes were reached, but
the squadrons closed in and setting the spurs into their horses
rushed headlong for the enemy. In an instant it was seen that,
instead of 200 men, the 21st had been called upon to charge
nearly 1500 fierce Mahdists concealed in a narrow, but in places
deep [dry watercourse]. In corners the enemy were packed nearly
fifteen deep. Down a three-foot drop went the Lancers. There was
a moment or so of wild work, thrusting of steel, lance, and sword,
and rapid revolver shooting. Somehow the regiment struggled
through, and up the bank on the south side. Nigh a score of
lances had been left in dervish bodies, some broken, others intact.
Lieutenant Wormwald made a point at a fleeing Baggara, but his
sabre bent and had to be laid aside. Captain Fair's sword snapped
over dervish steel, and he flung the hilt in his opponent's face.
Major Finn used his revolver, missing but two out of six shots.
Colonel Martin rode clean through without a weapon in his hand.
Then the regiment rallied 200 yards beyond the slope. Probably
80 dervishes had been cut or knocked down by the shock. But the

few seconds' bloody work had been almost equally disastrous for the Lancers. Lieutenant R. Grenfell and fifteen men had been left dead in the khor. It so happened that the squadrons on the two wings ('A' was one of these) had comparatively easy going and did not strike the densest groups of the enemy. Squadrons 'D' and 'B' fared badly, and particularly Lieutenant Grenfell's troop, of whom ten men fell with that officer. In their front was a high rough bank of boulders, almost impassible for a horse. They were cut down and hacked by the enemy. His brother, Lieutenant H.M. Grenfell, subsequently recovered his watch, which had been thrust through by a dervish lance point and had stopped at 8.40 a.m. Young Robert Grenfell was probably struck from behind with a Mahdist sword blade, and killed instantly as his charger was endeavouring to scramble up the wall of stones and rock. Mêlées were taking place to right and left, every trooper having any difficulty in getting out of the khor being instantly surrounded by mounted dervishes and footmen. Lieutenant Nesham in leading his troop was savagely attacked. His helmet was cut off his head, and he was wounded severely upon the left forearm and right leg. The bridle reins of his charger were cut, but he piloted the animal safely through. 'B' and 'D' squadrons lost respectively nine killed and eleven wounded, and seven killed and eight wounded. Lieutenant Molyneux, R.H.G., had his horse knocked over. He called to a trooper not to leave him, and the man replied, 'All right, sir, I wont leave you.' Together they had a busy time. Two dervishes attacked the Lieutenant; he shot one, but the other cut him over the right arm, causing him to drop his revolver. He then ran for it and got away. Lieutenants Brinton and Pirie received wounds. Private Ives of 'A' squadron picked up a wounded comrade in the nullah, and got chased and separated from his regiment. He reached the infantry covered with his comrade's blood. The latter was killed, but Ives was not seriously hurt.

Churchill, of course, provided his own version of the action. As the dervishes were sighted:

> . . . the trumpet sounded 'Right wheel into line', and all the 16 troops swung round towards the [enemy] riflemen. Almost immediately the regiment broke into a gallop . . .
> The fire was too hot to allow of . . . flank squadrons or

anything like that being arranged. The only order given was
Right Wheel into Line. Gallop and Charge were understood.

I went through the first 100 yards looking over my left shoulder
to see what sort of effect the fire was producing. It seemed small.
Then I drew my Mauser pistol and cocked it. Then I looked to my
front. Instead of 150 riflemen I saw a line nearly 12 deep – all in
a nullah (ditch) with steep sloping sides 6 foot deep and 20 foot
broad.

I was right troop leader but one. I saw we overlapped. I
was afraid we would charge into air. I shouted to Wormald
to shoulder and we actually struck the enemy in a crescent
formation. Result of our shoulder was this – my troop struck the
nullah diagonally and their increasing slope enabled us to gallop
through not jump it. Result we struck – faster and more formed
than the centre troops.

Opposite me they were about 4 deep. But they all fell knocked
[over] and we passed through without any sort of shock. One
man in my troop fell. He was cut to pieces. I had the impression
of scattered Dervishes running in all directions. Straight before
me a man threw himself on the ground, I saw the gleam of his
curved sword as he drew back for a ham-stringing cut. I had
room enough and time enough to turn my pony out of his reach,
and leaning over on the offside I fired two shots into him at
about three yards. As I straightened myself in the saddle, I saw
before me another figure with uplifted sword. I raised my pistol
and fired. So close were we that the pistol actually struck him.
Man and sword disappeared below and behind me . . .

The momentum of the charge carried the horsemen straight through the
front rank of defenders and, in most cases, out at the rear of the screaming,
slashing tribesmen. GW Steevens wrote:

Through everything clean out the other side they came – those
that kept up or got up in time. The others were on the ground
– in pieces by now, for the cruel swords shore through shoulder
and thigh, and carved the dead into fillets. Twenty-four of these,
and of those that came out over fifty had felt sword or bullet or
spear.

. . . Lieutenant Robert Grenfell's troop . . . when they burst
straggling out, their only thought was to rally and go in again.

The charge of the 21st Lancers at Omdurman was a military mistake that resulted in numerous casualties – wounding or killing almost a quarter of those involved. Though deadly – at least for those in the centre of the British formation – it lasted only 120 seconds.

'Rally, Number 2!' yelled a sergeant, so mangled across the face that his body was a cascade of blood, and nose and cheeks flapped hideously as he yelled.

And Churchill remembered:

> As soon as we got through I reformed my troop getting about 15 together and told them they would have to go back and perhaps again after that. Whereupon my centre guide said in a loud voice, 'All right sir – we're ready – as many times as you like.'
>
> I asked my sergeant if he had enjoyed himself. He replied 'Well, I don't exactly say I enjoyed it sir, but I think I'll get more used to it next time.' At this the whole troop laughed.

There was wild confusion as the Lancers re-formed and attempted to gather their wounded. Bennet Burleigh observed that:

Lieutenant Montmorency, having got through safely, turned
back to look for his troop-sergeant Carter. Captain Kenna
went with him. At the moment they were not aware that young
Grenfell had fallen. Lieutenants T. Connally and Winston
Churchill also turned about to rescue two non-commissioned
officers of their respective troops. They succeeded in their
laudable task. Surgeon-Captain Pinches, whose horse had
been shot under him on the north side of the khor, was saved
by the pluck of his orderly, Private Pedder, who brought him
out on his horse. Meanwhile, Captain Kenna and Lieutenant
Montmorency, who were accompanied by Corporal Swarbrick,
saw Lieutenant Grenfell's body and tried to recover it. They
fired at the dervishes with their revolvers, and drove them back.
Dismounting, Montmorency and Kenna tried to lift the body
upon the Lieutenant's horse. Unluckily, the animal took fright
and bolted. Swarbrick went after it. Major Wyndham, the second
in command of the Lancers, had his horse shot in the khor.
He was one of the few who escaped after such a calamity. The
animal fortunately carried him across, up, and beyond the slope
ere it dropped down dead. Lieutenant Smith, who was near,
offered him a seat, and the Major grasped the stirrup to mount.
Just then – for these events have taken longer in telling than
in happening – Montmorency and Kenna found the dervishes
pressing them hard, both being in instant danger of being
killed. Swarbrick had brought back the horse, and Kenna turned
to Major Wyndham and gave him a seat behind, then leaving
Grenfell's body they rejoined their command. Proceeding about
300 yards to the south-east from the scene of the charge, Colonel
Martin dismounted his whole regiment, and opened fire on the
dervishes. Getting into position where his men could fire down
the khor, a detachment of troopers soon drove away the last
of the enemy. Thereupon a party advanced and recovered the
bodies of Lieutenant Grenfell and the others who had fallen in
the khor.

Private Wade Rix, who was in the thick of the fighting, described the
aftermath of the charge:

Once out of the shambles the scene was one of confusion. Many
horses were dead, others were trotting around riderless, some

were in a distressing state standing with their heads down, most of them streaming with blood from the many gashes received from the fearsome double-edged swords. Mr. Churchill wanted the men to charge the enemy again but the Colonel wisely forbade it, instead we formed line, wheeled round to face the enemy's flank, dismounted and opened up a sustained rifle fire. This was more than they could stand and they finally retreated.

That Churchill asked if his sergeant had 'enjoyed' the action may seem callous, but what must be remembered is that cavalry charges, though practised in training and performed on manoeuvres, were extremely rare in modern battle. To take part in one was the dream of every ambitious mounted soldier. It was an experience they expected would produce a surge of exhilaration, a crowning moment in their service. Now they had done it. They could assess their feelings, and the price paid by their comrades for this moment of heady excitement. Lieutenant RN Smyth was one of those involved in clearing up the grisly remains of those who had not survived:

After we saw the complete success of work we revisited the scene of the charge. I was told off to get six men of my troop to collect our dead. The less said or written about that the better. It was a ghastly sight. The tears streamed down my cheeks & I was physically sick. It was terrible. At this present moment I don't wish the morn' repeated, it cost too dear. I have always wanted to be in a charge & have got my desire & am satisfied.

We appear to be the only lot who had real hard fighting & suffered to any extent . . . It was an experience, & what struck me most was that you always hear that there are cases in every action where some men want dash & courage, in this instance I can't quote ONE. I would if I could because I value the statistics. As far as cavalry goes it is the biggest thing since Balaklava & I am proud of belonging to the 21st Lancers. Wise or unwise, it was a brave deed nobly done, &, as Colonel Martin said, he was so proud & pleased that it had happened, as it proved that cavalry still existed & that we did not come here to play at mounted infantry.

And Churchill had another item to add to his list of military adventures:

I am glad to have added the experience of a cavalry charge to my military repertoire. But really though dangerous it was not in the least exciting and it did not look dangerous – at least not to me. I suppose it was the most dangerous 2 minutes I shall live to see . . .

An official statement from Lieutenant General Francis Grenfell, commanding officer in Egypt, captured a mood that was both sombre and proud of this pointless and unplanned attack:

The heavy losses in killed and wounded in the 21st Lancers is to be deeply regretted. But the charge itself, against an overwhelming force of sword and spear men over difficult ground, and under unfavourable conditions, was worthy of the best traditions of British cavalry.

The infantry officer Lieutenant Ronald Meiklejohn gave the reaction of the rest of the army:

We hear the charge was a great error, and K. is furious. They lost over 1 officer and 20 men killed, and 3 officers and 40 [men] wounded, and 100 horses, and were not able to undertake the pursuit of the Khalifa, as Kitchener intended. Their fire, however, drove the enemy on to the Gyppy brigades, who wiped them out.

The Lancers' 21 fatalities (nearly a quarter of the regiment were killed or wounded) contributed to an Anglo-Egyptian total of 48 dead and 434 wounded. Dervish losses were difficult to count, but most estimates put the number of dead at between 10,000 and 11,000.

This action has often been described as the last cavalry charge in history, or the last in British history, but this is nonsense. There were to be similar events in South Africa and in World War I, while the last cavalry charge involving British troops is thought to have taken place as late as 1941, in the Middle East. They were, however, rare even by 1898 because they simply cost too many lives.

To people at home, the charge had fulfilled the expectations of a public that expected glory, sacrifice and victory from its soldiers. Esme Wingfield-Stratford was a boy at the time of Omdurman. He recalled the outlook that influenced him (and a large section of the population) when news of the battle reached Britain:

To anyone born in the twentieth century it must seem incredible that there was actually a time, within living memory, when war was regarded in the light of a glorified test match – a thrill of all thrills, more to be looked forward to than feared. Not that I think there was any urgent desire to take on a European Power, that would be rather too much of a good thing. The ideal arrangement would be a jolly, imperial war once every two or three years, with an occasional frontier scrap between whiles – a war involving no risks to anyone except Tommy Atkins, who accepted them with his pay; but war on a large enough scale to call for a sensational deployment of imperial force. Just such a model war as the one to avenge Gordon, staged by the up-to-date superman Kitchener, culminating in a record-breaking holocaust of a relatively unarmed enemy by scientific weapons, followed by a touching parade service at the death-place of the Christian martyr.

War, in fact, at its best, with special correspondents, including a bumptious young Subaltern called Churchill. To keep one posted up in every stage of its progress. And the prospect of an even bigger and more spectacular show that old Joe could be trusted to produce, after the necessary interval, entitled *The Avenging of Majuba*.

That was how we boys looked at it, and how most of the grown-ups, to the best of my experience and belief, looked at it too. War was the sovereign remedy for the boredom of a safe existence, and the Empire overseas the spiritual macrocosm of the one in Leicester Square.

The battle was seen by some as a 'holocaust', or at least a massacre, because the dervishes were mostly armed with primitive weapons and were largely killed with modern ones. These critics had presumably forgotten the implacable nature of Kitchener's opponents and the fact that British-led troops had twice been defeated – and put to the sword. They had never seen what dervishes did to those they killed.

Even a badly wounded dervish was likely to lunge at any soldier who went close enough to assist him, and that is one reason why the enemy wounded were left to die. This neglect caused a good deal of outrage among British observers – not least Churchill himself, whose history of the campaign was to include some very sharp comments on Kitchener's attitude to the defeated enemy. Some of those lying on the battlefield were given water but not medical attention, and it is probable that the army's medical services were simply not adequate to deal with casualties on this scale. Nevertheless, Bennet Burleigh recounts that injured dervishes were not completely ignored:

The large number of the enemy who for days had survived shocking wounds, to which a European would have instantly or speedily succumbed, was appalling. These wretched creatures had been seen crawling or dragging themselves for miles to get to the Nile for water or into villages for succour. Food and water were sent out to them by the Sirdar's orders on the day after the battle, when it was seen that the natives gave neither heed nor help to other than their own immediate kinsmen upon the field. Of wounded dervishes over 9,000 were treated by the British and Egyptian Army Medical Staffs, although the doctors' hands were busy enough for two days with our own sick and wounded.

The Mahdi's elaborate mausoleum, a conspicuous landmark set on the riverbank, had been heavily shelled by the gunboats, which had blown large holes in its beehive-shaped dome. His body, buried in a table tomb protected by an elaborate wrought-iron screen, was exhumed on Kitchener's orders and flung into the Nile. The skull was apparently taken by the Sirdar as a souvenir, and Kitchener considered having a drinking-vessel made from it. This idea was so outrageous that Queen Victoria wrote him a stiffly worded letter of rebuke, while Churchill again gave vent to pungent criticism in his book about the war. Denouncing this as a 'wicked act of which the true Christian, no less than the philosopher, must express his abhorrence', he told how:

By Sir Herbert Kitchener's orders the Tomb had been profaned and razed to the ground. The corpse of the Mahdi was dug up. The head was separated from the body, the limbs and trunk were flung into the Nile. Such was the chivalry of the conquerors!

Kitchener alleged that the Mahdi's skull was subsequently returned to the Sudan in an empty kerosene tin. Whatever the truth, it is perhaps understandable that it should be demonstrated with brutal finality that the Mahdi's cause was lost and that his cult would no longer be allowed to threaten the peace of the region. The Khalifa, who had escaped the battle, remained at large until he was killed in a skirmish with Anglo-Egyptian forces two years later. It was to take a decade after Omdurman before the last vestiges of the dervish rebellion were wiped out.

Churchill lingered for a few days after the battle and deepened his acquaintance with the correspondent GW Steevens. A fellow journalist, Lionel James, recalled Steevens' assessment of him:

'Churchill will go far!,' he said, 'he has every property that makes for success. He has blood, brain, rich friends behind him, and audacity. That is enough for the first lap. We have to see if he has judgement. His method of exploiting his publicity capital suggests at any rate considerable business capacity.'

However impressed some people were with his drive and determination to find adventure, his behaviour was both noticed and condemned at home. The periodical *Modern Society* published an article on 21 January 1899 that stated:

Some months ago we stated in these columns that jobbery was never more rampant nor favouritism more unblushing than it is at the present time in the War Office, and if proof were needed it may be found in the manner in which Lieutenant Churchill of the 4th Hussars has been allowed by the authorities to pursue his military career since he first joined the Army, some four years ago. It would be interesting to know how many days' duty with his regiment this young officer has performed during this time.

At an early period after joining the Army, Lieutenant Churchill brought his name before the public by participation in a discreditable scandal which occurred in the 4th Hussars. Almost immediately after this episode, and before his drill and training could have been properly completed, Lieutenant Churchill was allowed to proceed to Cuba on leave of absence, in order to witness the struggle between the Spanish troops and the insurgent Cubans, instead of completing his education as a cavalry officer by the performance of the duties of his position.

Since then the life of this enterprising and favoured young officer would seem to have been spent anywhere but with his regiment, and as a newspaper correspondent he has given the public the advantage of his ripe experience in the criticism of the conduct of our wars on the North-West Frontier of India, and in Egypt.

It is difficult, therefore, to understand of what possible use Lieutenant Churchill can be to the regiment in which he holds a commission, but this may possibly be explained by the announcement in the newspapers that he is about to proceed to India with the 4th Hussars for the purpose of taking part in a polo tournament in which that gallant regiment is shortly to compete. Surely this is not only a case of playing at polo but playing at soldiering, and it is high time for the War Office to interfere.

Churchill was sufficiently stung by rebukes of this sort (and there were several) to write to the editor of the *Army and Navy Gazette*. This letter was published on 11 February 1899:

'A General Officer' is apparently so annoyed and alarmed that 'a subaltern with less than four years' service is acting as a special correspondent here, there and everywhere,' and that I am that individual only increases his dissatisfaction. He asserts that the question of my position in the Army is being discussed daily in all Service clubs and that 'the young men are evidently more concerned than the older ones' at my proceedings.

What are the restrictions which govern the actions of a junior officer? The first and the last is that he should give satisfaction to his official superiors. Now if a Lieutenant misbehaves himself there is a powerful machinery designed to wheel him into line. If he is not subjected to this process the conclusion is that his official superiors do not think that he has acted improperly, and if he has given satisfaction to his official superiors he has done his duty. And if he has thus correctly conducted himself then there is no reason why either the junior ranks or 'A General Officer' should disturb themselves.

Nevertheless, he continued to be the subject of considerable resentment.

RETURN TO INDIA

Churchill returned to India with two objectives: to win the regimental polo championship and to get on with his book. The regimental history describes what happened regarding the first of these:

To win this cup had been the Regiment's ambition since it landed in India. It was a tough proposition, as the cup had never been won by a regiment from southern India. By 1899, however, when Churchill returned from his travels, the Regiment felt it was ready.

The tournament was held at Meerut, which entailed a fourteen-hundred-mile train journey. The party – the players, reserves, native servants and thirty ponies – stopped for a fortnight at Jodhpore for final practice. The night before they left Churchill slipped on some stone stairs and dislocated his right shoulder. He presumed, naturally enough, that he would be out of the team, but after grave consideration the team captain decided to play him in spite of his injury. It was felt that even if he could not hit the ball, his knowledge of the game and their teamwork would give a better chance of success than playing a reserve.

Churchill played extremely well, scoring two goals with his injured arm. The lead passed from one team to the other and back. He recalled: 'I have never seen such strained faces on both sides. You would not have thought it was a game at all . . .' But his team won – the first and last time a southern Indian regiment was to do so.

This was his final act before departing the 4th Hussars. He was given an affectionate send-off:

> The Regiment were very nice to me when I departed for home, and paid me the rare compliment of drinking my health the last time I dined with them. What happy years I had had with them and what staunch friends one made. It was a grand school for anyone. Discipline and comradeship were taught, and perhaps after all these are just as valuable as the lore of the universities . . .

His book on the campaign, *The River War*, was written with customary speed and thoroughness, so that it was ready for publication in November 1899. This was in every way a finer work than *The Malakand Field Force* had been. It was much bigger, as befitted a larger subject, and thus ran to two volumes of 464 and 500 pages. It appeared in an edition of 3,000 and cost 36 shillings, making it far too expensive for many people to afford. Churchill did not want to impress only the rich; he needed the voters in their scores of thousands to be able to read his views and marvel at his deeds, and thus sought the release of a cheap edition as soon as possible. In 1902 a popular, single-volume version, with much of his pontification removed, was ready.

Professor Keith Alldritt has analysed the book:

> Though similar in design to its predecessor, *The River War* is, in literary terms, a very much more substantial and considerable work. It has more narrative interest and suspense; it has some

of the qualities of epic. It is informed by a great amount of background reading and research. The book involved not merely the writing of some nine hundred pages but also a very large amount of research work. Churchill clearly found it necessary to find out for himself and for the reader the historical context of what was one of the most important experiences of his life.

But *The River War* is not made up of a culling and reproducing of pieces of information from other texts. In his use of sources the 24 year-old author shows himself to be a writer of considerable imaginative powers. His method is that of a serious historical novelist; he takes the received evidence and transmutes it so that the reader receives it as experience rather than fact. In reading the first of the two volumes, which deals with events prior to Churchill's arrival in the Sudan, it is very easy to forget that the author did not witness what he presents and that what we are reading is an imaginative reconstruction from other literary works . . .

A review in an American periodical, *The Nation*, stressed some weaknesses as well as the strengths of such a precocious narrative:

Our author is not at his best when describing the campaign in which he took part. Not unnaturally he dwells at too great length on the incidents, sometimes trivial, of which he was an eye-witness. His account of the battle of Omdurman, especially, suffers for this reason.

While this may be true, the book is praised for its scrupulous fairness. It is critical of Kitchener, though these references were toned down and largely exorcized by the second edition because of the author's political ambitions, and it describes the Mahdi's life and career with respect and objectivity. It was a work of considerable maturity, impressive had it been written by someone twice his age. By the time it appeared, he was already involved in the last of his colonial adventures.

6
SOUTH AFRICA, 1899–1900

A year or two before the outbreak of the Boer War, Churchill had written in a private memorandum:

> **Sooner or later, in a righteous cause or a picked quarrel, with the approval of Europe, or in the teeth of Germany, for the sake of our Empire, for the sake of our honour, for the sake of the race, we must fight the Boers.**

Although war in South Africa was looking increasingly likely, he was no longer hunting for opportunities to get into action. He felt that his exploits on the North-West Frontier and the Sudan had given him enough of a reputation and he was now impatient to begin in politics. He resigned his commission in the spring of 1899 and returned to England from India. In July he stood as Conservative candidate in a by-election at Oldham in Lancashire and came third, losing to the Radical candidate by 1,149 votes. He resigned himself to waiting for a similar opportunity, but he was not destined to be idle for long, for war broke out that autumn and gave him another, more significant chance of finding military glory.

South Africa had been a theatre of potential conflict for most of Churchill's lifetime. It was now to become the scene of one of Britain's longest, most expensive and most humiliating colonial wars, a sad end to Victoria's reign (she was to die before it was over) and a fatal blow to the complacency that had come to characterize Britain's stewardship of Empire.

Settled by the Dutch in 1652 and bought by Britain in 1806, the huge territories on the southern tip of Africa retained a population of fiercely independent Dutch-speaking Protestant farmers: the Boers (the word means simply 'farmer', or 'peasant'). Never having been reconciled to British rule, the Boers had abandoned their homes and marched hundreds of miles inland to establish new states beyond the reach of Britain. The 'Great Trek' of 1835–7 became a national epic that defined the Boer sense of identity ever afterwards. The hardships involved in crossing mountain ranges, rivers and vast plains, and of fighting the hostile inhabitants of these regions, in every way mirrored the experiences of American pioneers, but with an additional dimension of ideology. This migration had been undertaken not in search of wealth or living space, but to protect their freedom from interference.

The two neighbouring independent Boer republics – the Transvaal and Orange Free State – were not left alone for long. In 1843, Britain added to its possessions the territory of Natal between Orange Free State and the Indian Ocean. In 1877 the Transvaal was annexed by Britain, which was intent on grouping its colonies in the area into a single unit: a Union of South Africa. The Boers had no intention of tolerating this and they took up arms.

BOERS AT WAR

Like any frontier people, the Boers were tough and resilient. Boer farmers were superb marksmen, could live in the saddle for days or weeks, and knew their own country well enough to live off the land and to disappear when hunted. They began by besieging British outposts and garrisons, including the city of Pretoria, so that relief columns had to be sent to the rescue. In their first major encounter, at Bronkhorst Spruit on 20 December 1880 with a column of British troops that was marching to Pretoria, they shot down almost half the force.

A few weeks later, in fighting at Laing's Nek, they similarly decimated a British frontal assault (in which, incidentally, colours were carried in battle for the last time in British history). Worse was to come. While talks sought to end hostilities the impatient British commander, Sir George Pomeroy-Colley, decided to occupy the strategic Majuba Hill overlooking Laing's Nek. This was a strong position, albeit held without artillery. Nevertheless it was attacked by Boer troops on 26 February 1881. Their deft use of cover and unerring marksmanship enabled them to capture the summit and take a terrible toll of the defenders, who were driven in confusion down the farther slope. The defeat caused a howl of anguish in Britain and a desire for revenge that was to simmer for a generation (Churchill's essay on the problem was to include the phrase: 'Imperial aid must redress the wrongs of the Outlanders; Imperial troops must curb the insolence of the Boers'). For the moment, however, there was peace. Negotiation granted internal independence to the Transvaal in 1881 and three years later this was broadened to full independence. The Transvaal became the South African Republic.

Shortly afterwards, in 1886, gold was discovered there. As happened elsewhere in the world, the result was an influx of prospectors to the region.

In this case, most of them were British, and their presence began to alter the character of this Boer nation. The inhabitants feared they would soon be outnumbered by 'Uitlanders' (foreigners). It is not difficult to imagine how the morality of a gold-rush mining camp will have offended the dour sensitivities of a Calvinist state. To curb any political influence that weight of numbers might lend them, Paul Kruger, the country's president since 1883, extended the period of residence that qualified citizens to vote from five years to 14. Inside and outside the Republic there were British who looked for an excuse to annex it. One of them was the vastly wealthy and influential Cecil Rhodes; another was the high commissioner to Cape Province, Sir Alfred Milner. If discontent could be maintained, an excuse for intervention might present itself. After the accidental shooting of a drunken British prospector by a policeman, Queen Victoria received a petition bearing 21,000 signatures asking for annexation, but this incident was not enough to light the spark.

Rhodes believed that an armed invasion of the Republic would provoke an uprising by Britons living there. This bold act would be aimed at winning sufficient power for Uitlanders to vote for union with the British territories. At the end of December 1895, with his connivance, a body of horsemen largely recruited from his British South Africa Company, and led by his friend Doctor Leander Starr Jameson, galloped over the border under cover of night – an action that came to be known as the Jameson Raid. Rhodes was not the only one convinced that British Uitlanders were a persecuted minority. Back in Britain the Poet Laureate, Alfred Austin, wrote:

> Let lawyers and statesmen addle
> Their pates over points of law:
> If sound be our sword and saddle
> And gun-gear, who cares one straw?
> When men of our own blood pray us
> To ride to our kinfolk's aid,
> Not heaven itself shall stay us
> From the rescue they call a raid.

The expedition was an embarrassing farce. Within three days the participants had been cut off, rounded up and put under guard. There had been no uprising in support of them. Whatever sympathy its members might have had for Rhodes and his motives, the British government hastily dissociated itself from the action. Jameson was put on trial and imprisoned, and Rhodes had to resign as prime minister of Cape Province.

All these events had done was to make a collision seem inevitable to both sides. At Kruger's request negotiations took place to defuse the tension but Milner, who represented Britain, was determined to see that they failed. He asked London to send troops to Natal so that they could make a show of strength on the border, and these were largely brought from India. There were 15,000 of them.

For their part, the Boers were ready for war. Their 'army' consisted largely of mounted riflemen and virtually all were citizen volunteers (the only professionals were the gun crews of the artillery), but they were able to muster about 40,000 of these. Each of the 40 districts within the Republic and the Free State was obliged to contribute a 'commando' – a unit of up to 500 men – and any male over the age of 16 was liable for conscription. These commandos were highly mobile and had all of the skills necessary to wage guerrilla war. They were armed not with farmers' shotguns but with effective modern military rifles (Mausers, which were superior to the British Army's Lee-Metfords), for their country's wealth enabled them to be well equipped.

Seeing the futility of further talk, Kruger issued an ultimatum to Britain stating that troops must be withdrawn from his border and that some sort of disinterested arbitration be established for dealing with sensitive issues. Britain ignored these requests and the silence that met his ultimatum, issued on 9 October and expiring two days later, was taken by the Boers as a declaration of war.

As with another conflict 15 years later, the British public assumed it would be over within a matter of weeks. Yet this period of time went by and there were no successes to celebrate. The Boers invaded Natal and quickly controlled about a quarter of it. The British suffered a costly defeat at Elsin. Bodies of troops and civilians found themselves besieged in three cities: Kimberley, Ladysmith and Mafeking. These were all remarkably civilized affairs and none of them was an unbearable ordeal, at least for the white population. At Ladysmith the Boers allowed the defenders to establish a hospital outside the town, and on Christmas Day sent plum puddings to the garrison. At Mafeking the senior British officer, Robert Baden-Powell, shortly to become founder of the Boy Scout movement, had ordered immense amounts of provisions in advance. Rationing was therefore relatively gentle and a well-organized social life kept morale extremely high. At Kimberley, Rhodes himself was among the besieged. The Boers conducted these operations with leisurely informality. For most of the time, they simply ensured that those inside could not get out, and otherwise left them alone.

While the sieges went on, the British Army continued to fare badly. At the end of the year there were three crushing defeats within five days – a period that was dubbed 'Black Week'. On 10 December, a column led by Sir William Gatacre (who had been at Omdurman) failed to seize a Boer position at Stormberg and, owing to confusion, left 600 men to face capture. The next day another force, composed of Guards and Highlanders, assaulted a ridge at Magersfontein that was in Boer hands. Their enemy normally deployed at the top of ridges, where British artillery could pummel them before the infantry attacked up the slopes, but the Boers had developed a new tactic. This time they were dug in at the bottom of the ridge where their opponents had not thought to look for them, and their own rifle fire, at close range, mowed down the advancing troops with such devastating effect that the attackers broke and ran. This was the worst defeat suffered by British troops for over a century.

The third battle was at Colenso on the 15th, when a force led by the Commander-in-Chief, Sir Redvers Buller, attempted a frontal attack on Boer-held heights above the Tugela River. Two batteries of guns – a dozen in all – were moved so far forward that the Boers were able to capture ten of them. A gallant attempt was made to save them by an infantry lieutenant, the Hon. Frederick Roberts, who was the son of Field Marshal Lord Roberts. Like his father, he won the Victoria Cross, but his was posthumous.

Buller was superseded as commander-in-chief by Lord Roberts, a vastly experienced officer affectionately nicknamed 'Bobs'. He brought with him the hero of the Sudan, Kitchener, as chief of staff. In Britain, press and public hoped desperately that colourful personalities and expert leadership – a touch of genius, perhaps – would make the difference. The country was deeply shaken by these huge reverses and baffled as to how they could have come about. Victory had been taken for granted and failure was simply unthinkable. As Queen Victoria famously put it, 'We are not interested in the possibilities of defeat. They do not exist,' though they clearly did exist and had to be faced.

It was into this atmosphere of unmitigated gloom that the news broke – a few days before Christmas 1899 and like some heaven-sent gift to the nation – that Winston Churchill, who had escaped from a Boer prisoner-of-war camp a fortnight earlier, was free.

WINSTON ON THE SCENE

Churchill had arrived in South Africa in mid-October, now a fully fledged journalist and not a serving officer. Through his detailed process of self-education, he knew a good deal about the background. He was anxious to get to the potential theatre of conflict and others were equally anxious to send him there. In September he had received an invitation from the newspaper magnate, Alfred Harmsworth, to go as the *Daily Mail*'s correspondent. Through his friendship with Oliver Borthwick, the son of the *Morning Post*'s proprietor, he found a lucrative alternative. With one book to his credit and another about to be published, he was able to command generous terms, and he did. The *Post* agreed to pay him £250 a month for four months, and £200 a month thereafter (the war was, after all, expected to be short). In addition all his expenses were paid and he was given copyright of everything he wrote. This, as he liked to boast, was the highest remuneration yet given to a correspondent.

His preparations included obtaining from the colonial secretary a letter of introduction to Sir Alfred Milner. This time he expected not only to observe the fighting but also to interview those who directed events. He laid in provisions for the trip: his son was later to write that 'Churchill never believed that war should be needlessly uncomfortable' and he ordered, from a St James' Street wine merchant, more than 70 bottles of various beverages. These included vintage wines, whisky, vermouth and *eau de vie*. Though this may seem like pretentious luxury, we must remember that he expected to be away for several months and that this quantity was therefore not unreasonable. In a climate where water might be unsafe, wine and whisky would be useful alternatives. Churchill was accustomed, when campaigning, to dine with officers, and would therefore have been used to drinking liqueurs in a tent.

He sailed on the RMS *Dunottar Castle*, which took the Commander-in-Chief, Sir Redvers Buller, as well as other correspondents, to the war. The ship called at Cape Town on 31 October. While Buller and his staff stayed on board for the onward journey to Durban, Churchill landed and took the quicker route by train. As soon as he arrived he began to meet, or to hear of, old friends. Reginald Barnes, who had gone with him to Cuba, was recovering from a wound aboard a hospital ship. Colonel Ian Hamilton, now a general, was among those trapped inside Ladysmith. Leo Amery, whom he had thrown into the Harrow swimming-pool, was now correspondent for *The Times*. Even without these familiar faces, Churchill was unlikely to feel lonely in South Africa; he had brought with him his valet, Thomas Walden, and in addition much of his family would join him at the war. Before it was over his brother Jack and his cousin 'Sunny', Duke of Marlborough, would be serving as soldiers, while his mother and the Duchess, Consuelo, would be managing a hospital ship; another female cousin would be besieged in Ladysmith.

Churchill's escape from an inadequately guarded Boer prison brought him international fame. Here he is featured in a series of popular photographs of the war. He is dressed not in uniform but in the practical, quasi-military outfit of a correspondent.

Unable to reach Ladysmith because the Boers had severed the line, he pitched camp in the railway-yard at Estcourt, some 40 miles to the south. He and Amery shared a tent, hosting dinners amid the sidings and the clanking, hissing locomotives. Churchill was characteristically impatient to get to Ladysmith, but in the meantime he was well positioned. Through Estcourt station came all the supplies, troops and rumours relating to the war in that area. He spent his days exploring the surrounding landscape – on horseback or in a hired carriage – in search of copy for his dispatches and staring at the Boer encampments through field-glasses. The war was quiet and he conceived the ambition to smuggle himself into Ladysmith. He offered to pay £200 to anyone who would guide him there, but nothing came of the scheme. Another of his old friends, Captain Aylmer Haldane of the Gordon Highlanders, was in command of another armoured train which had been making regular runs on the line to Colenso, and he invited Churchill to take part in a patrol. He remembered:

I told him what I had been ordered to do and, knowing that he
had been out in the train and knew something of the country
through which it would travel, suggested that he might care
to accompany me next day. Although he was not at all keen he
consented to do so, and arranged to be at the station in time for
the start.

The journey was to have fateful consequences, though at the time it
seemed so routine that Amery, who was also invited along, stayed in bed.
Years later, when writing about Churchill, he recalled:

We shared a tent at Estcourt, from which, while I overslept, he
caught the armoured train whose fate – admirably recounted in
My Early Life – led to his capture by Louis Botha and his escape
from prison in Pretoria.

The armoured train was a military nonsense. It ran at that time, every two
days or so, for distances of 20 miles or more northwards towards the Boer
positions. Its task was to search the countryside for enemy units as well
as making a show of strength. It was more elaborate than the train on
which Churchill had travelled in Cuba. At the front was a flat-car carrying
a seven-pounder naval gun with a crew of five sailors. This was followed by
two steel-sided trucks filled with infantry who could fire through vertical
rifle-slits. The engine and tender were in the middle, then there were two
more armoured trucks and a guard's van containing a track-repair crew.
The Boers were skilled at sabotaging the line but they did not destroy
it, for they appreciated its value to themselves in a future advance. The
damage they did could therefore usually be rectified quickly and easily, but
constant maintenance was necessary.

The train was slow-moving and noisily ostentatious and its movements
were predictable. The 117 men aboard it thought it a 'death trap'. It could
easily be cut off by simply blocking the track behind it, and was extremely
vulnerable to artillery placed on nearby hills or embankments. The train
set off at 5.30am and arrived without incident at the small township of
Frere. From there, Haldane reported their progress by telegraph to his
colonel at Estcourt, but the train then went on without awaiting a reply.
In fact Boer patrols had been sighted and at that moment were only four
miles away. There was going to be trouble.

Haldane later said that Churchill's zeal had led him to push farther on
in the hope of engaging with the enemy. At the next station, Chievely,

there could be no doubt that they had found them. On the hills ahead were a large number of horsemen and there could be no further progress. Telegraphed orders told them to retire and this the train began to do. The Boers opened fire with rifles and field-guns and the sailors responded with their seven-pounder. The enemy, however, had laid the ambush carefully and did not expect the train to escape. What happened next is described in an account of a talk that Churchill gave at his old school the following year, as reviewed in the *Harrovian*.

MR CHURCHILL'S LECTURE

On Friday, October 26th, Mr Winston Churchill gave a most interesting lecture in the Speech Room on his experiences in the South African War. The lecturer, who was received with loud applause, gave an account of the armoured train at Chievely, and his own imprisonment and escape. As a correspondent of the *Morning Post* he was on board the train which went on to reconnoitre between Estcourt and Chievely. Captain Haldane was in command of this train which, as the picture on the screen showed, was defended by thin plates, which were only bullet proof, and could not withstand shells.

They reached Chievely without seeing any of the enemy, but on their return journey as they turned a corner of the line they saw a commando of the Boers posted on a hill about 60 yards off. The sailors loaded the one little toy gun which they had, the enemy opened fire with two large field-guns and a maxim, the engine-driver put on full steam, and the train dashed at high speed round the corner of the hill into a large stone considerately placed on the line by the enemy.

The trucks took up different positions on the line, one remaining half on and half off the rails; the Boer guns at once changed their positions, again opened fire, and speedily smashed our gun. Then the men worked at clearing the line, and at last the engine and tender passed the overturned truck, and the way home lay open. The engine was a sorry sight with water spurting from the tanks, the fire-box in flames, and wounded clinging on everywhere. The soldiers who were left behind then made for some houses about 800 yards distant, but one man waved his handkerchief and the Boers galloped down and called on all the men to surrender.

This they did, and so became prisoners of war, meanwhile Mr

Churchill, who after travelling some 500 yards on the engine had jumped off to take part in the fight, found himself in a cutting with no soldiers and two Boers in sight. He at once made for the houses, but as he said owing to slackness about football and other games at Harrow, he was unable to go any pace at all; finding no cover and seeing a mounted Boer in front he surrendered himself, and with the other prisoners was finally moved to Pretoria.

Churchill's own role in the skirmish was, in fact, rather more important than this description suggests. As the train ran backwards picking up speed, it came under increasingly heavy fire. Exploding shells filled the air with flying shrapnel and the stench of cordite, and a Maxim gun opened up at close range. Through a curtain of smoke and fire, the train ran downhill with increasing speed. It rounded a corner and crashed into the boulder, as the Boers had intended. The rear car was tipped down an embankment, the armoured car behind it also capsized and spilled its crew. The next armoured car swung round and jammed across the track, blocking any movement by the rest of the train. Though Haldane was in charge, Churchill recovered more quickly, and effectively took control. Under heavy and continuous fire, he ran forwards to the engine where the driver, Charles Wagner, was injured, and urgently persuaded him to try getting it going again. Since the line was blocked, he asked for 20 volunteers to heave the derailed truck out of the way, but the firing was so intense that only nine crept out of their scanty cover and began to work. Churchill urged them on with the extraordinary statement: 'Keep cool, men, this will be interesting for my paper.'

His valet, Thomas Walden, met the driver shortly afterwards and recorded his reaction to the incident:

He told me all about Mr Winston. He says there is not a braver gentleman in the Army. The driver was one of the first wounded, and he said to Mr Winston: 'I am finished.' So Mr Winston said to him: 'Buck up a bit, and I will stick to you,' and he threw off his revolver and field-glasses and helped the driver pick 20 wounded men up and put them on the engine. Every officer in Estcourt thinks that Mr Winston will get the V.C.

The tender could now get through, but the engine was too wide and became stuck. Worse, the couplings had broken and the cars in front of the engine were now stranded. Sizing up the situation, Haldane ordered that the wounded in these should be transferred to the locomotive and tender. Laboriously this was done, under Churchill's supervision, with the injured men propped or draped wherever there was space. As rifle and cannon fire kept whistling overhead or smacking off the trucks, the engine, having built up steam, attempted to ram the disabled car out of the way, and with a hideous shriek of tortured metal it succeeded. With unwounded soldiers crouching alongside for cover, it began reversing the half mile back across the river to Estcourt station. It was on fire, and water was pouring from its bullet-holed tanks, yet it picked up speed and, with Churchill among those crowded on the footplate, began to leave behind both the Boer attackers and those defenders who could not keep up with it. The remains of the train pulled into Estcourt station, but Churchill was determined to re-cross the river and help the survivors. Unwilling to abandon them, he ran across the bridge to see what could be done.

He was in a cutting and ahead of him he saw two armed Boers. He dodged up the bank and they fired at him. Now he was in open ground, but a single mounted Boer was galloping towards him with a levelled rifle. He described what followed:

> Suddenly on the other side of the railway, separated from me by the rails and two uncut wire fences, I saw a horseman galloping furiously, a tall, dark figure, holding his rifle in his right hand. He pulled up his horse almost in its own length and shaking his rifle at me shouted a loud command. We were 40 yards apart. That morning I had taken with me, correspondent-status notwithstanding, my Mauser pistol. I thought I could kill this man, and after the treatment I had received I earnestly desired to do so. I put my hand to my belt, the pistol was not there. I was quite unarmed. Meanwhile, I suppose in about the time this takes to tell, the Boer horseman still seated on his horse, had covered me with his rifle. The animal stood stock still, so did he, and so did I. The Boer continued to look along his sights. I thought there was absolutely no chance of escape, if he fired he would surely hit me, so I held up my hands and surrendered myself a prisoner of war.

Churchill had been armed with the same Mauser pistol he had carried at Omdurman. He would have attempted to escape if he had had any chance of success. He gave himself up and at once informed his captors that he was entitled to be treated as a non-combatant. Fortunately for him he remembered that in his tunic pockets were the ammunition clips for his pistol, and managed to dispose of them. They carried vicious soft-nosed bullets.

This episode was the most important combat experience of Churchill's life and demonstrated immense bravery, even though he had no business to be carrying arms or taking part in an operation. Had he been dealing with an enemy more ruthless than the Boers, who after all had seen him struggling with the engine, he might have been shot at once. He was deeply fortunate that his experience of capture was at the hands of chivalrous and easygoing opponents. Given his transparent ambition and his fixation with winning medals, it is tempting to be cynical about his actions on that day. He made no secret of the fact that he 'performed' in battles for the benefit of those watching. Here the situation had been desperate, however, and there was no time to think about the implications of what he was doing. He undoubtedly possessed great personal courage, a virtue enhanced by the desire to dominate situations and to set an example. Churchill was largely responsible for the rescue of the wounded, one of whom later wrote home that:

> **Churchill is a splendid fellow. He walked about in it all as cool as if nothing was going on. His presence and way of going on were as much good as 50 men would have been. After the engine got clear he came about ½ a mile on it and then got off and coolly walked back to help the others . . .**

Misinterpreting a conversation he had some years later with the great Boer politician Louis Botha, who became prime minister of the Transvaal, Churchill came to believe that Botha himself had been the horseman who captured him that day. This was untrue. Botha was in charge of the men involved in taking him prisoner, but the most likely candidate was an officer called Field Cornet Sarel Oosthuizen. Since Oosthuizen was killed in the war, confirmation is not possible. The two other Boers involved were thought to be brothers-in-law Dolf De La Rey and François Changuion.

The prisoners were marched off in pouring rain. Skirting Ladysmith, they travelled to the railhead at Elandslaagte. Churchill, who had no hat, was kindly given an army field cap. For him the prospect of forced inactivity was unbearable, and he was already protesting loudly his right to be released. He did not perhaps realize that his social position rather than his non-belligerence was a deciding factor in the Boers' treatment of him.

Because of his aristocratic background (he was generally believed by foreigners to be titled) Churchill was a celebrity as soon as news of his capture reached the outside world. A contemporary Belgian postcard showing British survivors of the ambush detraining en route to captivity points him out, dressed in civilian clothes, though he has his back to the camera, with the caption: 'Arrival at Pretoria of the prisoners from the wrecked train at Estcourt (Lord Churchill at left in cap).'

This status, together no doubt with a good deal of bluster of the 'Now look here!' variety, caused him to be treated as an amusing curiosity. In response to his demand that he be released as a non-combatant, a Boer Field-Cornet replied, with what sounds like good-natured derision: 'We are not going to let you go, old chappie, although you are a correspondent. We don't catch the son of a lord every day.'

It was largely for the same reason that Churchill was not immediately court-martialled and shot, although he spent an anxious interlude while his fate was being decided. A photograph records this moment: separated from the other prisoners, he stares disconsolately back at the camera.

ESCAPE

It was a 30-year-old officer, the Cambridge-educated Jan Smuts (decades later, as prime minister of South Africa, Smuts would be one of Churchill's closest allies), who decided that the obstreperous correspondent should be imprisoned as a belligerent. News of the armoured train incident having been telegraphed all over the world, the Boers could read in newspapers as easily as anyone else the stories told by British survivors. These made it clear that he had been active in the fighting and was therefore lying in an attempt to gain his freedom. A letter from a Boer officer, Captain FW Reitz, gave a view of Churchill's escapade from the other side:

> Full reports [have] appeared of the active and prominent part taken by the newspaper reporter Winston Churchill in the battle with the armoured train at Frere Station. Churchill called for volunteers and led them at a time when the officers were in confusion. According to *Volkstem Standard & Digger News*, he now claims that he took no part in the battle. That is all lies. He also refused to stand still until Field Cornet Oosthuizen warned him to surrender. He surrendered only when he aimed his gun at him. In my view Churchill is one of the most dangerous prisoners in our hands. The Natal papers are making a big hero out of him.

He was sent with the other captured officers to the States Model School in Pretoria, which had been adapted for the purpose. The Boers were not strict jailers and life within this compound was agreeable enough. Several prisoners, however, including Haldane, began planning to escape. It was inconceivable that Churchill, pushy and longing to get out as he was, could be kept out of any such plan. The account of his lecture at Harrow resumes the story of his life after capture:

> Mr Churchill then showed us some pictures of the States Model
> Schools where the prisoners were shut up . . . After having been
> some time in the prison Captain Haldane and he made a plan
> of escape, by which they were to climb the wall of the schools
> into a deserted garden from which they hoped to escape through
> the town. A good night came, Mr Churchill clambered over the
> wall and waited for Captain Haldane, and he did not appear, but
> whispered through the wall that he could not make the attempt
> as the sentry was watching.
>
> Mr Churchill was desperate; he had no compass, little food, no
> knowledge of Dutch or Kaffir. His companion urged him to climb
> back in again, but he decided to make the attempt. We must feel
> sympathy for Captain Haldane in his disappointment, but it is a
> relief to know that he managed to escape later, by hiding in the
> schools after the prisoners had been moved elsewhere.
>
> Mr Churchill then walked out of the town till he came to a
> railway station; there he lay down in a ditch just beyond the
> platform, expecting that he would be able to board the train
> before it got up steam.
>
> Everything happened as he thought; a train came in, stopped,
> and slowly started again; he jumped up and climbed into a coal
> truck, and saw the head of the engine-driver standing out against
> his furnace. Till the next stoppage he lay wondering whether the
> man's face had been turned against him or not, but as he was
> undisturbed he recovered his spirits; just before it grew light,
> as the train went up a steep incline, he jumped down and rolled
> into a ditch. All day he lay up; at night he wandered on to a spot
> where he hoped to board another train, for he observed that they
> passed every three hours.
>
> Hour after hour passed till he realised that the trains did
> not go there at night. He stumbled off in pursuit of a light
> he saw in the distance, determined to throw himself on the

mercy of the first man he met. On arriving at the light he found himself in a small settlement at the head of a coal mine. Choosing one of the houses at sundown, he knocked and waited, pondering what to say to the owner. – Here Mr Churchill digressed a little to give the School some excellent advice on the art of lying with success. – On the owner's appearance he began a story about going up country to join his uncle's commando, and skylarking on the train and rolling off it. He was led in and given some food. Further enquiries followed and he confessed everything. The owner of the house, Mr Harrison, told him that he was the only Englishman in the place and that he had stayed to look after the mine. He hid Mr Churchill in the coal-mine stable, after getting rid of two Boers for want of patriotism, and on the sixth day he was put in a load of wool that happened to be going to Lourenco Marques. Arrived there he was escorted to a steamer for Durban by the British residents with loaded revolvers, and so back to the British lines before Ladysmith.

The lecture was illustrated with some good photographs, those of the guns at Ladysmith being especially interesting. After the usual vote of thanks by Dr. Wood, the School, led by Mann, gave three hearty cheers for their old schoolfellow. In conclusion, we can only say that Mr Churchill accomplished a difficult task with great taste, for he gave a most interesting account of his adventures without magnifying their importance in proportion to the rest of the war.

The circumstances of Churchill's escape have been closely studied in South Africa. An article by a local historian, AM Davey, provides detail of both the place and the event:

At about a quarter past seven on the evening of the 13th December, 1899, Winston Churchill clambered over the corrugated iron screen that bounded the eastern side of the yard of the State Model School and escaped to freedom . . . The night of the 13th was well chosen for the escape as the moon rose at about a quarter to eight: full moon fell due on the 17th December. The time of escape is important and luckily the Rev. Adrian Hofmeyr, an Anglophile Cape Colonial and an inmate of the officers' prison has mentioned it as 7.15 p.m.

Churchill puts it as half-way through the dinner hour which began at 7 p.m.

On the day following the escape Advocate Schagen van Leeuwen and H.W. Zeiler, a judicial commissioner, were appointed to enquire into the circumstances of the get-away. Sworn statements were submitted by the guards, other responsible officials and a few of the officer prisoners . . . It seems that there were usually nine guards on duty around the building or in the ground with a few others on call. The afternoon and evening watches were from 4 p.m. to 8 p.m., 8 p.m. to midnight and midnight to 4 a.m. By some quirk of fate there were only eight guards at the time that Churchill scaled the iron screen at the back of the closets in the yard and there was no guard at the important position at the south-eastern corner of the ground in Skinner Street. After 8 p.m. there was a sentinel at this strategic point, Jan H. Montgomery. This guard saw nothing but Churchill states that when he walked out of the garden of the adjoining house into Skinner Street the man was five paces away. Churchill, after climbing the screen lay doggo in the garden next door 'for an hour' waiting for his friends, Haldane and Brockie to join him but they were unable to do so as the guards were on the alert. Churchill was warned verbally by his friends inside the ground that no-one else was able to join him. Another guard, C.F.C. Landman, stated that he saw Lieutenant Grimshawe and two others near the fence at ten minutes to eight and when Grimshawe tried to peer over the fence the guard said 'Go back you b—!' In evidence before the committee Captain M. Lonsdale stated that on coming out after dinner between seven and eight he heard Churchill had escaped: he thereupon went to the spot and saw Churchill on the other side. It therefore seems that when Churchill emerged into Skinner Street it was well after 8 p.m. and the guard had been changed in the time that he was crouching in the garden next to the ground of the school.

Davey explained how the friendship had been instrumental in bringing Churchill to this particular theatre of war:

Haldane had aided an eager Churchill to accompany one of the military expeditions on India's North West Frontier: it was Haldane who invited Churchill to join the military in the armoured train sally to Chieveley: Haldane who persuaded the Republican officials at Pretoria station that a newspaper correspondent ranked as an officer and should therefore not to be sent to the racecourse camp for captive non-commissioned officers and men: it was also Haldane who wrote to the Commandant-General on the 19th November affirming on his honour as an officer that Churchill was a correspondent and a non-combatant. The third member of the trip was Regimental Sergeant-Major Brockie of the Imperial Light Horse: he was taken prisoner by the Boers about the same time as Churchill and Haldane but not in the armoured train affray. A Johannesburg 'Uitlander', Brockie knew a little of Dutch and Native languages and was therefore considered a valuable ally in an escape project.

AA Roberts was a student in 1910 and lived at the hostel at Prospect House next to the States Model School. The northern end of the school was assigned to the students and he then understood that Churchill had been confined in the large room across the north end of the building.

Forty-two years later, said Davey, Roberts was the Union's High Commissioner in Canada and met Churchill at a luncheon in Ottawa on 12 January 1952. He asked him several questions about his Boer War adventures:

Sir Winston was 'in great form' and was emphatic in recalling that his room was entered by going up the steps of the main entrance, turning left along the passage and entering the last door in the passage to the left i.e. the third room north-west, from the main entrance. It will be seen that this indication is also totally at odds with the 'Zeiler' sketch-plans and is yet extremely close to Haldane's description. If, after half a century and the dynamics of two world upheavals, Sir Winston's recollections err to the extent of the width of one room (which seems to be the case) it is nevertheless a remarkable feat of memory and a valuable aid to our conclusions. Sir Winston could not recall the Cullingworth family from which the prisoners received news signals but it seems from Haldane's account that this episode was of later date than the time of Churchill's imprisonment.

Davey noted that the security system in force before Churchill's escape was somewhat easy-going:

> Commandant Opperman who Churchill describes as 'an honest and patriotic Boer' had only been in charge for a month. The guards, mainly ex-policemen, were, one presumes, of middle age and unfit for commando service. Roll-call was never held so that Churchill had been gone for 12 hours before his absence was discovered. The officer prisoners were allowed to wear plain clothes and possess substantial sums of money. No regulation forbade their sleeping on the verandah or walking in the ground until the small hours. There was another startling disclosure: two private soldier prisoners, Cahill and Bridge, who acted as servants to the officers and were in tents, had earlier in the month escaped via the same route, viz. over the screen behind the lavatories. Although they had been recaptured the guards had thought it inadvisable to report the incident to their superiors!
>
> In a telegram received in Pretoria on the day before Churchill's escape, the Commandant-General vigorously opposed any suggestion that Churchill be included in a proposed exchange of prisoners. Ever since the armoured train affair General Joubert, backed by Commandant Danie Theron, had insisted that Churchill was a dangerous prisoner who should be watched closely. Louis de Souza, Joubert's deputy in Pretoria, told the 'Zeiler' committee that after the escape he received a letter from the Commandant-General in which the latter said that Churchill's proffer of parole or to leave Africa for the duration of the war could be accepted. This seems to be a reference to a sarcastic letter that Joubert wrote at Volksrust on the 12th December. (This letter shows a rather reluctant change of view on the part of the Commandant-General: he said that he would raise no further objection provided the Government was satisfied that Churchill would abide by his offer and that he would tell the truth about his experiences. Joubert added a thrust of disbelief as a postscript – 'Will he tell the truth? He is sure to prove to be his father's son in this respect'.) After Churchill's disappearance an angry Joubert insisted that all correspondence be published.
>
> A determined effort was made to recapture Mr. Churchill. Descriptions were posted and the well-known reward notice was

issued. Suspicion of complicity fell on several people and some were put over the border, but the guards had not been bribed nor was there any evidence of other outside assistance. The escape project [was] termed a 'primitive' but the simple and direct plan succeeded where a more devious one might have failed.

Next, Davey retraced Churchill's steps after he had turned his back on the confines of the State Model School:

He was wearing an old felt hat and was clad in a civilian brown suit. In his pockets were four slabs of chocolate and £75 in cash. Walking down the centre of Skinner Street in an easterly direction he came to the small stone bridge across the Apies on which he rested. Having crossed this he walked southwards 'half a mile' towards the railway using the stars as a guide as he had no compass. Where he came on the railway it seemed to turn northwards – probably near Mears Street station. He then followed the line. 'The night was delicious', he tells us feelingly. 'A cool breeze fanned on my face and a wild feeling of exhilaration took hold of me.' Two hours' walk brought him in sight of a station, and at a point 200 yards from the platform he 'jumped' the train that took him on the next stage of his adventure. Haldane who memorized the names of all the stations on the Delagoa Bay line and their distances says that Churchill boarded the goods train at Koedoespoort.

An extraordinary angle on the escape is provided from an unexpected source. In 1959 a senior army officer, Field Marshal Lord Ironside, told the following story to an officer in the Royal Army Medical Corps:

I knew Winston Churchill very well as, in the early days of the Boer War I was out there serving with a Special Force and working largely on my own as I spoke German and Afrikaans fluently, and by this means helped to increase my pay being a somewhat impecunious Gunner Subaltern. I took on a Basuto servant, and soon learnt his language. In my roving job I developed scouting techniques and got to know of the movements and strengths of the Boer Commandos. This information I passed on to the British Staff, and, I believe, it impressed General Baden Powell of the value of scouting;

and this no doubt led him to the founding of the Boy Scout movement after the War.

At about the turn of the century Lieut. Winston Churchill came out to South Africa and to the war as a correspondent and reporter for the London *Morning Post,* and not as a Hussar officer. Churchill heard about my experience of the country and Boers.

We met, and got to know each other well, both of us being young ambitious regular officers. He told me he wanted to get up to the Boer Commando at Pretoria in order to get a good story for his newspaper, and if possible contact his friend Captain Haldane, Royal Sussex Regiment, relative of Lord Haldane, the War Minister. Captain Haldane was a P.O.W. in Pretoria. I told Winston it would be foolhardy if he went on the armoured train, as it was likely to be ambushed and derailed, and that he would become a P.O.W. himself. Churchill however was stubborn, and said he was damn well going to have a try and added, 'If I should get captured then Tiny, you as an up-and-coming adventurous young officer can come and get me "out of the bag!"'

Well – Churchill went in the armoured train, was ambushed, and was captured by the Boers and put in prison in Pretoria.

I felt I ought to do something about it, so I raised some funds from the British community in Cape Town, bought a Vortrek Wagon and team of oxen, and with my Basuto boy trekked up to Pretoria disguised as a Boer. I hadn't any definite plan of action, but I had a stroke of luck when, at a prayer meeting or some such function, I met and got to know a young Boer woman. After I had got to know her well, I confessed I was not a Boer but a British Officer; that I was not spying, but was on a delicate mission; this was to try and get the release of a certain young man of an aristocratic British family, and who had been captured. This was Winston Spencer Churchill of the Marlborough family. He, Winston, I explained, was a journalist out to get war news and a story for the World, and he was not spying or fighting the Boers. I now had to think up a fictitious story in order to impress her, and this was, that young Churchill was engaged to a lady – daughter of an English aristocrat – and was due soon to be married. It was essential this marriage should take place soon as the young woman, due to indiscretion, was pregnant, and had come out to Cape Town for the wedding.

Failure to get married would bring disgrace to the young woman and to two noble families. I appealed to her to help another woman in distress.

I was successful in arousing her sympathy, and through her I got a message in to Winston Churchill; the jailer was 'hoodwinked' and Churchill's escape made possible. We got him away, and so to the railway where Churchill stowed himself away amongst the bales of fodder and other goods.

The story of this adventurous rail journey is told by Churchill in his book, *My Early Life*.

There is no way of proving this story, and Ironside (an extremely able and respected career officer) was a very private man of whom no biography was ever written. He and Churchill were friends and colleagues (Ironside was Chief of the Imperial General Staff at the beginning of World War II) and it is suspicious that, in an association that continued for many decades, neither of them ever mentioned the event. The escape has been analysed in detail and no commentator has considered the possibility that the fugitive received assistance at this stage. Ironside's account also contains obvious errors: Haldane, for instance, was in the Gordon Highlanders, not the Royal Sussex.

It is true, however, that Ironside, nicknamed 'Tiny' because he was six foot six, was fluent in several languages and undertook covert operations for the British. A tribute to him in the *Royal Artillery Journal* mentioned that:

> He served throughout the South African War and, as by then he spoke Afrikaans well, in 1902 was given the task, after the conclusion of the war, of getting the Boers back to their farms which the British Government would restock. He thought that the best way of doing so was to be a Boer himself. He therefore bought a complete set of Boer clothes and . . . acquired a Cape cart, horses and two native drivers and proceeded to find and direct Boers back to their farms. Quite naturally they accepted him as a Boer.

It is plausible that he arrived in Pretoria and kept the States Model School under close observation. He might have smuggled in a note or, having worked out the most likely escape route, might have been waiting, over a period of nights, to rendezvous with anyone who got over the wall. Although Churchill describes walking through the streets until he came to a railway siding, might he instead have been able to avoid this highly risky part of his escape by being concealed in a cart and delivered to a train by someone who knew the local geography? An intriguing possibility.

A PRICE ON HIS HEAD

Though most of the British press treated the escape as heroic, there were also detractors. The *Daily Nation* expressed a view that was held by a number of officers who regarded honour as all important. Not only was Churchill seen as having broken his word, he had also made life more difficult for those still in captivity:

> Mr Winston Churchill's escape is not regarded in military circles as either a brilliant or an honourable exploit. He was captured as a combatant, and, of course, placed under the same parole as the officers taken prisoner. He has, however, chosen to disregard an honourable undertaking, and it would not be surprising if the Pretoria authorities adopted more strenuous measures to prevent such conduct.

The Boers' attempts to recapture him included a reward of £25 – an insignificant sum for such a voluble and high-profile prisoner – and his description was widely posted:

> Englishman, twenty-five years old, about five feet eight inches tall, indifferent build, walks with a forward stoop, pale appearance, red-brownish hair, small and hardly noticeable moustache, talks through his nose, and cannot pronounce the letter s properly.

An unpublished memoir by a South African, Sir George Anderson, which was written in 1965, contains this account of the escape:

> My father was on the staff of the High Schools of Johannesburg and Pretoria. He explained that the latter was in the buildings of the old Dutch school where the British prisoners had been confined for a while. He wrote his memoirs in the early part of the war, and died in 1943
> It was from the same school that the present Prime Minister, Mr Winston Churchill, made his escape. I was given the story of his adventures by the father of one of my pupils, by name

Howard, who was manager of a coal mine at Witbank on the Delagoa Bay line and with whom I used to stay . . .

Howard himself was sitting up late that evening when there was a knock on the door. On opening it, he was confronted by what seemed more like an apparition than a human being. After verbal fencing on both sides, Howard invited his visitor to enter. The intruder protested that he was famished. On being taken to the larder, he began to eat the butter neat as it was the only form of food readily available.

After refreshment, Howard concealed Churchill at the bottom of his mine shaft, but impressed upon him the need for caution and for not disclosing his presence in the mine. Churchill was as good as gold save for a solitary lapse when, then as now, he could not resist a cigar. A native, sniffing the fragrant aroma, looked down the shaft and ran in terror to Mr Howard protesting that he had seen a spook. Howard subsequently brought up wool and loaded it on a truck with Churchill beneath; after a perilous journey the truck, together with its precious cargo, reached Lourenco Marques and safety.

The author concludes with these observations:

Howard's story also refutes the allegation that Churchill, in making his escape, let down his confederates in the escapade. Churchill was most particular to tell him that he was much worried by what might have happened to them that he himself had waited for them for some time in the adjoining garden, but that they had not appeared. Howard promised to send out trusty emissaries to intercept them should they come his way.

Eventually Major Haldane and Captain le Mesurier were intercepted by Howard and enabled to escape. Their story was that, after having failed to negotiate the railing, they resumed their previous efforts to make an underground tunnel beneath one of the classrooms. They remained underground for some days and then found that the other prisoners had been moved elsewhere. Their escape therefore became comparatively easy.

I took early steps to follow up their story. The trap door had been screwed down by the unimaginative Public Works Department, and on opening it I found the tunnel exactly as the two prisoners had left it. Their implements, which had been purloined from the school gymnasium, were still there; so also were their pyjamas, playing cards, tins of bully beef and so forth . . .

Churchill's later accounts of his escape make light of the danger and exhaustion involved. In reality he very nearly gave up, and might well have surrendered to any Boer he met rather than die needlessly in the open. Lionel James recalled that, shortly afterwards, Churchill talked 'in confidential vein' about his experiences:

> By climbing on freight cars at night, and by crawling in shadows, Churchill had accomplished some part of his journey to the Portuguese Frontier; but at last even his brave heart was beaten. Starving and dead beat, he came to the conclusion that it would be better to return to Pretoria and imprisonment than to die of exhaustion and exposure on the veldt.

His gamble, however, paid off, and on 21 December, 1899, Churchill telegraphed his employers, the *Morning Post*, from Lourenco Marques:

> I am weak but I am free. I have lost many pounds but I am lighter in heart. I shall also avail myself of every opportunity from this moment to urge with earnestness an unflinching and uncompromising prosecution of the war.

While his adventures were obviously exciting, and his escape made headlines around the world, Churchill was by no means the only young man of his age and background to be at the centre of great events. During the Boer conflict, almost every edition of his old school's magazine had a prominent section on 'The War', or 'Harrovians in the Transvaal' in which Old Boys provided descriptions of the fighting they had witnessed, and there were even reports from more exotic scenes of strife – one account was sent from the Foreign Legation at Peking and described the Boxer siege. Some scaled greater heights of fame than Churchill: his friend JP Milbanke won the VC, as did another Old Harrovian, WN Congreve. Others shared the same danger, or had equivalent experiences that commanded interest as much as his. In December 1899 the magazine linked his name with that of his later Cabinet colleague:

> Two Old Harrovians, Messrs. Winston Churchill and L.M. Amery, are acting as War Correspondents in South Africa. The former,

who represents the *Morning Post*, was the only correspondent in the armoured train which was derailed by the Boers on November 15th. All accounts of that unfortunate event are unanimous in their praise of Mr Churchill's gallantry. He was taken prisoner with most of his companions. Mr Amery, *The Times* correspondent, distinguished himself by a night ride through the lines of the Boers besieging Ladysmith. It is satisfactory to know that he was not wounded.

Winston Churchill, however, was now more famous than all of them. He recalled in his memoirs: 'I found that during the weeks I had been prisoner my name had resounded at home.' And another of Gough's pencilled observations states that:

It was about this time that Churchill met me outside Dundonald's tent. He showed me some cuttings, not in the least abashed, and said: 'Look at these – you see people are talking about me already.' He did not seem to mind what they said so long as he got the publicity.

BACK TO THE FRAY

Churchill did not return to England. The war was still going on, and he was anxious to get to the fighting. Within a month of his escape he was back in front of Ladysmith and, while still a correspondent for the *Post*, had been given an unpaid commission in the South African Light Horse. As has been seen, not all senior officers disliked him, for his zeal and courage could charm and impress. His personal friends included several of his military superiors such as Bindon Blood and Ian Hamilton. Now the Commander-in-Chief, Sir Redvers Buller, became one of his admirers, telling his wife: 'He really is a fine fellow, and I must say I admire him greatly. I wish he was leading regular troops instead of writing for a rotten paper.'

Churchill also arranged a commission for his brother, and Lady Randolph and Jack arrived in South Africa in January. She had raised the sum of £40,000 over a period of two months from American donations to this British war effort, and with characteristic energy had insisted on bringing the ship to its destination herself. The Duchess of Marlborough, who as a fellow American was also involved in fundraising for the ship, saw this kind gesture as the beginning of a trend that would continue:

The South African war, which began in 1899 and ended in

1902, gave me my first experience of war work when, with Lady
Randolph Churchill and other American women, I helped
to equip and send out a hospital ship to Cape Town. This
ship, called the *Maine,* was the precursor of an endless tide of
American generosity, which reached the high mark in World War
II. Lady Randolph went out on the ship to join her son Winston
... The resistance the Boers were putting up proved unexpectedly
successful and alarm at the English casualties and more
especially at the loss of British prestige was becoming general.

One of the first patients aboard Lady Randolph's hospital was her younger
son, who was shot in the calf during the first skirmish in which he was
involved. JB Atkins, a correspondent who had accompanied Winston
Churchill throughout the conflict, remarked, 'It seemed as though he had
paid his brother's debts.'

In the same month one of the war's fiercest battles was fought at
Spion Kop, a strategic point on the hills overlooking the Tugela river
that separated Buller's troops from Ladysmith. If it could be captured,
the British would have broken the back of the Boer defences. The setting
for this encounter was described afterwards in a book on the war by the
Prussian General Staff:

The summit of Spion Kop is, as it were, strewn with boulders of
all sizes, in the spaces between which grows short, coarse grass.
Where there is any soil it is shallow. In plan the surface may be
compared to an equilateral triangle with its apex on the North
and its base on the South. It is not absolutely flat, but slopes
gently downwards from the South towards the centre, and from
near that point rises again towards the edge on the northern side.
From this elevated edge the mountain slopes steeply towards
the valley of the Blaauwbank in several terraces. The result of
this configuration is that the field of fire from the centre of
the plateau is limited towards the North by the edge of the
mountain, and that it is quite impossible for rifles placed at the
centre to produce any effect whatever on the northern slope. The
slopes in all other directions, and specially that on the South
towards the Tugela, fall away steeply from the summit. On the
south-western angle the ascent is made easier by several terraces
which combine to form a chain of high points stretching along
the East of the Spion Kop stream towards Trichardt's Drift ...

Churchill used his memoir to give his account of the advance:

> **Three days later we attacked the line of heights beyond Ventner's Spruit. We trotted to the stream under shell fire, left our horses in its hollows and climbed the steep slopes on foot, driving back the Boer outposts. Following sound tactics we advanced up the salients, stormed Child's Kopje and reached the general crest line with barely a score of casualties.**

Once again, General Gough bursts the balloon: 'Gross exaggeration. There was practically no resistance. Any casualties were only caused by some shell-fire.'

Churchill's narrative continues: 'The tongue of land encircled by the river included on our left Hlangwane Hill, assaulted by the South African Light Horse.'

Gough comments: 'This assault never even reached the foot of the heights and in any case it was the squadrons of the Natal Carbineers and the Imperial Light Horse which came under fire, not [Churchill's regiment] the South African Light Horse.'

British troops initially scrambled to the top without heavy losses, but once at the top they found themselves fatally exposed. Without effective cover and unable to dig more than eighteen inches into the ground, the men were shot down by the score. Even their inadequate trenches were open to Boer rifle fire from nearby peaks that the British commanders had not thought to secure, and so they came under fire from four directions. Their own artillery, hampered by mist, fired on their positions, aiding a determined Boer counter-attack. For a whole day they remained on the hilltop, their only cover the piled-up bodies of their comrades and suffering from thirst, hunger and lack of ammunition, as well as incessant bullets and shrapnel. Communications with the commander, Sir Charles Warren, were difficult and confused.

Churchill's unit had not been committed to the battle, but in his correspondent role he had climbed near the summit during the afternoon, taken in the difficulties and shortages, and gone to report these to Warren. Throughout the following hours he returned to the top of the hill to urge the officers there to hang on and to tell them that provisions were on the way. It was too late. Colonel Alec Thorneycroft, the most experienced of the officers on the summit, had been in the fighting for over 23 hours. He had made the decision to abandon the hill and, although other officers objected, he had his way and the troops slunk away from the barren, corpse-strewn peak. There had been 1,733 casualties. Churchill was to write: 'The scenes on Spion Kop were among the strangest and most terrible I have ever witnessed.' German observers were to conclude:

> In this fighting at close quarters the Boers had certain advantages: they found better cover behind boulders and at the sharply defined edge of the plateau, than the British had in their defective entrenchments; and they hardly suffered at all from Artillery fire. Besides this, they knew how to snatch moments of repose in the course of even the heaviest fighting; generally only a part of their men were firing in the foremost line while the remainder, retiring into dead angles and behind large masses of rock, drank their coffee in perfect comfort. The result was that the Boers always had men in fresh trim available for the repulse of any rush forward made by the British. On the call, 'There come the Khakis', everybody able to use a rifle reappeared in the firing line . . . Sometimes the British, sent forward from the rear-most sections, could be actually seen as they advanced into the firing line; sometimes when they crawled along the ground they reached the front without being seen at all. Although many of them gradually fell asleep, the fire of the Boers never entirely ceased; they waited for the moment when a British helmet should be seen somewhere, to overwhelm it with fire from all sides, so they soon ceased to appear. A few weak attempts of isolated groups to rush forward in a bayonet charge were crushed from the very outset. At the same time our line was getting thinner every minute the afternoon advanced; we had lost not a few of our men, and many unscathed men even crept back to the rear.'

Unbeknown to them, the Boers had also given up. They too had suffered exhaustion, thirst and hunger on the heights, and they had marvelled at the endurance of the British soldiers, which had persuaded many of them that they could not win. Throughout the day there had been a steady trickle of Boers down the slopes, though enough remained to keep the fight going. During that night they thought they had lost possession of the hill, and they were astonished the next morning to find the summit deserted. German observers concluded that, in a battle in which both sides became weary and dispirited, victory for the Boers – who had reoccupied Spion Kop – had hinged on the personality of the commanders. Louis Botha's greater determination had been decisive.

Buller in the end outflanked the hill, and a number of other obstacles. In weeks of hard and costly fighting, at Hussar Hill (where Jack Churchill was wounded), Monte Cristo, Colenso and Hart's Hill, the Boers were gradually driven back until they abandoned Ladysmith. They retreated into the Transvaal and fighting in Natal was thus over. Churchill had not been with the first troops to enter Ladysmith on 28 February – he was with the cavalry in the rear of the relieving column – but he attended a celebration dinner that evening at which he greeted his old friend Ian Hamilton, who had cheerfully survived the 117-day siege.

Churchill's account of the final advance states that: 'On the 15th the whole army marched from its camps along the railway to Hussar Hill and deployed for attack.' While Gough recalls that: 'The advance began on the 14th, but Churchill was then sight-seeing with his mother and being shown around in Durban.'

Churchill concludes his description of the relief of Ladysmith with a colourful image of the army's advance:

> The Boers were in full retreat, and the dust of the wagon-trains trekking northward rose from many quarters of the horizon.
> All day we chafed and fumed and it was not until evening that two squadrons of the South African Light Horse were allowed to brush through the crumbling rearguards and ride into Ladysmith. I rode with their two squadrons, and galloped across the scrub-dotted plain, fired at only by a couple of Boer guns. Suddenly from the brushwood up rose gaunt figures waving hands of welcome. On we pressed, and at the head of a battered street met Sir George White (commander of the garrison), faultlessly attired. Then we all rode together into the long-beleaguered, almost starved-out Ladysmith. It was a thrilling moment.

Gough's memory of the scene was a good deal more prosaic:

> A totally inaccurate account and pure fabrication.
> 1. We certainly did not see the dust of the retreating wagons.
> 2. Neither Churchill nor [as mentioned in his account, Lord] Dundonald 'chafed and fumed' all day to get on. The advance started about noon. A few Boer patrols immediately held it up and Dundonald did nothing but wait till they went away. He never attempted to attack.
> 3. South African Light Horse never rode in that day, and the

squadrons that did ride in under my orders were officially not allowed to do so. They went on in spite of definite orders to retire from Dundonald. None of those who first entered 'galloped' at all. Our last advance of three miles across the plain of Ladysmith was a somewhat majestic walk. Dundonald and Churchill may have galloped 6 miles when they received my message that we were inside the defences. They were both heated, somewhat breathless and rather excited when they finally burst into Sir George White's dining room. They never met Sir George in the street.

4. Two guns did not fire at us – only one gun and that only fired one shell.

It is understandable that Churchill should have exaggerated the excitement and danger of the fighting, since this would not only make for a more interesting narrative but enhance his own heroic stature. Though these passages were written thirty years after the war, they demonstrate a characteristic that applies throughout his personal memoirs – he makes no attempt to be objective. The reader, in return for being entertained by splendid prose and warm humour, is expected to accept his opinions and prejudices, and his personal view of events.

The Boers were offered an amnesty by Lord Roberts, but there was plenty of fight left in them and the fact that Britain would not recognize the independence of the Boer republics stiffened their resolve. Though the sieges were lifted (Mafeking was relieved on 17 May after 217 days) the Boers carried on a mobile guerrilla war.

After some weeks in Ladysmith, Churchill travelled north to see more fighting. He attached himself to a force of Imperial Yeomanry, commanded by his old regimental colonel, John Brabazon (now a brigadier general). Intent on taking part in any scrap that was going, Churchill took off one day with a party of mounted scouts to head off a group of Boers that had been sighted some distance away. They were in pursuit, but when they halted to cut their way through a wire fence, the enemy opened fire and they had to make a hasty retreat. Bullets whistled around Churchill and, as he tried to mount his bucking, terrified horse, the saddle slipped and he was left alone, on foot and within easy rifle range. He takes up the story:

Most of the Scouts were already 200 yards off. I was alone, dismounted, within the closest range, and a mile at least from cover of any kind. One consolation I had – my pistol. I could not

Churchill's brief service with Montmorency's Scouts *(above) provided one of his most dangerous moments of the war. Despite his egotism, he remembered the courage of others and, tried to see that it was suitably rewarded – as he did in the case of the trooper who saved him.*

be hunted down unarmed in the open like I had been before. But a disabling wound was the brightest prospect. I turned and, for the second time in this war, ran for my life on foot from the Boer marksmen, and I thought to myself,' 'Here at last I take it.' Suddenly, as I ran, I saw a scout. He came from the left, across my front; a tall man, with skull and crossbones badge, and on a pale horse. Death in Revelation, but life to me!

I shouted to him as he passed: 'Give me a stirrup.' To my surprise he stopped at once. 'Yes, get up,' he said shortly. I ran to him, did not bungle the business of mounting, and in a moment found myself behind him on the saddle.

Then we rode. I put my arms around him to catch a grip on the mane. My hand became soaked with blood. The horse was hard hit, but, gallant beast, he exerted himself nobly. The pursuing bullets piped and whistled – for the range was growing longer – overhead. 'Don't be frightened,' said my rescuer, 'they won't hit you.'

I said, 'You've saved my life.' 'Ah, but it's the horse I'm thinking about.' That was the whole of our conversation.

In 1906, when he was a member of the government, Churchill had the heroism of his rescuer brought to official notice. Trooper Clement Roberts was awarded the Distinguished Conduct Medal.

By the end of May, British forces were approaching Johannesburg from the west and south. Churchill, with Hamilton to the west, needed to send some dispatches by telegraph, though the only facility for doing this was with the other body of troops on the far side of the city. Carrying his own and some military messages, he disguised himself as a civilian and, in company with a Frenchman who acted as guide, cycled through Johannesburg from one side to the other. Though he experienced no serious danger, this was the second occasion during the war on which he could have been shot if captured, this time as a spy.

At the beginning of June he achieved a particular satisfaction when he accompanied British troops into Pretoria. With his cousin Charles, the 9th Duke of Marlborough, he made directly for the prison in which his erstwhile comrades were confined, and personally ran the Union Jack up the flagpole there.

He had a more thorough grasp of the war than many serving officers. E Craig-Brown, one of his old Sandhurst contemporaries, remembered meeting him in unusual circumstances:

> I was sent with warm clothing from Bloemfontein for the 21st Brigade of Infantry, which had arrived from the east with only thin khaki clothing. The train started north – I didn't know where to tell the train to go, as no one knew where the 21st brigade was. At a siding somewhere north of Bloemfontein, I saw Churchill standing in a field – he was no longer in the army then – so I got out and told him my difficulty. Churchill knew exactly where the 21st Brigade was, so the clothes were delivered thanks to him.

He took part in one final action. Hamilton set out to dislodge an entrenched Boer force to the east of Pretoria, which threatened the city's security. It was inconclusive fighting, lasting two days, and ended, as was so often the case, with the Boers melting away to resume the fight elsewhere, though the possession of Diamond Hill meant that the city could not be recaptured by them, and as a tactical victory it was therefore decisive. Hamilton described in his memoirs how:

> Winston gave the embattled hosts at Diamond Hill an exhibition of gallantry for which he has never received full credit. My column . . . lay at the bottom of a grassy mound. The crestline was held by the Boer left. The key to the battlefield lay on the summit but nobody knew it until Winston, who had been attached to my column by the High Command, somehow managed to give me the slip and to climb this high mountain. He ensconced himself in a niche not much more than a pistol shot directly below the Boer Commandos. From this lofty perch Winston had the nerve to signal me, if I remember right, with his handkerchief on a stick, that if I could only manage to gallop up at the head of the Mounted Infantry we ought to be able to rush the summit.

He continues, writing from the perspective of World War II when his protégé had reached another sort of summit. Interestingly, Hamilton identifies the reason why, though he won a number of campaign medals, Churchill never received a gallantry award of any sort, despite his often-demonstrated bravery:

> Persistent efforts were made by me to get some mention made or notice taken of Winston's initiative and daring and of how he had grasped the whole lay-out of the battlefield; but he had two big dislikes against him – those of Bobs and Kitchener. And he had only been a Press Correspondent – they declared – so nothing happened. As it was under me at Gudda Kalai that he had enjoyed a brief but very strenuous course of study in the art of using ground to the best advantage either for attack or defence, this made me furious with impotent rage and I would like the numbers of penmen who are making good copy out of Winston every day to bear this in mind: that he had his full share of bad luck as well as of good before he reached his present high perch on the political Diamond Hill . . .

PERSPECTIVE

Though the war would drag on for a further two years, and Kitchener's policy of starving Boer guerrillas of support by shutting their families in 'concentration camps' (a policy applied with success by the Spaniards in Cuba) would earn Britain international odium, the war was over for Churchill. He sailed home on the *Dunottar Castle* in July, to write a history of the campaigns and to launch his political career. Many people had noticed him and were already preserving their memories of him against the day when he would achieve high office. General Sir Hubert Gough, for instance, wrote:

> The incidents I have related of Churchill's early days may not show him as a very pleasant and popular young man, but one can recognize in them his energy, his capacity for emotional excitement, which could stir him so deeply and which were the foundations of his power for leadership. That quality eventually was to make him the greatest war leader, not only of his time, but perhaps of all time. Certainly no one can call a whole people to great emotional resolutions and courageous effort unless he himself is fired by deep emotions, as Churchill is.

Evelyn, Viscountess Byng, who was the wife of his commanding officer in the South African Light Horse, also recalled him:

> Of all the odd people who passed through the Light Horse during the earlier part of its existence, the oddest was my husband's galloper (personal courier) – a young carroty-headed ex-Hussar subaltern, snub-nosed, impish, brave to the point of foolhardiness, but certain of delivering the goods – a youth named Winston Churchill, whose fate was to be, twenty-two years later (as Secretary of State for the Colonies), to offer my husband the Governor-Generalship of Canada. He gave us a dinner before we sailed for the Dominion and said to me with a chuckle, 'Well, I don't think anybody ever cursed me as heartily as "Bung" did in the Light Horse days!' No doubt he deserved the cursing, for discipline never appealed to him; but I remember during his political eclipse, when he was a voice crying in the wilderness, Julian said, 'We haven't seen the last of Winston. Wait till this country is in a jam and wants a strong man to lead – then watch out.'

While these memories were recorded some decades after Churchill's youth, a detailed contemporary appraisal of him as a young man was written by the author and artist Mortimer Menpes for a book on the Boer War. Here is a snapshot of Winston Churchill at the moment his military career ended and his long political pilgrimage began:

> Among the correspondents there was Mr. Winston Churchill. What is there that has not been said about him? One has heard that he is this, that, and the other; that he was a tornado, a storm bird, a young man in a hurry; that he was a calm phlegmatic person, with an iron will and an audacious heart. I myself found him a very sympathetic individuality; not arrogant, not an egoist, but a good listener, and modest.
>
> ... At first, Mr. Churchill strikes one as being in a great hurry. His movements are quick; his manner is brisk and determined, and even a little brusque. At moments he falls into silence and apathy, until one touches upon a subject that interests him deeply, when he bursts out into a torrent of eloquent and enthusiastic conversation. He talks brilliantly, in a full clear voice, and with great assurance. He can be either epigrammatic or sarcastic, and is often both.
>
> I should say that he is more brilliant as an orator than as a conversationalist. At times, even in solitude *à deux*, he seems to be addressing a large audience, or a deputation meekly waiting upon him to learn his views. I have heard him talk upon almost every subject – South Africa, the War, his escape from Pretoria – all with the greatest ease and facility, but not carelessly. I noticed that his conversation is never careless.

With an artist's eye, Menpes penned a vivid sketch of the physical appearance of this brisk, brusque, thorough and self-assured man:

> His countenance wears rather a grave expression; it is purely intellectual, and has a slight resemblance to that of Lord Rosebery. The rest of him is rather short, broad-shouldered, almost stubby; perfectly still and tranquil. Altogether his face – or is it his body? – seems to belong to someone else. His frame makes you think that he is a little apathetic; but his face decides you that he is alert and wide-awake, and it is just the same with his manner. By his conversation you would think him perhaps a little too pleased with himself; but by his actions you are quite sure that deep down he is modest.
>
> He is always dressed with care and precision; his clothing,

whether khaki or broadcloth, is of the latest fashion, and remarkable only for its great simplicity; he wears nothing that would compel attention.

His hands are of a very good shape, and, like few men, he knows exactly how to hold them. Mr. Churchill is very energetic when he talks . . .

Mr. Churchill is a man who might be unpopular because of his great cleverness. He is too direct and frank to flatter, and would never consent to efface himself in order to give added and unmerited value to the quality of others. On the whole, he struck me as a man who, in certain circles, might be termed unpopular, and accused of an arrogance which, to any but a jaundiced vision, would appear for what it undoubtedly is, frankness and perfect manliness.

Churchill's return to England coincided with the end of the war's first phase. There were no further battles, simply an inconclusive guerrilla action that offered no glory or excitement. Kitchener, now commander-in-chief, set out to crush the Boers by the same methods the Spanish had used in Cuba. He divided the country into sectors and controlled it with a network of blockhouses. He also had the farms of Boer sympathizers burned and, as the Spaniards had done, had thousands of civilians interned in 'concentration camps.' Theoretically these were simply refugee camps, but inadequate facilities led to rampant disease and a soaring death toll. This in turn resulted in an international outcry and in widespread condemnation in Britain, where public opinion had turned against the war. Exhaustion, and impatience to reach a settlement, were common to both sides, and in May 1902 hostilities ended in negotiation. The Boers were offered generous financial compensation, and self-government within the Empire.

7
AT THE ADMIRALTY, 1900–1915

In July 1900 Churchill was back in England. His writing, and his wartime escapades, had made him so well known that his political career could soon begin. Eleven different constituencies asked him to represent them as Unionist (Conservative) candidate, but he chose the scene of his former defeat, Oldham, and this time won by 222 votes in the so-called 'khaki election' on 1 October, called by the government in a successful bid to capitalize on the patriotic mood of the country.

In the same month the publication of Ian Hamilton's *March* completed his two-volume work about the war, following *From London to Ladysmith via Pretoria*. Unlike his previous books, these did not constitute a history of the conflict. They were memoirs of his own experiences, the text as always being built around his newspaper dispatches. The books were well received, though *The Harrovian* reviewed the first volume somewhat harshly:

> *London to Ladysmith via Pretoria* is an interesting book. Much of it even those of us who do not take the *Morning Post* have read before, for Mr Churchill has the knack of getting himself copied by other papers; and his terse, vigorous style, and the confident courage which he has in his opinion merit quotation. Written as the book is in a series of letters to a paper, it is bound here and there to be a little contradictory. We find ourselves again, as England was for four months or so, relieving Ladysmith so frequently and so prematurely that the process is apt to become wearisome. So many 'keys' were found that ended only in deadlocks. Again the book is not, and could not be satisfying; for example the terrible muddling at Spion Kop disclosed in the dispatches has little place in Mr Churchill's account.
>
> We find ourselves ever asking why this and why that – questions to which the newspaper correspondent can give no answer. Yet as a clear account of the operations, as a defence of the general in command, as a picture of modern war in

a cramped and difficult country, as a record of difficulties doggedly overcome, the book is good. It is certainly not a matured judgement, but it is a brilliant impression . . . The one chapter describing the wrecking of the train, and the hawling [*sic*], bustling, shoving and struggling under fire to get the engine clear of the derailed trucks is a piece of vigorous description, in which the author played a distinguished part, and tells us of it modestly and engrossingly.

In the wider world his second volume was treated more sympathetically. The *New York Times* said:

In a considerable degree, Mr Churchill is qualified to do serious military writing. He is a man of talent, courage and boundless energy. He has seen real war as a soldier. He is practised in observing, arranging and presenting military facts . . .

Not even the short time between winning the election and taking his seat in Parliament was wasted. Churchill shrewdly spent it building up his assets on a lecture tour of Britain and North America that proved highly lucrative and brought him considerable prestige. In the USA, with Bourke Cockran's connections, he was feted everywhere. Mark Twain introduced him to a New York audience with the words: 'His father was English and his mother is American. Behold – the perfect man!' More important than this flattery was the sum he earned: £14,000. This, quickly invested, was to underpin his first years in politics, for it would not be until 1911 that Members of Parliament received any salary. After that they were paid only £400 a year, so a man without private means could still not afford to be an MP.

In his maiden speech, made less than three weeks after his arrival, he annoyed his own party and pleased the Opposition by stating: 'If I were a Boer I hope I would be fighting in the field.' In later speeches he attacked the 'Army Estimates' – the defence budget – just as his father had done with unfortunate results. Despite having been a soldier, Churchill did not blindly support spending on the armed forces. He attacked the Secretary of State for War, St John Brodrick, over a proposed increase in troop numbers:

If this vast expenditure on the Army were going to make us absolutely secure, I would not complain. But it will do no such thing. The Secretary of War knows that if we went to war with any great Power his three corps would scarcely serve as a vanguard. If we are hated, they will not make us loved. If we are in danger, they will not make us safe. They are enough to irritate; they are not enough to overawe. Yet, while they cannot make us invulnerable, they may make us venturesome. And we shall make a fatal bargain if we allow the moral force which this country has so long exerted to become diminished, or perhaps even destroyed, for the sake of costly, trumpery, dangerous military playthings on which the Secretary of State for war has set his heart.

THE CONVICTION POLITICIAN

Conviction (and he soon became known for a refusal to compromise his personal convictions for the sake of party unity) caused him to make this sort of attack on the very Government of which he was a member. His political beliefs placed him on the left of his party, and he had more in common with many Liberals than with his own colleagues. His continuing criticism made him increasingly unpopular on the Government benches, to the extent that Members would walk out of the Chamber when he rose to speak. The most important issue on which he was at odds with them was Free Trade (unrestricted commerce between nations, without protective tariffs), which he supported while the Government favoured Protectionism. This caused him, when entering the Chamber on 31 May 1904, to go and sit on the Liberal benches instead of the Government's – the famous 'crossing the floor' that brought him the hatred of Conservatives for decades afterwards.

Having changed his political colours and found a Liberal seat, he was soon to gain promotion to the Cabinet. The general election of 1905 brought a Liberal government into power. The following year, Churchill published a two-volume biography of his father. Now Liberal Member for north-west Manchester, he first achieved office as Under-Secretary of State for the Colonies, and became a privy councillor – a member of the ancient and illustrious advisory body to the sovereign. He toured East Africa, an experience that he published as a book entitled *My African Journey*. After a second Liberal win, he became President of the Board of Trade, a quaintly named post equivalent to Trade and Industry Secretary or Secretary of State for Commerce. Having lost his seat in Manchester, he became MP for Dundee. He also married Clementine Hozier, whose patient and unflagging support throughout his stormy career was to prove the greatest blessing he received from Fate.

An aspect of his visit to Africa, to which he went in a warship, is described by his private secretary, Edward Marsh. It illustrates not only the conservatism that traditionally characterizes the officer class but the way in which Churchill could use his charm when he wanted:

> I joined Winston at Malta, and we sailed from thence in the
> second-class cruiser *Venus*, which would otherwise have been
> doing her gun practice. The officers were annoyed at losing
> this opportunity of self-improvement for the sake of conveying
> a Liberal, or as they put it, Radical, Under-Secretary through
> the Red Sea (most naval officers are touchingly Tory) but the
> captain, Cecil Chapman, asked two of them each night to dine in
> his cabin, and Winston, putting forth his powers of seduction,
> had them all at his feet by the time we landed at Mombasa.

His friend Violet Asquith, the daughter of the Prime Minister, described him as he was at this time:

> What did he look like in these early years? It is difficult to
> convey a true impression of his physical appearance. He did
> not, like Mr Gladstone, 'look the part' of the Great Man
> as popularly imagined and depicted. There was nothing
> immediately arresting or impressive either in his stature or
> his features. He was not carved in stone or cast in bronze but
> rather moulded in a lively clay.
>   Action or speech transformed him. The clay became a mobile
> and translucent mask through which his inner being shone,
> transforming it with light and fire. It then assumed an infinite
> variety of Protean shapes – in turn that of an orator, a pugilist,
> a statesman, or a Puckish schoolboy cocking defiant snooks at
> all authority. Every emotion was faithfully reflected. His was a
> face that could not keep a secret. His personality thrust its way
> through so forcibly that his features seemed irrelevant trappings
> of his intrinsic self.

He became Home Secretary in 1910, and within months had won the long-lasting hatred of the trade unions by ordering the Metropolitan Police, supported by troops, to break up a strike by coal miners at Tonypandy in South Wales. He also used the army against striking railwaymen. His attitude to domestic disquiet, which was to treat it as a minor military campaign, was demonstrated even more clearly in January 1911 at the 'Siege of Sidney Street', in which a gang of Eastern European anarchists (an ominous precursor of the terrorism that was to characterize the later 20th century) shot four policeman and barricaded themselves into a house in London's East End. This time Churchill approved the use of armed police and soldiers to seal off the street. After shots were exchanged, the anarchists' lair caught fire. Churchill, who had arrived by car to supervise events in person, refused to allow fire engines to put out the flames, and the defenders perished.

The Illustrated London News reported this event with a mixture of deference and amusement:

> ### The Home Secretary as director of the 'battle' of the East End
> Mr Winston Churchill arrived on the scene of the extraordinary 'battle' in Sidney Street shortly after half-past eleven, and at once took active part in the direction of operations, arranging, in consultation with the officers, the tactics of police, Scots Guards, and firemen. The Home Secretary was by no means unwilling to take risks of being hit; but was at last persuaded to occupy a position less exposed than the open street. He did not leave the fighting area until three o'clock – that is to say, until after the search of the ruins of the burnt house which had been under siege had commenced. Thus he was present when heavy fire was exchanged between the desperadoes and when the military on duty were reinforced by a detachment with a machine gun, when the house took fire, and when Horse Artillery arrived with guns.

He was much criticized for his behaviour in this incident. Many of his colleagues found it extraordinary that a Cabinet minister should swagger about like a minor Napoleon, and criticized him for usurping the authority of police chiefs at the scene. His meagre *gravitas* was not enhanced when he responded to a reproach by saying, 'Oh, don't be cross, it was such fun!' Cinema crowds who saw his top-hatted figure on newsreels, peering from behind rifle-toting soldiers, either hooted with derision or booed lustily.

FIRST LORD
At this stage of his career he became preoccupied with social legislation and worked closely with the radical Chancellor of the Exchequer, David Lloyd George, to produce in 1910 the controversial 'People's Budget' that

Churchill's sense of adventure led him to visit the scene of the Sidney Street siege and, as the most senior official present, to take control of the situation. He was never intimidated by the threat of violence or terrorism, and sometimes carried a revolver for protection.

would raise income tax to pay for a wide range of social reforms, including old-age pensions and unemployment and sickness benefit. The latter was Churchill's special concern and he was responsible for the first Labour Exchanges in which the unemployed could look for work. This was the height of Churchill's infamy in Conservative eyes. He was effectively ostracized by society and barred from all country houses except Blenheim. When the House of Lords blocked Lloyd George's budget, Churchill was among those who successfully fought for a Bill to curtail the veto power of the Upper House. In October 1911, however, he acquired even more important concerns. Prime Minister Asquith gave him the post he had coveted for the last few years: First Lord of the Admiralty.

During this period of hectic activity he did not lose touch with the army. In Britain, where conscription was unknown, there was (as there still is) a strong tradition of part-time, voluntary military service. He belonged to a cavalry unit, the Queen's Own Oxfordshire Hussars, that was almost a personal fiefdom of the Churchill family. Many years later the story of the regiment and of his connection with it would be told in a tribute paid to him by the Territorial (Reserve) Army:

It was a visit to Oxford in 1835 by Queen Adelaide, wife of William IV, that provided the Oxford Yeomanry with a royal title and colour, the latter mantua purple, her favourite. Originally the title was the Queen's Own Oxford Cavalry but later the Queen's Own Oxfordshire Hussars.

The Churchill family have been members of this regiment for nearly 150 years. Lt. Col. Lord Churchill was in command in 1817; the Duke of Marlborough in 1845; and another Lord Churchill in 1857.

A Duke of Marlborough served with the regiment in the Boer War and it seemed quite natural, therefore, that in 1899 the young Winston Churchill, having left the South African Light Horse at the end of that war and become Member of Parliament for Oldham, should maintain his interest in the army by joining the local yeomanry regiment. Thus began a close association which was to continue until his death 65 years later.

At this time the regiment was organized on a four squadron basis centred on Oxford, Woodstock, Henley and Banbury. Competition for officer vacancies was keen and Captain Churchill's position was no sinecure, nor did he wish it to be. From the day of his joining until the start of the First World War his presence was very much in evidence, in the night marches, the exercises at Churn and elsewhere, and in the camps at Blenheim. Nor was he the only member of his family serving with the regiment at this time. A photograph taken in 1910 shows four members of the family together, all serving (Col. The Duke of Marlborough, KG; Major Viscount Churchill, GCVO; Major Winston Churchill, MP (Home Secretary); and Capt. John S. Churchill. As a result of his labours he was promoted Major in 1905.

It was in his Yeomanry uniform that he was frequently to be seen as Home Secretary in 1910 attending military exercises. It must have caused some surprise when he arrived thus attired to watch manoeuvres with General French and subsequently when he was in official attendance upon Kaiser Wilhelm II, in Germany; perhaps he felt on this latter occasion that a uniform would give him better standing in Prussian eyes.

Another account recalls:

> After the [Boer] War a great advance was made and the lessons
> of South Africa began to be taught in earnest. The annual
> training was increased to fourteen days and took place under
> canvas in many of the beautiful private parks of the county,
> which were generously lent by their owners. Recruiting improved
> in every way and the farmers sent their sons to join. These
> young men were splendid material. They could shoot and ride
> and many of them brought their own horses. Working dress
> improved and the blue serge superseded the stable jacket and
> was in turn superseded by khaki. The War Office began to take
> a more intelligent interest in the yeomanry. Under the command
> of Sir Robert Hermon-Hodge, now Lord Wyfold, the efficiency
> of the Regiment grew rapidly. The strength of the Regiment
> increased and several young officers joined. The friendly rivalry
> with the neighbouring county developed, and a fierce battle
> took place every year against the Royal Bucks Hussars. This
> necessitated night marches and bivouacs. Among the officers
> who joined at this time were Mr Winston Churchill, who had
> seen service in five campaigns, and Mr F.E. Smith, now Lord
> Birkenhead. The connection of these officers with the Regiment
> was of considerable service in influencing the fate of the
> Regiment in 1914.
>   Many distinguished Generals visited the Regiment. Sir John
> French and Sir Ian Hamilton were always ready to give their
> help. Regular staff officers fresh from the Staff College came
> down and made suggestions to the C.O. and the squadron
> leaders.
>   In 1908 the War Office instituted a new organization of the
> Territorial Forces, by which the county associations managed the
> affairs of their own Territorial regiments.
>   In 1909 a small book was issued to the members of the
> Regiment, marked secret. In it was given, down to the smallest
> detail, the secret orders to be carried out in the event of a
> mobilization order being issued, and it is interesting to place
> on record that when [in 1914] the telegram 'mobilize' was sent
> out, the instructions in the little book, issued years before, were
> carried out almost to the letter with ease and punctuality.
>   The Duke of Marlborough became Colonel, and through his

After leaving the army and entering Parliament, Churchill continued his military life by serving as a cavalry officer in the Reserve Forces. This enabled him to progress through the ranks from lieutenant to major – the rank he still held in 1915 when he went to Flanders.

hospitality the squadrons continued to train under the shadow of the Great Duke's monument in Blenheim Park. One year the whole Brigade of Bucks, Berks, and Oxfordshires camped in the park. Half the county came to see a brigade field-day, and in the evening a ball was given at Blenheim Palace. On another occasion Major Winston Churchill – then First Lord of the Admiralty – took the Henley and Woodstock Squadrons to Portsmouth, where they were shown the latest Dreadnoughts and the dockyard.

During these years the Regiment was nearly always up to strength and it was the ambition of many to be allowed to join. These were pleasant years for members of the Regiment to look back to. With a Cabinet Minister to intercede at times with the Secretary of State for War, and Second Lieutenant F.E. Smith to answer conundrums of inspecting generals, the Regiment throve.

The fact that Churchill wore this regiment's uniform on official visits to Germany caused a certain amount of hilarity among the British public. On two occasions – in 1906 and 1909 – he was invited by Kaiser William II to attend the annual manoeuvres of the German armies. This was a major event in the military calendar. Each autumn it was held in a different part of Germany and attended by the whole Court as well as a multitude of foreign guests, attachés and military observers. The mock battles that occupied each day were followed in the evenings by full-dress banquets and even operatic performances. Since observers such as Churchill were expected to watch the manoeuvres from horseback, he no doubt decided that his Yeomanry uniform was the most practical form of dress, though as a mere major he would scarcely have looked impressive amid the glitter of generals and field marshals. To a hostile British press, however, this was merely more schoolboy play-acting. A cartoon by Edward Tennyson Reed captured the widespread perception of him as absurdly flamboyant and self-important. It depicts him, gorgeously clad in a busby and Hussar uniform – and thus more elaborately dressed than the Kaiser – saying to William:

> Now mind, your Majesty, if any point should arise during the Manoeuvres that you don't quite understand – that you can't get the hang of – don't hesitate to ask me! Remember, I shall never be thinking too deeply to be disturbed by *you*. Any topic, mind! Strategy and tactics; anything that worries you about the Empire – all the same to me, you know – put you right in a moment.

In fact, Churchill's German visits were less flippant and more thought-provoking. They provided a chance to examine and evaluate the colossal military force that would soon be ranged against his own country:

> In the Review that preceded the manoeuvres 50,000 horse, foot and artillery marched past the Emperor and his galaxy of kings and princes. The Infantry, regiment by regiment, in line of battalion quarter columns, reminded one more of great Atlantic rollers than human formations. Clouds of cavalry, avalanches of field guns and – at that time a novelty – squadrons of motor cars completed the array. For five hours the immense defilade continued. Yet this was only a twentieth of the armed strength of the regular German army before mobilization; and the same martial display could have been produced simultaneously in

every province of the Empire. I thought of the tiny British Army, in which the parade of a single division and a brigade of Cavalry at Aldershot was a notable event. I watched from time to time the thoughtful, sombre visage of the French Military Attaché, who sat on his horse next to me absorbed in reflections which it would not have been difficult to plumb. The very atmosphere was pervaded by a sense of inexhaustible and exuberant manhood and deadly panoply. The glories of this world and force abounding could not present a more formidable, and even stupefying, manifestation.

Yet for all its majesty, the German armies lacked the all-important experience of real warfare that Churchill's contemporaries possessed:

Like others in the handful of British officers who in various capacities were watching the operations, I had carried away from the South African veldt a very lively and modern sense of what rifle bullets could do. On the effects of the fire of large numbers of guns we could only use our imagination. But where the power of the magazine rifle was concerned we felt sure we possessed a practical experience denied to the leaders of these trampling hosts . . . Besides South Africa I had also vividly in my mind the Battle of Omdurman, where we had shot down quite easily, with hardly any loss, more than 11,000 Dervishes in formations much less dense, and at ranges far greater than those which were now on every side exhibited to our gaze. We said to ourselves after Omdurman, 'This is the end of these sort of spectacles. There will never be such fools in the world again.'

THE GROWING MENACE
By the time Churchill returned three years later, he found the atmosphere distinctly more ominous:

The manoeuvres at Wurzburg showed a great change in German military tactics. A remarkable stride had been made in modernizing their infantry formations and adapting them to actual war conditions. The dense masses were rarely, if ever, seen. The artillery was not ranged in long lines, but dotted about wherever conveniences of the ground suggested. The whole extent of the battlefield was far greater. The Cavalry were hardly at all in evidence, and then only on distant flanks. The Infantry advanced in successive skirmish lines, and machine-guns had begun to be a feature. Although these formations were still to British eyes much too dense for modern fire, they nevertheless constituted an enormous advance upon 1906. They were, I believe, substantially the formations with which the German Army five years later entered the Great War, and which were then proved to be superior to those of their French opponents.

His interest in these impressive bodies of troops was more than academic, for like many men in governments across the Continent he knew that a European war was inevitable some time within the next few years. It was also clear that Germany and Britain would be enemies.

The two nations had traditionally been friends, and their royal families were closely linked, but this friendship was now superficial and insincere. Germany's growth into a major power could not avoid threatening Britain's influence and interests, and Germans saw Britain as intent on denying their country the status it had earned. Rivalry had become especially bitter at sea, for Germany, which already had Europe's biggest army, was rapidly expanding her navy to match Britain's in size. This armaments race had started in 1898 when Germany's massive shipbuilding programme had begun, and had been given added urgency in 1906 by the British development of the dreadnought, a type of battleship so large and powerful that it made all existing battleships obsolete and the race had to start again. Both sides protested that they needed the ships to protect their overseas trade and colonies, but neither would reduce the size of their fleet, because the other had not done so.

In 1904 Britain had made an alliance with France – the 'Entente Cordiale' – and three years later had joined France's military pact with Russia to create the 'Triple Entente'. Germany was already bound by treaty to Austria-Hungary and was able to make alliances with Bulgaria and the Ottoman Empire. The opposing camps were thus forming. In an atmosphere of brooding tension, mutual suspicion and oversensitive national honour, any minor crisis or international incident could set off the conflagration, for as Churchill was later to write of this period, 'The vials of wrath were full.'

War almost broke out in 1911, when tribes in southern Morocco rebelled against the Sultan and requested French assistance. Germany feared that, once on the spot, French troops would remain permanently. Because Germany believed she had a right to some influence in that part of the world, the Kaiser dispatched a gunboat, the *Panther*, to

Agadir, where it remained for some months as a bargaining counter (the justification for this was that local German merchants had asked for protection, even though there were none in the territory). The Berlin government made it clear that, if Germany were to be deprived of her share of influence in Morocco, she expected to be compensated elsewhere in the world with some gift of territory. The matter was eventually settled by negotiation. However ludicrous this bargaining with theoretical rights to other countries' territory may seem today, it was an important aspect of international diplomacy at the time. The '*Panther*'s leap', as it became known, sent shockwaves through the chanceries of Europe. It demonstrated not only Germany's belligerence but also the irresponsible nature of the Kaiser.

It was in the wake of this incident that Churchill was put in charge of the Royal Navy. The title 'First Lord of the Admiralty' would translate as Secretary of the Navy. Franklin Roosevelt was to serve as Assistant Secretary of the Navy in the US Government, and this shared nautical past gave the two men important common ground when they met in 1941 (Churchill's letters to the President were to be signed 'Former Naval Person'). The post of First Lord existed until 1964 when a centralized Ministry of Defence came into being. It was a position of considerable influence, for the Royal Navy was much bigger, and for national defence more important, than the army. While the day-to-day running of the navy was entrusted to an experienced professional sailor known as the First Sea Lord, overall control was vested in a political appointee whose job was to represent the navy in Parliament and liaise between the Service and the government. The majority of First Lords had been aristocrats and were usually decades older than Churchill, for the post had often been seen as a suitable climax to a long political career. To be put in charge of this government department was therefore a great privilege, as well as colossal responsibility, for a man of 37.

That he appreciated this was not in doubt. To have reached this height after only 11 years in the Commons was meteoric progress. Small wonder that, in the memoirs of a blasé young man of the time, this story is told:

> Mischance had it that, through my very presence, on fleeting occasions, in the ante-rooms of Government, I got glimpses of things that I was not man-of-the-world enough to accept. I ought, I see now, to have been sympathetically amused when I came down to dinner before the other guests at a week-end party, and caught a newly appointed First Lord of the Admiralty leaping over the dining-room chairs singing:

Yip-i-addy, i-ay, i-ay,
Yip i-addy, i-ay,
I don't care what becomes of me,
I'm the First Lord of the Admiraltee'
Yip-i-addy, i-ay, i-ay

But at the time, when the German Navy was undergoing swift
and sinister enlargements, I thought this a lamentable exhibition
by a statesman alone with his thoughts.

The post had been given to Churchill by the Prime Minister, Herbert
Asquith, while he was staying at Asquith's house in Scotland. It was not
a simple matter of offer and acceptance, however. Churchill had long
coveted the Admiralty, and indeed regretted that he had not 'pushed' for
it even earlier in his career. He lobbied hard for it against competition
from Lord Haldane, a much more experienced public servant who had just
completed a series of energetic and effective reforms at the Admiralty's
army counterpart, the War Office. Moreover, the office was already held
by a dedicated and efficient First Lord, Reginald McKenna, who had
no desire to leave it. What had impressed Asquith was Churchill's acute
understanding of military essentials in an international climate that was
becoming almost daily more ominous.

Churchill had been appointed to a body called the Committee for
Imperial Defence. He had, in any case, a nature that led him to meddle in
matters outside his own department, and the fact that the Home Office
was partly responsible for national security gave him the necessary excuse
to involve himself in war preparations. For instance, he had discovered,
and quickly rectified, the fact that no guard was placed on the magazines
in which stores of naval cordite were kept. A few acts of sabotage could
therefore cripple the country's maritime war effort. More significantly,
that August he had written and circulated to the committee an appraisal
of how he thought a European war would develop after its outbreak. This
was disregarded by a number of the senior military figures, one of whom
(the Director of Military Operations) called it 'silly' – yet it predicted with
uncanny accuracy what actually happened in 1914. He wrote:

The balance of probability is that by the twentieth day [following
mobilization] the French armies will have been driven back
from the line of the Meuse and will be falling back on Paris
and the South. All plans based upon the opposite assumption

ask too much of fortune. Four or six British divisions in these great initial operations would be value to the French out of all proportion to its numerical strength. France will not be able to end the war successfully by any action on the frontiers. She will not be strong enough to invade Germany. Her only chance is to conquer Germany in France.

By the fortieth day Germany should be extended at full strain both internally and on her war fronts, and this strain will become daily more severe and ultimately overwhelming, unless it is relieved by decisive victories in France. If the French Army has not been squandered by precipitate or desperate action, the balance of forces should be favourable by the fortieth day, and will improve steadily as time passes.

Churchill's friendship with a recent First Sea Lord also gave him a good deal of insight into the navy's nature and problems. Admiral Lord Fisher was an irascible and difficult little man, but he had a single-minded devotion to modernizing the Royal Navy that had transformed it during the previous 20 years. He had been responsible for introducing the submarine and the dreadnought, and 13.5in guns instead of the previous 12in. He had also refocused the efforts of the navy from the south coast (for centuries the enemy – France or Spain – had come from the south) to the North Sea to face a foe from the east, with new bases at Rosyth and Scapa Flow. His work had about it a sense of urgency because he, too, knew with certainty that war was coming. In 1906 when the dreadnought had been introduced, Fisher had predicted that it would take Germany eight years to widen the Kiel Canal sufficiently to accommodate this new type of ship (which the Germans rapidly introduced). This would therefore be completed by the summer of 1914. They would then take in the harvest, and declare war. His estimate was wrong by only a matter of weeks. Churchill shared his passion for creating a navy that could meet the challenges of the age, and Fisher provided him with expert opinion as to how this could be achieved.

Churchill's new sphere of activity was impressive indeed. The author Jan Morris describes his department as it was at the time:

The Admiralty in those days was far more than a mere service department. It was one of the most influential organizations in Europe – a very ancient and peculiar corporation, as *The Times* once called it. It was an idiosyncratic world of its own, immensely important to the social and economic structure of the nation, and handling about a fifth of the British government's total expenditure. Besides being the chief industrial patron in Britain it designed and made for itself an astonishing variety of things, torpedoes to chamber pots, and entire towns like Portsmouth, Chatham and Plymouth were in effect its fiefs. It had its own intricate hierarchy, honouring traditions all its own, and bound by life-long friendships and enmities. It spoke its own stately language, surviving even into modern times: 'Their Lordships desire to express their gratitude for all the benefits thus bestowed upon the Royal Navy,' is how the Admiralty thanked the Chinese dock workers of Hong Kong, when the dockyard was closed in 1959. Its political chiefs were always noblemen – until 1908 no First Lord of the Admiralty ever sat in the House of Commons.

It was once quipped about Churchill that he never wondered if he was big enough for a job, but rather whether the job was big enough for him. Violet Asquith recalled the change wrought in him by his appointment to the Admiralty:

> He felt to the quick the traditional glamour of his new office, the romance of sea-power, the part that it played in our island history, the conviction that it was today the keystone of our safety and survival. He revelled in its technology and enjoyed its symbols . . . It was a joy to see him buoyantly engaged in his new context, tasting complete fulfilment. I remember telling him that even his brooding had assumed a different quality. He travailed almost with serenity. 'That is because I can now lay eggs instead of scratching around in the dust and clucking. It is a far more satisfactory occupation. I am at present in the process of laying a great number of eggs.' He then enumerated the various tasks which faced him: the creation of a Naval War Staff; the forming of a joint strategy for the navy in close union with the Army; the urgent need to increase the gun-power and the speed of the new ships and to prepare against a sudden attack by Germany as though it might come next day.

It is unlikely there had ever been a more energetic First Lord. He inspected every ship and every naval base in Britain, or within reach overseas. He studied gunnery and observed firing practice, and as a result was responsible for increasing the power of naval guns from 13.5in to 15in. Of vital importance, he converted the navy from coal power to oil. This ended the fleet's dependence on overseas coaling stations and relieved sailors of the filthy and unpopular job of 'coaling' but it brought a new dependence on an overseas fuel. To support this oil-powered navy he had to urge the government to buy control of Persian oil and he succeeded in doing this just in time – in June 1914.

Also significant was his championing of aircraft for the navy. The Royal Naval Air Service was created partly under his initiative, and he even went aloft himself to experience this potential new weapon. Work was undertaken to develop naval airships, fast boats and submarines at the Vickers' shipbuilding yards in Barrow-on-Furness. A member of the staff there recorded his impressions of Churchill, who made an inspection one day. His experience was probably typical of those who encountered the First Lord when he was preoccupied, or was otherwise not bothering to be charming:

> Monday, September 8th (1913)
> Winston Churchill visited the works, the *Enchantress* anchored in Morecambe Bay and he went up in a tug, being expected at 10 and not arriving till 12. He went around . . . making several thoroughly impractical suggestions as to small details, and being very rude to Vickers directors about their lateness in delivering the boats: then went over all the submarines on the building slips, after which lunch, about 2 p.m.

Curiously, he also ordered naval engineers to examine the idea of armoured cars that could be used against trenches. Though derided as 'Winston's folly', this was the birth of the tank.

MILITARY INNOVATOR
Churchill aroused serious hostility among the German public (he was earning the beginnings of a reputation, which was to be evoked until the defeat of Hitler, that he was an implacable enemy fixated with their destruction) when he made a speech in Glasgow in February 1912. At a time when the German parliament had voted for increased expenditure on its navy, he said:

> The British Navy is to us a necessity and, from some points of view, the German Navy is to them more in the nature of a luxury.

The Royal Navy had never encountered a First Lord with such restless energy, curiosity and enthusiasm. He constantly visited ships and bases, asking questions, inspecting equipment, and soliciting opinions from all ranks. This approach earned him both dislike and respect.

Our naval power involves British existence. It is existence to us; it is expansion to them.

A memory of him as First Lord was written by a young man who was later to make his own mark on history. Lord Mountbatten, one of World War II's great commanders, was a child when he first met Churchill. His father, the German-born Prince Louis of Battenberg, was an extremely effective First Sea Lord who worked in tandem with Churchill until after the outbreak of war, when anti-German feeling led to his resignation. Mountbatten and Churchill were similar in several important respects. Both were overwhelmingly ambitious, both sought to vindicate their fathers, and both were deeply interested in technology and modernization. In spite of this, their acquaintance did not begin on a promising note, as Mountbatten recorded:

It was to clear up the mess which had been revealed during the Agadir Crisis (the sending of the *Panther* to North Africa) that

Winston Churchill first came to the Admiralty as First Lord in October 1911.

Two months later my father returned to the Admiralty as Second Sea Lord, and in that position initiated many of the new and overdue personal reforms which were carried out during Churchill's period of office.

But Churchill's chief task was to set up something against which Fisher had always firmly set his face – a real Naval Staff, to prepare strategic plans and integrate them with War Office plans, so that we should never find ourselves in such a ridiculous position again. My father always believed in this, and he was Churchill's strongest backer – against, I need hardly add, the usual stiff opposition which innovators encounter in Britain.

It was during this time – I was eleven years old – that I first came to know Winston Churchill. He would often walk home with my father after a day's work, and call at our house. He was very good with young people, very friendly, and would talk to me as though I was grown up. I wasn't sure what to make of him. My mother told me he was unreliable – because he had once borrowed a book and failed to return it. Later I formed the same conclusion myself, when I was a cadet at Osborne, and he came down to inspect us. He asked whether we had any complaints, and whether there was anything he could do. Rather boldly, I got up and said, yes, there was something; he could get us three sardines each for our Saturday supper, instead of two. This he promised to do, but the third sardine never materialised, so that I knew he was unreliable!

He certainly fluttered the dovecotes as First Lord. During his first eighteen months he spent 182 days at sea – something no First Lord has done before or since.

He upset a great many people. There were complaints to the Admiralty that he undermined naval discipline by consulting lower ranks without reference to senior officers. He disgusted his Radical friends by no longer talking of 'bloated armaments', but instead backing the Navy's demands for money. And he made the King furious when he proposed to name a new battleship the *Oliver Cromwell*.

But his achievements were great. He improved Lower Deck conditions, increased the prospects of promotion to

commissioned rank, and brought forward younger officers
– among them Sir John Jellicoe and Sir David Beatty.

A significant step forward was his speeding up of work on the
new North Sea bases – Rosyth and Cromarty and Scapa Flow.
These were absolutely vital, in view of the German menace; but it
takes time and money to build naval bases, and time was running
short.

In December 1912 my father became First Sea Lord, and the
most fruitful period of his association with Churchill then
began. Together they started a Naval War Staff – but that again
is a long job. You can't produce a large number of fully trained
staff officers overnight.

Churchill and my father revised the war plans, this time taking
the Army into account, and they decided on the strategy of
distant blockade that was adopted from the moment war was
declared. But beyond a doubt the most important thing that
they did together – with tremendous consequences – was their
decision not to hold the normal annual manoeuvres in 1914.
At my father's suggestion they decided instead to have a Test
Mobilization of the Reserve Fleet, something that had not been
done before, to find out just how effective our arrangements were
for bringing the Navy quickly up to strength in time of war. This
extraordinarily valuable exercise took place in July 1914, and the
whole mobilization worked without a hitch.

Churchill's stewardship of the Admiralty was as resented by some senior
naval officers as his war correspondent career had been by their counterparts
in the army. The First Lord was expected to take a nominal interest in the
Service, to defer to the advice of senior officers as a matter of course and to
leave them largely alone. Never one to let deference or tact get in his way,
Churchill made enemies all over the Senior Service. He was particularly
criticized for asking the opinions of junior officers and ratings in front
of their superiors, an abominable breach of discipline. However, he was
forgiven a great deal owing to the zeal and energy with which he pushed
the navy's interests in Parliament. Among the useful innovations he made
was a close studying of the potential enemy's fleet: he had a giant map of
the world hung on the wall of his office and the position of every German
ship was marked on it every day, no matter where in the world it was. He
created a useful working relationship with Fisher and with Prince Louis of
Battenberg, who became First Sea Lord in 1912.

Their work paid off. In July 1914 the Home Fleet was on manoeuvres, but when this training period came to an end Churchill and Battenberg did not release the men from service. The crews remained aboard their ships, and when hostilities commenced at the beginning of the following month, Prince Louis was able to send the signal: 'We have the drawn sword in our hand.' Thanks in no small part to Churchill's constant improvement of the service, the Royal Navy was ready. Churchill sent the North Sea squadrons to their battle stations.

Events moved quickly during those hectic few days. The cause of the war was the assassination, on 28 June 1914, of the heir to the Austrian throne by Serb extremists. Austria-Hungary, for whom this provided an excuse to deal with a troublesome smaller neighbour, sent a stiff ultimatum to Belgrade. Russia then mobilized her forces to protect her fellow Slavs. Austria declared war on Russia; and Germany, owing to treaty obligations, did so too. Because her war plans forced her to attack France first (and France was bound by treaty to help Russia), Germany also declared war on the French. The attack began, but German strategy – the Schlieffen Plan – dictated that her troops must march through a neutral country, Belgium, in order to take the French armies in the rear. Britain was obliged by treaty to go to the aid of Belgium, and in any case did not want to see the strategic Channel ports in German hands. His Majesty's Government issued an ultimatum to Germany requesting withdrawal from Belgium. When this expired at 11pm (midnight Berlin time) on 4 August, Britain was committed to the great European conflict.

Churchill was in his room at the Admiralty, within earshot of Big Ben, as the last minutes of peace ticked away. As the boom of the bell sounded, and was followed by cheering from the crowds in Whitehall, he signalled to British fleets all over the world the order they had been waiting to receive:

Commence hostilities against Germany.

THE OPENING PHASES

When the war began in 1914, the Royal Navy was at sea and prepared for action. The German fleet (with the exception of some raiders that were destroyed at the Battle of the Falklands that December) was in port, and would remain there until the ships came out to meet their rivals at Jutland two years later. On the whole, the Royal Navy was not destined to play a decisive role in the war, and the potent weapon that Churchill and Fisher had forged did not give him scope for command.

Churchill did, however, make one command decision that was to have far-reaching consequences by imposing the 'distant blockade' on Germany. To cut the German homeland off from overseas imports, the Royal Navy sowed minefields across the English Channel just south of Ostend, and across the North Sea from the coast of Norway to the Shetland Islands. (These barriers would remain in place until the spring of 1919, causing increasingly severe shortage and hunger in the enemy countries.)

The British Expeditionary Force landed on the Continent during August, and the presence of these seasoned troops immediately helped to stall the German drive towards Paris. Nevertheless, the fighting was severe and the Channel ports were vulnerable. Lacking enough soldiers the Commander-in-Chief, Lord Kitchener, asked Churchill to send Marines to Flanders to distract the Germans with a show of force. Churchill was clearly itching to get involved in the war and was already making visits to see the scenes of conflict. The First Lord had obviously promised Kitchener more than he could deliver, as one of his Marines, Lieutenant RHWM Empson, suggested in a letter to his family:

> There are high hopes of us going in a month or so – Winston
> is a notorious blabber, & if he starts saying he's got 4,000
> magnificent Marines ready! K of K [Kitchener of Khartoum]
> won't wait for the Naval Division, but we will go. Did you hear
> that he went to France on Friday for the day? He had a special
> train down here, crossed to Havre in the 'Sentinel' and came back
> the next day.

Some Marines in fact landed in August. Their task was to make frequent, ostentatious movements around Antwerp and Ostend to make the Germans think the area was alive with British troops. Having no horses, they used armoured cars for this. The enemy was able to immobilize these by digging trenches across the roads, so Churchill suggested that one car in every reconnaissance group should carry planks for bridging. Then he began to think about the development of a trench-crossing vehicle. The birth of the tank had come a stage nearer.

Although inundated with volunteers, the army faced an acute shortage of trained men. The war had begun so quickly that there had simply not been time to create a body of skilled troops large enough for the tasks Britain had to carry out. One solution during those first months was the 'Royal Naval Division', a motley collection of men combed out from any number of sources but substantially made up of sailors, though including large elements of volunteers without military experience, such as miners from Tyneside. Many of the officers were retired Regulars. Though the unit used naval ranks and nomenclature, its members never fought at sea. They were a hybrid form of infantry. They were also at the disposal of the Admiralty, which made them in effect Churchill's personal troops. They certainly saw themselves in that light. A song the division sang comments on the multifarious origins of the men and the thrown-together nature of their unit, which was based at the Crystal Palace in south London:

> So there we were, a merry crew,
> Winston Churchill's Army
> Hyde Park talkers
> Swell shopwalkers
> Cooks and waiters
> Wearing gaiters
> Good ole Palace Army

In fact the Royal Naval Division was to develop, remarkably quickly, a noticeable discipline, cohesion and even glamour, and would go on to become one of the most well-known British units of World War I. That was still in the future, however. Many of its members were hopelessly lacking in training and experience when the Division was ordered to Antwerp by the First Lord to help to defend the city.

Another body of troops whom he threw into the fray was his Yeomanry unit. The Territorial Army's magazine was later to record that:

> As First Lord of the Admiralty, in 1914, he was precluded from active service but this did not prevent him retaining his interest in his regiment. He was primarily responsible for the formation of the Royal Naval Division, and it can hardly be a coincidence that the only Territorial unit within this force was his own. Perhaps he felt the Navy needed a little stiffening.
>
> Thus the QOOH [Queen's Own Oxfordshire Hussars] was the first territorial regiment to see action in the First World War, although the London Scottish and the HAC [Honourable Artillery Company] had landed in France a few days earlier. Before they left England Sir Winston dined with the officers and surprised the more optimistic of them by telling them that they were in for two years of war at least. In his final telegram to them before their departure he sent his best wishes and added that

Members of the Royal Naval Division, travelling in naval trucks, pause in the Flemish town of Furmes during their highly-mobile show of strength in the first weeks of the war. As a unit they were as swashbuckling and unconventional as their founder.

they were in for 'a jolly good show'. They were soon in action in the defence of Antwerp when his brother, Maj. Jack Churchill, commanded a squadron.

This opening phase of the war still had something of a Victorian unreality about it. JFC Fuller, an officer involved with the shipping of Churchill's comrades to Belgium, remembered the paraphernalia that went with them:

> I remember when the Oxfordshire Hussars embarked, they brought with them a vast quantity of kit: tin uniform boxes, suitcases and cabin trunks, as if they were on their way round the world. Someone questioned the loading of this baggage, whereupon a red-faced Major burst into my office in a towering rage: 'This is simply damnable!,' he shouted 'Winston said we could take 'em, and now one of your prize B.F.s says we can't . . .' After having ascertained what the First Lord of the Admiralty

had sanctioned . . . all were loaded and, I believe, a week later were unpacked by German hands.

If the Belgian government, which had withdrawn to Antwerp, could be persuaded to hold out there for as long as possible, British forces might be able to halt the Germans outside it and save this vital port. Regular British troops were falling back through the city as the attempt to contain the enemy in that corner of the Continent was failing. Describing a scene that was to be eerily echoed by the retreat towards Dunkirk 26 years later, Lt Empson wrote:

> You have seen pictures of Lille. I was at the battle there and saw the burning town. Antwerp when we passed through it on our retreat was like hell. You can't picture the misery. And the fire looked awful. The Germans blew up the bridge 5 minutes after the last of us were over. Nothing is in the paper. It has been kept out but there will be an enquiry and someone will have to answer for it. Winston I expect.

LOSS AND CRISIS

Churchill had been entrusted by the Cabinet with the task of persuading the Belgians to hold on. They probably had not envisaged that he would carry this out with quite such enthusiasm, but he saw an opportunity not only to stall the German advance but to direct operations. He offered to resign from the Admiralty in order to take up a military command, and asked to be made a general. The War Office would not hear of this, so he simply used his authority as First Lord to go to Antwerp to supervise the defence. This was Sidney Street writ large.

But this was not to be his finest hour. Antwerp was doomed and, although he browbeat King Albert into holding out for several days as the Germans closed in, he could not save the city once it was attacked in earnest. Resistance continued between 3 and 7 October 1914, but by the 8th the surviving British forces had been evacuated and the Germans had reached the sea. Not all got away. Apart from suffering heavy losses, the Royal Naval Division had lost 1,500 men through internment; they had been obliged to retreat into the neutral Netherlands, where they remained incarcerated for the rest of the war.

Those who encountered Churchill during this crisis, either in his office at the Admiralty or in Antwerp, recalled two equally pronounced characteristics: his ruthless, impatient demand for efficiency and, the other side of the coin, his quixotic but touching appreciation of the efforts of others. AA Gordon, a retired officer working for a Belgian relief fund, reported:

> It was known that the Naval Division had hurriedly left their camp near Dover, and were insufficiently trained and equipped, and were not even in possession of maps of the district in Belgium they were to defend. I was the fortunate owner of five excellent maps, two of which I had given, at his request, to the First Lord on 5th October. When he saw me next day he asked me to procure twenty further copies. I at once applied to the Military Governor, who could only furnish me with six. I then unsuccessfully tried the Minister of War and every conceivable office, and eventually learnt that the cartographer had left the city – I think for Ghent – taking his blocks and stores with him. I implored one prominent official to get word through to wherever the cartographer was to send at once fourteen maps to me by fast car. I then went to the St Antoine and handed the six copies I had gathered to the First Lord, explaining that was the total I could collect in Antwerp. He said, 'How many did I ask you to get for me?' to which I replied, 'Twenty.' 'Well go and get the remaining fourteen.' To say I felt annoyed and hurt after all my efforts is expressing myself mildly. I left things as they were in the meantime, hoping that the urgent message to the cartographer had got through and that further copies would thus arrive . . . Mr Winston Churchill left for England late on 6th October. When shaking hands and bidding me good-bye he said, 'We are very grateful for your good work,' and I need not say that he rose a hundred per cent in my regard!

Later in London he encountered the same reactions:

> On Monday, 12th October, I was asked to take official papers to the Admiralty and elsewhere in London and I left Ostend at one o'clock . . . On reaching Dover a special train was in waiting, as also a telegram for me asking me to go and see the First Lord at the Admiralty immediately on our arrival in London. I got there by 7.30 p.m. and was at once shown into the Minister's room, where I spent an half an hour giving an account of all that had happened since he had left Antwerp six days previously. He was

most interested and kind and plied me with many questions, finishing with a request that I would write out for him a full report of all that I had told him. I asked him when he would like the report, expecting a few days' grace, to which he replied, 'Early to-morrow.' I was at a loss how I could manage this, but I was able to procure the help of a good friend, Miss Grace Boyce – a wonderful lady shorthand-typist who had done much work for me in the past – and we commenced our task at Apsley House at 11.30 p.m. and completed it by 4 a.m. next morning, and the report was delivered at the Admiralty before 9 a.m., together with copies for the Prime Minister (Mr Asquith) and the Minister for War (Lord Kitchener) which I had been directed to provide at the same time.

Churchill returned to London to face a storm of criticism for deserting his vital post at the Admiralty in order to rush off on what seemed a juvenile outing – or would have done had it not wasted so many lives to no purpose. He already had a reputation for political inconsistency and for putting his own advancement before other concerns. Now he had demonstrated a rashness and lack of stability that was to prejudice many senior military figures against him and would seriously hamper his strategic schemes during the rest of the war. Yet Antwerp had not been entirely a failure. If he had not gone there, and had not persuaded the Belgians to hang on, and had the city therefore fallen several days earlier, the British Expeditionary Force would not have had time to take up positions to stop the Germans at Ypres, where they succeeded in containing them. Without Churchill's delaying action, the Germans would have swept through the rest of Belgium without meeting effective resistance, and more of the Channel coast would have been in their hands.

Churchill continued in office and presided over a highly efficient department. When Battenberg resigned in October, Churchill brought back the 73-year-old Fisher as First Sea Lord and procured another previous incumbent, Admiral Sir Arthur Wilson, as Fisher's deputy. Their experience and wisdom compensated for his own preoccupation with the wider war.

One aspect of this that continued to engage him was the development of the armoured vehicle. This would be the mongrel offspring of a tractor and an armoured car, for it would have caterpillar treads for traversing in mud and for crossing trenches. He proposed the building of prototypes for what he called a 'land cruiser' and tried to interest the War Office. It proved that an officer, Colonel Ernest Swinton, had had the same idea and Churchill urged the development of his ideas too. The War Ministry, however, felt the concept was impractical and research went no further. Not to be discouraged, Churchill ordered the Navy to experiment instead. Forming an aptly named 'Land Ships Committee' in February 1915, he authorized the spending of nearly £70,000 of Admiralty funds on prototypes. As he later wrote:

> The matter was entirely outside the scope of my own Department or of any normal powers which I possessed. Had the tanks proved wholly abortive or never been accepted or used in war by the military authorities, and had I been subsequently summoned before a Parliamentary Committee, I could have offered no effective defence to the charge that I had wasted public money on a matter which was not in any way my business and in regard to which I had not received expert advice from any responsible military quarter. The extremely grave situation of the war, and my conviction of the need of breaking down the deadlock which blocked the production of these engines, are my defence; but that defence is only valid in view of their enormous subsequent success.

In the meantime, 'Winston Churchill's Army' was still being built into an effective force. The Royal Navy had taken over the huge glass-and-iron Crystal Palace exhibition hall on a hilltop overlooking south London and converted it into a shore-base in which everything, as is naval custom, was run as if it were a ship at sea. (The Crystal Palace is long gone – it was destroyed by fire in 1936 – but the ship's bell of HMS *Crystal Palace* is still displayed in the grounds.) A member of the unit, Basil Rackham, recalls life in this establishment:

> The Crystal Palace was then training depot for the Division. So I joined 'D' Company of the Hawke Battalion. It was an extraordinary set-up. We worked entirely to naval routine, marching out in liberty boats. That is to say that you couldn't just walk out of the door, you had to put your name down for a certain liberty boat. You were there formed up and marched out of the Palace, which I suppose was rowing ashore. The training was physical fitness, marksmanship, drill and general discipline and really not much else.

We felt tremendously that we were part of the Navy, we had great esprit de corps and were very proud. But people who had been in the RNVR before the war were very disappointed that they were not going to sea. Later in the war the Naval Division established a tremendous name for itself and was one of the six divisions which were specially mentioned by the Germans as knowing that when one of these divisions were present there was going to be an assault, one of the top divisions, as it were. We had a terrific sense of identity and had a great advantage as we had our special training centres, you never left the Naval Division, whereas the army chap might go anywhere, so we were much more of a family.

The most famous member of the division was undoubtedly the poet Rupert Brooke, who came to know the Churchills through his friendship with Edward Marsh, the First Lord's private secretary in the Home Office and the Admiralty. Brooke described a period of training at a camp in Dorset which was visited by the First Lord, his wife and Marsh:

Hood Battalion, Blandford,
18 February, 1915
Even yesterday – Winston's visit – barely damped me. What a day! A real Blandford day of the milder kind, mud, rain, and a hurricane. First old Paris (the Commanding Officer) put the review off, because of the weather (but that was after we'd stood out a battalion of Lears, in the pitiless storm, for half an hour). Then Winston turned up and demanded something. We were hurried out to an extemporized performance, plunging through rivers and morasses. It was like a dream. At one point I emerged from the mud, with my platoon, under the wheels of a car, in the midst of a waste. And in the car were what I thought were two children, jumping about clapping their hands whistling and pointing. It was Eddie and Clemmie – Eddie came to luncheon – and was divinely civilian. It is rumoured Winston was 'pleased' and impressed by our (2nd Brigade) superiority to the other Brigades and that we shall go out as a Brigade.

This meant that the men would be sent to a theatre of operations as a unit and not split up and assigned wherever there were gaps in the ranks of other brigades. Churchill knew their destination. By 1915 the Western

Front was in stalemate. Continuous attempts by each side to outflank the other had extended the opponents' trench systems from Switzerland to the sea. As these were consolidated, it became clear that frontal assaults by either side would be suicidal. There was no prospect of a quick end to the war in western Europe. At the same time Russia, struggling on the Eastern Front and anticipating a major attack from Turkey, asked for help to distract the Ottoman forces.

THE DARDANELLES AND GALLIPOLI

Churchill had conceived the notion of attacking the Central Powers through the back door, or seeking, as he put it, the 'soft underbelly of Europe'. Britain controlled the Mediterranean, though the eastern end of it, and the straits leading north to the Black Sea, were held by Turkey. If these straits – the Dardanelles – could be forced by the Royal Navy, there would be immediate advantages: Britain and France could link up with their Russian and Romanian allies; Constantinople could be cut off from the rest of the Ottoman Empire and Turkey forced out of the war. Bulgaria and Austria could also be dealt with. Germany could thus be isolated and be made to fight on virtually all her frontiers. The straits were heavily mined and were defended by forts on both shores, but the navy, using minesweepers and with guns that could outrange those of the defenders, was expected to break through.

Fisher and Kitchener, together with other senior commanders, were inconsistent in their support of the scheme. Fisher began by giving strong backing, then became doubtful. Kitchener decided that the army should be involved. Other naval officers wanted a slow and careful attack in which gains could be consolidated. After some initial actions, the navy went in on 18 March 1915. The guns of their 16 warships, including the newest dreadnought, quickly put much of the Turkish defences out of action, but minesweeping could not be done effectively under heavy fire and was not carried through. Within a matter of minutes, three ships hit a minefield and exploded, with a loss of over 700 men. The naval commander, Admiral JM de Roebeck, decided that the straits could not be forced and ordered a withdrawal.

Churchill felt that the losses, huge as they were, were worth it if the objective could be achieved, but it was too late. The Turks were now fully aware of Allied interest in the Dardanelles and lost no time in improving their defences and dispatching reinforcements. Any chance of a swift campaign was now lost. The rivalry and indecisiveness of the Service chiefs had slowed down the operation, and the stubbornness of

Turkish defences made capture seem impossible. Churchill was to recall despondently:

> Hence forward the defences of the Dardanelles were to be reinforced by an insurmountable mental barrier. 'No' had settled down forever on our councils, crushing with its deadening weight what I shall ever believe was the hope of the world.

There would now have to be landings, with large numbers of troops attempting to capture the western side – the Gallipoli peninsula – in fighting that could become as much of a stalemate as the other fronts. Nevertheless, the die was now cast. The Royal Naval Division was to take part in this operation.

Rupert Brooke was delighted at the prospect of serving in this cradle of civilization, writing gushingly to his friend Violet Bonham-Carter:

> Oh Violet it's too wonderful for belief! I had not imagined Fate could be so benign. I almost suspect her. Perhaps we shall be held in reserve, out on a choppy sea for two months. I'm filled with confident and glorious hopes. I've been looking at the maps. Do you think perhaps the fort on the Asiatic corner will want quelling . . . and they'll make a sortie and meet us on the plains of Troy? Shall we have a Hospital Base (and won't you manage it?) at Lesbos? Will Hero's Tower crumble under the 15-inch guns? Will the sea be polyphloisbic and wine dark and unvintageable? Shall I loot mosaics from St Sophie's?

He was, of course, to do none of these things. He died of an infection while on the way to the Dardanelles. Perhaps this was as well, for there was to be precious little romance about the campaign.

Churchill's old friend Ian Hamilton was Commander-in-Chief of the Mediterranean Expeditionary Force. In his memoirs he explained how the campaign began to fall apart:

> After the naval attack had failed and the War Council had decided upon a joint naval and military attack upon the Gallipoli Peninsula, [Winston] did all he could to pilot it through the Cabinet and Committee of Imperial Defence; thus . . . the Navy became father and mother to the Expeditionary

Force throughout the landing operations and afterwards.
There were those, however, amongst his colleagues who were
more like the wicked stepmother in the fairy tale than any
legitimate parent. To them the Dardanelles was a 'side-show'
and Winston a discredited showman. So it came to pass in the
desperate see-saw of battle, when a prompt reinforcement by
quite a small contingent would have turned the scales in our
favour, there was a Cabinet crisis in full swing and my prayer for
help was not even considered by War Council for three weeks.
Remarking on this the Royal Commission on the Dardanelles
makes the following observations in their Report: 'After the
failure of the attacks which followed the first landing there
was undue delay in deciding upon the course to be pursued in
the future. Sir Ian Hamilton's appreciation was forwarded on
the 17th of May 1915. It was not considered by the War Office
or the Cabinet until the 7th of June. The reconstruction of the
Government which took place at the most critical period was the
main cause of the delay. As a consequence the dispatch of the
reinforcements asked for by Sir Ian Hamilton in his appreciation
was postponed for six weeks.'

Thus do politics cut across high strategy and Winston, who
saw that we might do at Gallipoli what was in fact achieved by
Allenby in Palestine two years later, i.e. the disruption of the
Turkish Empire and the opening of Germany's back door, found
himself before long out of favour and out of office . . .

Initial landings had met with ferocious opposition, including the large-
scale disembarkation of Australian and New Zealand troops on 25 April
1915. The Turks were brave, resourceful and stubborn soldiers, who won
the respect of their Allied opponents. The invaders were unable to gain
more than a toe-hold on the peninsula, and there the campaign settled
down to the same pattern of trench warfare that existed elsewhere. Violet
Bonham-Carter wrote:

Again and again when an advance was made at heavy cost there
were no reserves behind to follow up the thrust and push it
through. At best they were halted in their tracks, at worst driven
back over dearly gained ground. This gave the Turks a breathing
space to reform and reinforce themselves and strengthen their
positions. The Gallipoli campaign had . . . become a tragic

example of giving too little and too late. As Winston wrote:
'We have always sent two-thirds of what was necessary a month
too late . . .'

Basil Rackham, an officer in the Royal Naval Division, described what life
was like on the peninsula after trench warfare had set in:

> It was at night, that we got aboard a small ship of about 5,000
> tons and later landed on Gallipoli. We just walked through
> the ship and out at the side, onto a proper pier. We were met
> by people from the Hawke Battalion and were taken up to our
> camp, as the battalion was then in reserve. It was very much as we
> expected to find it.
>   The countryside I found myself in had lots of scrub. When one
> got over the cliffs Helles was like a great saucer, you could see
> all over the place. Straight up the peninsula was the Achi Baba,
> looking at you and before this, just a few ruins of the village of
> Krithia. Visibility was excellent, it was a wonderful sight and
> most days were lovely and sunny. You could see the whole area
> set out before you, over to Asia and the naval ships around in the
> blue sea . . .

The reality, of course, was not quite so beautiful, with disease, death and
constant shelling:

> At that time the flies were certainly still giving problems. Of
> course, it was trench warfare and so it was a question of finding
> the frontline. Well the frontline itself, I should say was about
> 5 miles in. We were then on the left, you might say opposite
> Krithia, but of course, when I actually joined the battalion they
> were in reserve. They were back in these so-called camps which
> were nothing more than holes dug in the ground and we got a
> few waterproof sheets and things of that sort and made up a bit
> of cover. The system was about eight days in the reserve, then you
> would move up to the Eski Lines, which were the second line of
> defence, not in touch with the Turks. You would spend about
> four or five days there and then you would do four or five days in
> the front line, until you went back to reserve.
>   The dead had to be dealt with on the spot because of the
> climate. There was no end of crosses where people had been

buried, they were interned rather roughly. As a young man it struck me about the futility of war, but it was one of those things that just had to be done and that was the price to be paid.

We got shelled from the mainland but there was nothing really to worry about at that time. There was a warning system for shelling by Asiatic Annie, which I think the French dealt with, but of course, we were on the very opposite flank to the French at that stage and we wouldn't hear it. But at that time the shelling from Asiatic Annie was very light.

You must realise that on the peninsula at Helles, you were always subject to shell fire, you might get it anywhere. But if you were in the reserve camp, which meant living under ground in dugouts, you were not able to move about much in the daytime because it would attract fire. We did have bathing parties, that went down and had a good wash and washed our cloths [*sic*] there.

When I arrived jaundice was very rife, there was no end of people with it, but this was not sufficient reason to be evacuated. It made people very lethargic, which didn't help matters. But as the weather got colder the jaundice became less of a problem.

Rackham soon came to know all about life in the trenches on the peninsula:

The trenches in Gallipoli were about seven to eight feet deep with a fire step, where you could get to see over the top. However, you couldn't show your head in the ordinary way as the trench lines were in some places only between twenty yards and one hundred yards apart. The communication trenches were much bigger and wider than those in the front line. We had field telephones on wire, but it was always getting cut. There was mining and of course, we did about a week up in the firing line and a week back in the camps and there was shelling certainly every time one went in. The state of morale was very high but those who had been there a long time were in pretty poor shape physically.

Not long after I got to Gallipoli, when in reserve, I paid a visit to Anzac. The impression I got was that there was no depth to it, and the terrain was terribly rough. And from the positions, I could not think how they existed. There was not a continuous line of trenches as this could not be, because of the landscape. It was so steep that I think at the Anzac they had better protection from shellfire, than we did at Helles. Because at Helles once you got up from the beach and over the cliffs you were exposed to the whole Turkish fire.

I remember, that I took part in a short raid of the Turkish trenches, in order to gain information and get an identification. We got into their trench and knocked out one Turk dragging him back, and handed him over to the intelligence people. They wanted to know who was there and what Division they belonged to. Their trenches were as deep as ours, but not riveted, or so well looked after and were very dirty.

The Royal Navy did bombard the Turks from the sea, but at this time they were very worried about submarines and as a result they sent out ships called Monitors with their great fifteen inch guns. They had great blisters on their sides, as had all the cruisers, these were supposed to explode the torpedo and not the ship. They were built out onto the side of the ship, like an extra wall. I think they were very effective.

The rosy picture of lovely sunny days, with ships decorating the blue sea, changed radically with the onset of winter:

I can't recall an official warning about likely storms of snow and ice, but as the winter advanced we all knew that it might well happen. When it did we were in the frontline and the conditions were simply terrible. Not, I think as bad as they were at Anzac where the trenches were almost literally flooded up to the top of the parapet, but we were well over our knees in water as nearly all the dugouts were simply flooded out. Snow made things even more difficult.

Some people had braziers but it was difficult to get any fuel as there were not many trees. We used bits of wood and pieces from the beach, that was all you could get. But this was very scarce, as everybody wanted it.

By the autumn it was clear that the Allies could not hope for success, and between December 1915 and January 1916 the troops were evacuated.

The process of casting blame had by then been going on in Whitehall for some time. Fisher, who had been emphatically in favour of the attack at the beginning, not only changed tack entirely but resigned as First Sea Lord and then put the responsibility on Churchill, calling for his dismissal. The Conservatives, who had been waiting a decade for the chance to take revenge, demanded his scalp. Asquith might have supported him, but he was putting together a coalition government, and Conservatives made it clear that they wanted Churchill jettisoned as a prerequisite of cooperation. On 26 May 1915, Churchill's career as First Lord came to an end. He was not expelled from Cabinet, however: Asquith allowed him to remain as Chancellor of the Duchy of Lancaster. This position, which has no equivalent in other countries, was an anachronism and a formality, the incumbent being the representative of a largely forgotten royal duchy. Even Churchill was shown in a cartoon asking: 'What is a Duchy and where is Lancaster?' Though he still had a title and the barest trappings of position, his effective political career was over.

8
FLANDERS AND AFTER, 1916

In political oblivion after the Dardanelles, Churchill sought refuge in action by returning to his original profession. With his detailed knowledge and wide experience he could have found half-a-dozen useful roles, but hatred of him by the Conservatives in Asquith's coalition would not allow him any position of prestige or responsibility. As in 1914, he asked for the rank of Major-General, and this was again refused. Field Marshal Lord French offered him command of a brigade, but this too did not come about.

It was difficult for the War Office to find him a niche. Experience as a junior cavalry officer in smaller conflicts did not fit him for the infantry and artillery war of the trenches, and his attempt at command in Antwerp was remembered as a failure. To the suspicion with which soldiers would regard a politician in their midst would be added the frank dislike with which a 'Radical' would be viewed by the officer class, while some senior officers had never forgiven his behaviour in the colonial campaigns. He was therefore not given – initially, at least – any significant authority. Late in 1915 he was posted to the 2nd Battalion, Grenadier Guards, 'under instruction', as a major, which was his rank in the peacetime Yeomanry.

WITH THE GRENADIER GUARDS
The Colonel's greeting when he arrived in Flanders – 'I think I ought to tell you that we were not at all consulted in the matter of your coming to join us' – indicated the hostility he might expect, yet in a very short time he won the respect of both officers and men, and was even briefly to become the unit's second-in-command, an event he described as 'one of the greatest honours I have ever received'. For one thing, he expected no favours. He respected those senior in rank and lived like any other officer. A natural sybarite when surrounded by luxury at home, he had the ability to shrug off discomfort and horror, whether this meant sleeping in waterlogged dugouts or seeing men blown to pieces. A history of the regiment describes their first impression of him:

One of the great events of the winter was the arrival in the 2nd Battalion of a fallen politician, Winston Churchill, on a month's attachment. He had particularly asked to come to the Guards but the Battalion's Commanding Officer was neither consulted or warned. Consequently Churchill was greeted with some suspicion. 'He had a very big kit and the Adjutant made him leave most of it behind.' At 9.30 p.m. on the day of his arrival he was taken round the 2nd Battalion line by Colonel Jeffreys through mud and water, and returned five hours later completely exhausted. However, he readily went out again on the dawn rounds from 6.30 a.m. to 9.30 a.m. when he declined to hear about the artillery fire plan and took to his bed. But by lunchtime he was back in terrific spirits, taking an interest in everything and quite captivated the officers. In the end, after insisting on spending a few days in the front line with No. 1 Company and hearing Colonel Jeffreys debrief a most successful patrol into the German trenches by Lieutenant Parnell and Sergeant Lyon, he quite won the confidence of the Battalion … Thus it came about that Winston Churchill became a life-long friend of the Commanding Officer, afterwards to be Colonel of the Regiment as General Lord Jeffreys.

In a letter to his wife Clementine he described his new surroundings:

Filth and rubbish everywhere, graves built into the defences … feet and clothing breaking through the soil, water and muck on all sides; and about this scene in dazzling moonlight troops of enormous rats creep and glide …

He had an extremely narrow escape during this period, which he recounted in his writings:

One afternoon when I had been about a week in the line with the Company, I sat myself down in our tiny sandbagged shelter to write some letters home … had written for perhaps a quarter of an hour when an Orderly presented himself at the entrance to the shelter and, saluting with Guardsman-like smartness, handed me a field telegram:
  'The Corps Commander wishes to see Major Churchill at four o'clock at Merville. A car will be waiting at the Rouge Croix cross-roads at 3.15.'

I had known General — personally for a good many years. But it was rather unusual to bring an officer out of the line, and I wondered what this summons could mean . . . However the order brooked no question, and in a rather sulky mood I put away my unfinished letter, arrayed myself in all my trappings, and prepared to set out on my trudge . . .

'You must take your man with you,' said the Company Commander, 'to carry your coat. It is always better not to be alone and he knows the way back in the dark.'

A few minutes later, they set out towards Rouge Croix:

We had scarcely got 200 yards from the trenches when I heard the shriek of approaching shells and looking round I saw four or five projectiles bursting over the trenches we had left. The firing continued for about a quarter of an hour, and then ceased. I thought no more of the matter, and toiled and sweated my way through the slush towards Rouge Croix. What on earth could the General want me for? It must be something important, or he would surely not have summoned me in this way.

At last I reached the rendezvous – a shattered inn at these exceptionally unhealthy cross-roads. There was no motor-car. I waited impatiently for nearly an hour. Presently there appeared a staff officer on foot.

'Are you Major Churchill?'

I said I was.

'There was a mistake,' he said, 'about sending the car for you. It went to the wrong place, and now it is too late for you to see the General at Merville. He has already gone back to his headquarters at Hinges. You can rejoin your unit.'

I said, 'Thank you very much. Would it be troubling you too much to let me know the nature of the business on which the General required to bring me out of the line?'

'Oh,' said the staff officer airily, 'it was nothing in particular. He thought as he was coming up this way, he would like to have a talk with you. But perhaps there will be some other opportunity.'

Churchill was furious at this cavalier treatment, but he had no choice other than to walk back to the trenches:

It was now nearly dark, and I had to begin another long, sliding, slippery splashing waddle back to the trenches. I lost my way in the dark, and it must have been nearly two hours before I got into Sign Post Lane. The cold rain descended steadily, and what with perspiration (for I was wearing my entire wardrobe) and the downpour, I was quite wet through. The bullets whistled venomously down Sign Post Lane, and I was glad when at last I came into the shelter of the breastworks of the line. I had still nearly a mile to go through a labyrinth of trenches. The sedentary life of a Cabinet Minister, which I had quitted scarcely a month before, had not left me much opportunity to keep fit. Tired out and very thirsty, I put my head into the nearest Company Mess for a drink.

'Hello,' they said, 'you're in luck today.'

'I haven't seen much of it,' I replied. 'I've been made a fool of.' And I made some suitable remark about the impropriety of Corps Commanders indulging their sociable inclinations at the expense of their subordinates.

'Well, you're in luck all the same,' said the Grenadier officers, 'as you will see when you get back to your Company.'

I did not understand their allusions at all. Having consumed a very welcome tumbler of whisky and water, I splashed out again into the rain and mud, and ten minutes later arrived at my own Company. I had got within twenty yards of my shelter when a Sergeant, saluting, said:

'We have shifted your kit to Mr —'s dug-out, Sir.'

'Why?' I asked.

'Yours has been blown up, Sir.'

'Any harm done?'

'Your kit's all right, Sir, but — was killed. Better not go in there, Sir, it's in an awful mess.'

I now began to understand the conversation in the Company Mess.

'When did it happen?' I asked.

'About five minutes after you left, Sir. A whizzbang came in through the roof and blew his head off.'

Suddenly I felt my irritation against General — pass completely from my mind. All sense of grievance departed in a flash. As I walked to my new abode, I reflected how thoughtful it had been of him to wish to see me again, and to show courtesy to a subordinate, when he had so much responsibility on his shoulders. And then upon these quaint reflections there came the strong sensation that a hand had been stretched out to move me in the nick of time from a fatal spot. But whether it was General —'s hand or not, I cannot tell.

PROMOTION TO PLUG STREET

His apprenticeship completed, he was promoted Lieutenant Colonel in December 1915 and given command of the 6th Battalion, Royal Scots Fusiliers, who were serving in a section of the line at Ploegsteert ('Plug Street'). This infantry unit was recruited from south-west Scotland. The novelist John Buchan, whose brother Alistair served with Churchill and was later killed, wrote an official history of the regiment. In it he said of this unit:

> The 6th Battalion, in the 27th Brigade of the Ninth Division, spent three months of 1916 in the Ploegsteert section of the front. Few incidents marked these months, the last of its existence as a separate unit, but it served under a most distinguished commander. Mr Winston Churchill had ceased to be First Lord of the Admiralty on the reconstruction of the Ministry in the early summer of 1915, and his energy of mind could not long be content with the nominal duties of the Chancellor of the Duchy of Lancaster. A soldier by profession, and a profound student of the military art, he went to France in the early winter of 1915, and at the close of the year was put in command of the 6th Royal Scots Fusiliers. The advent of so famous and so controversial a figure was awaited with a certain trepidation, but a week's experience of Colonel Churchill sufficed to convince doubters, and when the 6th Battalion was united with the 7th one of the chief matters of regret to its officers was that they must lose their commanding officer.

Many of its troops were farmers or miners, and its officers were more overwhelmingly drawn from the middle class than those he had encountered in any previous regiment. It is not known why this unit was chosen; it was probably just a convenient vacancy. In this instance he did not encounter the haughty dislike that had been evident on his arrival in the Grenadiers.

His adjutant, Captain AD Gibb, wrote a memoir after the war of

Churchill's time with the Battalion. It began by describing the rumour of his imminent arrival:

> One morning I fell in with the Transport Officer, and
> in exchanging rumours, he told me as a fact that almost
> immediately Winston Churchill was coming to take over the
> battalion. Not to be outdone I said I knew, and had further heard
> that Lord Curzon had been made Transport Officer . . . and was
> already in a position to teach him his job . . .

Many of the Scottish troops knew little about Churchill, or had only a vague idea of his identity and background. Gibb later observed that:

> Many of [the men] did not know even his name correctly: he was
> Lord Churchill, Viscount Churchill, Sir Winston Churchill, even
> the Duke of Churchill – but whatever his name was, his being
> there was a feather in their caps.

An officer in the same division, Lieutenant Colonel WD Croft, remembered that during divisional sports behind the lines in early 1916:

> There was a very strong field with teams from nearly every unit
> in the division. But the audience completely mobbed us; for the
> rumour had gone round, carefully fostered by his own battalion,
> that Winston Churchill, who had just joined the division, was
> a starter [for the cross country race]. Disappointment ran high
> when it turned out to be a common C.O. who had been mistaken
> for the famous man.

Though his name was known, many troops failed to recognize him. An account by CE Lyne, who was in that sector at the time, describes how his odd appearance caused confusion. He did not feel that the regiment's Glengarry bonnet suited him, and instead adopted a French Army steel helmet. This was all the more conspicuous because the British Army had not yet been issued with helmets at that time:

> About this period of static warfare rumours and gossip about
> spies became widespread, strange lights were reported flashing
> from church towers, German soldiers dressed as Belgian civilians
> were occasionally arrested. It was even reliably reported that train

loads of Russian soldiers were seen crossing England but not arriving at any known destination.

One day, Fawcett came into Battery Headquarters in a state of some excitement and said: 'I believe we have got a spy in our sector because I have just seen a bloke dressed in a Frenchman's steel helmet and queer garments and speaking in a gutteral voice, who said "This is a good place for an OP". 'Actually,' said Fawcett, 'I thought it was a bloody awful place, so I'm quite sure he is a spy, so let's go and arrest him.'

W. and I, who were the only ones in headquarters at the time, persuaded Fawcett not to, on the grounds that if he really was a spy he would hardly be likely to draw attention to himself by wearing queer garments, so we never did arrest him, which was just as well because we discovered that a Colonel Churchill, who was commanding a formation of 'Jocks', I believe the Sixth Battalion of Royal Scots Fusiliers, had been given a sector of the Plugstreet trenches.

We were none of us politically minded and the name Churchill meant nothing to us and in due course we became accustomed to the sight of Churchill in his queer attire on his way to and from the trenches from time to time. But we never got accustomed to his insatiable desire to 'stir up the Hun', which he used to do by calling up our gunners, usually between midnight and three a.m. to fire twenty rounds of high explosive at the German lines. It stirred them up all right but the shells they fired in return were not against the Jock trenches but against our guns and the inhabitants of Plugstreet and in the end, our peaceful life was completely disrupted and the French authorities had to clear the remaining civilians out of Plugstreet altogether. I managed to get hold of a picture of Churchill wearing the strange garments in which he had so startled Fawcett at the time when he came into our quiet area in Plugstreet. From this moment Plugstreet began to die.

The same article in the regimental magazine described how Churchill had arrived with a considerable entourage to take up his command of the battalion, and not all were ready to greet him so warmly at first:

It was a cold wet day in the winter of 1915 when Lt. Col. The

Lieutenant Colonel Churchill, Royal Scots Fusiliers, with his second-in-command Sir Archibald Sinclair. Even within the constraints of military uniform, Churchill achieved a striking individuality. The steel helmet he is wearing here is now preserved at Chartwell.

Right Honourable Winston S. Churchill, P.C. M.P., ex-regular cavalry officer and ex-First Lord of the Admiralty arrived at a dreary farm house near Meteren in north west France to assume command of the 6th Bn., Royal Scots Fusiliers, a unit of Kitchener's and Ian Hay Beith's 'First Hundred Thousand', and forming part of the 9th Scottish Division.

He came with an imposing cavalcade. Sir Archibald Sinclair [later Lord Thurso, Secretary of State for Air and leader of the Liberal Party], to be his Second-in-Command. Then four magnificent black chargers with two troopers from the Life Guards, a G.S. Limber with driver, batman and much luggage including a full-size enamel bath plus a contrivance to heat the water, all from the Grenadier Guards.

The officers of the 6th Battalion had been assembled to meet him, if not exactly to greet him, for his failure at Gallipoli was in everyone's mind. His stroke of genius and confidence in mobilizing the Fleet on his own responsibility before the declaration of war had not yet been fully understood and appreciated. We were nevertheless impressed to discover that he had considerably more campaign medals on his chest than anyone else we had seen.

At that time the 9th Scottish Division was in so-called 'rest' after three months of hell in the Ypres Salient.

Winston's first day was in every way noteworthy. After an exceedingly awkward lunch during which he glowered at every officer in turn and said no word he mounted one of his chargers and with 'Archie' and an unhappy adjutant in attendance went to a field where the Battalion was formed up for him to take over. Without waiting for a formal hand over he galloped up and bellowed out 'Fix Bayonets!' As the men were at the slope this order created a certain amount of confusion which was further aggravated when the new C.O. reverting to his early training as a cavalry officer ordered 'Threes-right-trot!'

But once the new commanding officer had been seen in action, the initial distrust quickly changed:

A few weeks later the Battalion went into the line near the village of Ploegsteert ('Plug Street', to the troops). The C.O. was magnificent. On the second night he had every man in the front line and ordered fifteen minutes' rapid fire. He gave the Bosch no peace and in no time his sector became one of the most unpleasant for the Hun from Switzerland to the Channel. We used so much ammunition that a seven days' silence had to be imposed.

In the field Churchill was utterly fearless and he had the faculty for making everyone feel that little bit braver than they actually were. Although he loved the good things in life he shared its hardships in battle with the officers and men he led and inspired. At that time he remarked 'Although an Englishman it was in Scotland that I found the three best things in my life: my wife, my constituency and my regiment.'

This time his fellow officers' reserve melted almost at once. Churchill intended to command an élite unit, and he set about creating one. He immediately insisted on higher standards of drill, smartness and cleanliness ('War is declared, gentlemen, on the lice!' became one of his most quoted sayings of this era). He posted sentries himself and explained to them in detail the purpose and importance of their work. He showed personal concern for every wounded man. He again ignored discomfort, his sole weakness being the importation of a tin bath which he allowed fellow officers to borrow. Gibb wrote:

> Nobody who knows the many uncomplimentary things which were said by the regular officers serving in the BEF regarding Winston Churchill as a soldier would ever have believed that they could be so extremely friendly, not to say forward, as some of them were while he was in command of his battalion . . . it is only just to admit that he improved us greatly. Meantime he improved on us. All the company commanders were invited to dine in the HQ mess and there learnt a little of the charm and courtesy of the man as distinct from the Colonel. No doubt he sought to win us, but for that he is only to be admired, and his capacity for coaxing and charming the best even out of the most boorish is a gift which I never ceased to wonder at. He materially altered the feelings of the officers towards him by his kindliness and by the first insight we thus gained into the wonderful genius of the man. And so he began a conquest which when he left us was complete – a complete conquest achieved in two or three short months . . .

His sector received some distinguished visitors, notably FE Smith and Lord Curzon (who did not become transport officer!). He also hosted several senior officers, to whom his manner could be a blend of respect and irony. One general criticized the exposed nature of his defences:

> 'Look here, Churchill, this won't do. There's no protection at all here for your men . . . it's dangerous, you know, positively dangerous.'
>
> 'Yes sir', he replied 'but, you know, this is a very dangerous war.'

As usual, his visitors included family members. At Blenheim a relic of one such occasion can still be seen, with the caption: 'Fragment of a 30lb shrapnel shell which exploded near the 9th Duke & Mr Winston Churchill during the First World War.'

The enemy, too, paid attention to his sector, according to Churchill's own theory:

> It was very noticeable that whenever we were in the trenches we had a lot of shelling, whereas our relieving battalion had things very quiet . . . This was in our view evidence, circumstantial, certainly, . . . to prove that the Hun knew Winston was there. But he would have none of this.
>
> 'I am just as well known in Germany as *Tirpitz* is in England and they don't like me there: they hate me. If they knew I was in the line here they wouldn't send over a few shells like this. They would turn on all their guns and blot the place out. They would love to do that.'
>
> I felt quite sure now that he was right, and yet the Germans must have known that Churchill had come out to Flanders. It was evidently not considered a fact of sufficient military importance to be censored in the newspapers, and knowing that he was out it is curious that they didn't find out, assuming they wanted to, exactly what part of the line he was in.

His lack of concern for his own safety was noticeable. Gibb recalled watching with him one night a German bombardment of their positions:

> As we stood on the fire-step we felt the wind and the swish of several Whizz-bangs flying past our heads which, as always, horrified me. Then I heard Winston say in a dreamy, far-away voice: 'Do you like war?'
>
> The only thing to do was to pretend not to hear him. At that moment I believe Winston Churchill revelled in it. There was no such thing as fear in him.

The regimental magazine later recorded John McGuire's account:

> When in command, Lt. Colonel Churchill personally made no fewer than 36 forays across No Man's Land to the enemy lines. The story is told by Mr John McGuire of Bellshill, Lanarkshire. McGuire was a corporal in charge of bombers and scouts and won the Military Medal for a single-handed attack on a machine-gun nest. He relates that one evening the Colonel approached him and said 'Do you feel like going out to-night, McGuire?'

'I strapped on a revolver and two mills Bombs,' says McGuire, 'and at midnight Winnie turned up with his adjutant. He wore his trench helmet, trench coat and Sam Browne belt with revolver. We topped the parapet and slipped through a gap in the barbed wire known only to scouts. Ten yards farther on I lay down on the second line of trench concertina wire enabling the other two to cross. From there we crawled on our stomachs across muddy ground punched with shell holes. Near the German lines we settled in a hole and listened to the Germans talking. After two hours we crawled home. This was the pattern for all our trips. While we were out our own side never fired but the Germans, worried by the silence, sent up verey lights and followed up with heavy machine-gun strafing. I often thought we'd 'had it', but Churchill showed no fear. He would smile and say, 'They know I'm here, McGuire, they know I'm here.'

The men were delighted with him. He was a new type of commander who took an interest in everything. He would inspect the feet of men on sentry duty. If their feet were wet he ordered dry socks for them. 'What were your father's politics?' he asked me once. 'Liberal,' I replied. 'A wise choice,' he commented.

I have never forgotten a concert in a barn where Churchill suddenly climbed on top of an old wagon. He could not sing for nuts, but in his deep nasal voice he belted out the old stable song: 'My old tarpaulin jacket.'

Mr McGuire summed up his memories of the Churchill he knew: 'I will always remember him for his warm humanity.'

Compared with the experience of many others, Churchill's time at the Front was quiet. His unit was involved in no battles although there was constant shelling and firing. He experienced no offensive, defensive or close-quarter fighting, though he had one or two hair's-breadth escapes from exploding shells – his headquarters was hit on three occasions. During his time with the regiment it suffered 138 casualties. Lieutenant Hakewell Smith, a fellow officer, remembered Churchill's coolness under fire:

He never fell when a shell went off; he never ducked when a bullet went past with its loud crack. He used to say, after watching me duck: 'It's no damn use ducking: the bullet has gone a long way past you by now'.

Aside from the everyday experiences of life in a war zone, Churchill found himself with little to do except administration and the constant inspection of his 200-yard-wide sector, which he diligently undertook, day and night, in his characteristic garb of waterproofs and blue French helmet.

After 100 days at the Front, Churchill's career as an infantry officer came to an end. The reason for this was that his post ceased to exist, as John Buchan explained:

> The amalgamation of the two battalions – due to the difficulty in keeping so many Scots battalions up to strength – took place in May [1916], when the combined unit became the 6th/7th Royal Scots Fusiliers.

Churchill was the commanding officer to lose his job. He was, in any case, impatient to resume greater responsibilities. Others, too, felt that he was wasted in the front line when his talents could have been better employed in government:

> . . . the order came that owing to heavy Scots casualties our 6th Battalion was to be amalgamated with our 7th. Churchill was junior to the C.O. of the 7th Bn. And so Haig sent for him and told him to go home and, through the House of Commons, [fulfil a more useful role].

Churchill was not the only one to lose his position. A number of other officers needed to find new employment, and his efforts to secure posts for them were greatly appreciated:

> I speak with all possible warmth and affection of him as the friend of his officers. This was most strikingly demonstrated in the last days of his command when he was anxious to find employment, congenial employment, for those who were to be thrown out into the cold when the battalions amalgamated.
>
> He took endless trouble: he borrowed motor-cars and scoured France, interviewing Generals and staff-officers great and small, in the effort to do something to help those who had served under him. No man was ever kinder to his subordinates and no commanding officer I have ever known was half so kind.

There was no doubt in the minds of his battalion that Churchill had been a great success as their commander. His courage, enterprise and concern for the welfare of his men made a lasting impression, and these qualities suggest that had he stayed in the army he would have had a highly successful career. Many men carried away pleasant memories of his time with the unit. Gibb wrote:

> An undying recollection will be of a lovely spring day in the courtyard of Lawrence Farm. The Colonel sat tilted on a rickety chair reading his pocket Shakespeare and beating time to the gramophone which was being assiduously fed by one of the servants.

Lieutenant Colonel Croft said that Churchill 'described himself as a cavalry soldier run to seed; all the same the Service lost a good soldier when Winston took to politics.' The Regiment did not forget him. In the next war he was appointed their Honorary Colonel, and a barracks was named after him.

A PERSUASIVE INFLUENCE

Churchill returned to the world of Westminster and Whitehall. He was still a member of parliament, his perspective on the war was useful and he therefore still had some scope for persuasion and influence.

The development of the 'Land Cruiser' had continued. It was now entirely an army concern and had a new name, the tank, as well as a unit called the Tank Corps (initially known as the Heavy Machine Gun Corps) to provide crews of mechanics and operators. Tanks were rhomboid in shape, designed for use in rough, uneven terrain. Some were adapted for bridging or other specific tasks. All were equipped for fighting, either singly or in groups. The Mark I tank carried a crew of eight, whose access was through hatches.

These vehicles were well suited not only to breaking through obstacles and enemy positions but for sheltering infantry, which advanced behind them. They were not without drawbacks. They moved very slowly (their top speed was under ten miles per hour) and were difficult to turn or manoeuvre. Their caterpillar tracks were not entirely proof against mud, and if they became mired in soft ground or cast a track they were helpless. They could, in any case, be vulnerable on their own, and only an attack en masse would enable them to be used to advantage. Unfortunately for the war effort, they were greeted with reluctance by many generals and their potential was not appreciated quickly enough. They were introduced to the battlefield in small numbers so that, although their early appearances provoked terror, the enemy soon became used to them and even captured some vehicles to adapt for their own use. The tank was used to best advantage at the Battle of Cambrai on 20 November 1917, where 10,000 prisoners were taken, but its potential as a weapon for making a massive breakthrough that would end the war was squandered by doubt and scepticism.

Churchill could, of course, claim a great deal of the credit for the creation of the tank. A number of other people were also considered to have influenced its development, however, and the matter was eventually the subject of a royal commission. The findings of this enquiry stated that:

> In the first place the Commission desire to record their
> view that it was primarily due to the receptivity, courage
> and driving force of the Right Honourable Winston Spencer
> Churchill that the general idea of the use of such an instrument
> of warfare as the tank was converted into a practical shape.

Churchill was easily persuaded to resume a managerial role in the war, and his military brain continued to be put to good use. When in May 1917 Asquith was replaced as Premier by Churchill's old Liberal colleague, David Lloyd George, he was given a job that properly matched his drive, his organizational ability and his commitment to winning: he was appointed Minister of Munitions. From his headquarters in the Metropole Building off Whitehall, he now headed an organization of 12,000 employees and was put in charge of producing not only munitions but artillery pieces, aircraft . . . and tanks. His pet project was now among his primary responsibilities. One who worked with him, General JDF Fuller, recalls the sphere in which Churchill now moved:

> In the autumn of 1917 Mr. Churchill, in a far-seeing and closely
> reasoned paper, set forth his views on the munitions problem
> of 1918. In it, so I understand, he pointed out that to attempt
> to exhaust the enemy's man-power could lead only to the
> exhaustion of our own, and that though 'blasting power' was
> required, without 'moving power' it was of little use; further, that
> the tank was the supreme instrument which could and would

re-establish movement on the battlefield. These statements were made a month before the Battle of Cambrai, which proved their correctness; yet three days after that battle, what were Sir Douglas Haig's opinions?

Because infantry units had already fallen so far below establishment, should Mr. Churchill's proposals be adopted not only would a large number of officers and men be required to man railway guns, trench mortars, tanks, etc.; but, further still, man-power would be used up in manufacturing these weapons. Turning to tanks, which seventy-two hours before had performed the star turn of the war, he considered, though they were valuable under certain conditions and to some extent for certain purposes, that as suitable conditions for their employment could not always or even often be found, their value was strictly limited. Further, that experience showed that methods of defeating a tank attack had already been discovered. Consequently, their place in the existing productions priority list, as agreed upon on August 20, 1917, should stand.

Did the War Office, then headed by Sir William Robertson, support these views? Yes. As regards tanks, it was pointed out that they absorbed large numbers of men in their manufacture and maintenance, and to exploit this machine to the prejudice of rifle power would end in exalting the servant above the arm it existed to assist and serve. Finally, it was recommended that our remaining resources of man-power should take precedence as follows: (1) Aircraft; (2) artillery and ammunition; (3) mechanical transport; (4) locomotives; (5) tanks; and (6) rope railways. That tanks were placed next but last to rope railways is surely one of the most delightful ironies in the history of this war.

In 1918 the stalemate on the Western Front was finally broken. The previous October the Bolshevik revolution had led Russia to pull out of the war. There was no longer an Eastern Front, and Germany could transfer a million men westward. The German High Command put all its effort into a final attack in the west (Operation Michael) in March. It was imperative to break through before the arrival of American forces in April. Initially the Germans were successful: they advanced 30 miles and the Allies lost 300,000 men in casualties and prisoners; but the Anglo-French armies held and Germany had used up her last

Churchill frequently visited military units, as this picture, taken in 1913, shows. As Minister of Munitions, he sometimes followed a morning's work in Whitehall with a flying visit to the fighting in France. Here, he has changed into jodphurs for travelling on horseback.

resources. Over the following months her forces had to give up increasing amounts of territory in the face of large and sustained counter-attacks. The strain of five years of war had in any case broken the spirits of her allies. Bulgaria, Turkey and Austria-Hungary began to sue for peace.

Finally, in November, Germany also made tentative approaches in the direction of peace, her back broken by the costly years of war. President Wilson, though the least experienced war leader, had stepped into the role of chief negotiator. His refusal to deal with the existing German government led to a revolution that deposed the Kaiser. In this upheaval a Communist revolution was barely avoided and a republic came into being. On 11 November an armistice ended the war.

For Churchill this had been a hectic period. A good indication of the duties and performance of his Ministry – as well as the wide range of fields in which he had to be an expert – can be gained from the contemporary press. The *Daily Chronicle* described the Ministry of Munitions as:

> . . . operating on a scale of unparalleled magnitude. It is easily the biggest business concern in the world. Its headquarters staff now numbers 15,000 persons and in the factories under its control 2,500,000 persons are employed. It now controls practically the whole of the raw materials available for industrial purposes in this country.
>
> Among the problems which the Ministry had to deal with last year were those arising from a deficiency in the supply of paper and, to a smaller extent, of other metals. The shortage in steel was dealt with by stimulating the home output of iron ore, and by an extensive scheme for the construction of new steelworks and rolling mills. Steps are being taken to develop all accessible mining resources within this country. At the same time steel users have been rationed, and economies in consumption instituted, and scrap metal carefully collected. The development of munitions production is now intensive. Owing to the immense scale of the present organization a considerable degree of substitution or internal modification is possible to adjust conflicting needs. Good examples are the turning over of projectile factories to gun repair work, and the work of the Machine Tool Clearing House, which transfers idle or semi-idle machinery to establishments where it is in greater demand. On the supply side the chief developments in 1917 were the extended programme of gun repair, the steadying of the output of gun ammunition, taking long views of future requirements, and building up suitable reserves, the elaboration of new programmes in regard to aircraft, aerial bombs, tanks, and machine guns.

A report in *The Times* of 9 October 1918 quotes a speech to munition workers in Glasgow in which Churchill explains the importance of the department's work:

> Mr Churchill spoke at some length on the nation's war activities. Today, he said, our Navy was overwhelmingly powerful. We were carrying countries as well as keeping ourselves fit and in the highest state of warlike industrial activity. We were carrying the greater part of the American

Armies who were hastening over to succour their brothers and comrades. (Cheers). We had the largest army in the field at the present time. (Cheers). We were carrying on four separate large campaigns and several smaller ones, and in every theatre they had been cheered by success. Valiantly as our allies had fought in the earlier days, the main burden had fallen upon us for the last two years, during which the British Forces had had heavier losses than any other army. We had had more men killed than any other army, and we had made more captures. Our military achievement was one of the most prodigious and formidable spectacles ever seen. (Cheers).

As regards industrial effort, we had an absolute right to be satisfied with what had taken place, but a further effort was needed. It was the last spurt which would give us decisive victory. Mr Churchill proceeded: All kinds of military machinery will be required next year. It is a delusion to suppose that the present open warfare will require less munitions than the close local fighting of the trenches of previous campaigns. On the contrary, it will require more. We have fired in recent weeks a heavier tonnage of shells per day than in any previous period in the whole of this struggle. For nearly 15 days in succession we hurled more than 10,000 tons of shells per day from the muzzles of our guns upon the enemy. (Cheers). Do not suppose that this great volume of fire has been directed upon them without result. I was shown the other day in France an order captured by our armies from General Ludendorff to his artillery commander in which he says, 'In a single month the enemy by their fire have destroyed 13 per cent of the whole of our artillery.' (Cheers). That is nearly one-sixth in a single month. That was the result of the generous supply of shells which we were able to give to our troops, and the industrial organization of this country combined with the aerial observation which indicated continually to our skilled gunners the targets on which they hurled their fire. (Cheers).

As well as supplying Britain and her older allies, he was responsible for providing all the ammunition used in France by the American Expeditionary Force. He did this to such good effect that he was awarded the Distinguished Service Medal by the United States government.

ARMISTICE

The Armistice officially came into effect at 11 am on 11 November 1918. Unlike the celebrations a generation later, which were decreed in advance, this occasion was spontaneous, and mass public demonstrations did not begin until certainty that the war was over had sunk in. The joy and relief in contemporary accounts of the celebrations in Central London are unmistakable. Miss WL Kenyon recorded in her diary:

November 11th, Monday
Truly the most wonderful day in my life for it's the end of the war! We were hoping for the news, as the Germans had to give their answer to our armistice terms by 11 a.m. today. Still, there was always the chance that they might fight on. But at 11 the maroons boomed out as for an air raid warning, and we knew it could only mean one thing.

In a trice even this road was bustling with people and gay with flags. I was just starting out anyhow and finally got to Oxford St. PACKED. Buses, lorries, private cars, crowded to overflowing with cheering, flag-waving mobs. Truly a marvellous sight. I'd meant to return by bus, but that was out of the question, for which I was afterwards glad, as my walk brought me past Buckingham Palace where was a cheering orderly crowd – a seething mass of people, and a few cars which had been rash enough to approach were covered with people inside and out, including bonnets, wheels and mud guards!

I had the luck to be there when the King, Queen, Princess Mary, Duke of Connaught and another woman came on to the verandah amidst deafening cheers.

Then at 7.30 there was an impromptu service at St. Gabriel's which was packed. Now at 10.30 the sound of cheering and singing still drifts into my room where I sit with the light on and the BLIND UP! Our first tangible proof on this side of the water that hostilities are over.

It was a wonderful feeling this morning to walk up those cheering streets, and yet I kept having to swallow a lump in my throat – one can't forget even today, the suffering which has brought this great day. And the light-hearted way in which we entered this war on that 4 of August – oh such ages ago! Seems inconceivable. Please God that the 'great tribulation' which we have come through may make us more ready and more fit to 'serve Him day and night.' And then the sacrifice will not have been in vain.

A young man stationed in London, W Ellams, wrote:

> My word I believe they made a fine mess of Trafalgar Square on Monday last. Our instructor was telling me that some Australian soldiers & a few Tommies, started a fire by taking the hand-cart of an errand-boy, pinched some oil and away it went, after they got a tarboiler (used for guarding the road under repair) the old watchman's hut (who was guarding the road under repair) & lots of other things, in the end they started pulling up the wooden roads. They also threw a German gun on the fire . . .

For Winston Churchill, the war ended in the same way that it had begun, with the chimes of Big Ben. This time he heard them not from the Admiralty but from the Ministry of Munitions a few yards away in a hotel commandeered for use as Government offices. In his book, *The World Crisis*, he recalled:

> On the morning of the Armistice at the eleventh hour I stood at the window of my room at the Hotel Metropole waiting for Big Ben to tell that the war was over. Suddenly the first stroke of the chime. The broad street beneath me was deserted. Then the slight figure of a girl gesticulating distractedly darted from the portal of a nearby building. The bells of London began to clash. From all sides streams of people poured out, hundreds, thousands, pushing hither and thither screaming with joy, a seething mass of humanity. The tumult grew like a gale. Flags appeared as if by magic. After fifty-two months of gaunt distortion, suddenly and everywhere the burdens were cast down.
>
> My wife arrived and we decided to go and offer our congratulations to the Prime minister. No sooner had we entered our car than twenty people mounted upon it, and in the midst of a wildly cheering multitude we were impelled slowly forward through Whitehall.

The world order in which Churchill had grown up was finished. A new era, with its attendant problems, had already begun. Even with his own exalted sense of destiny, Winston Churchill could not have guessed the part he was fated to play.

9

BETWEEN TWO WARS

TOTAL WAR

The Great War had brought an end to the era of Victorian confidence. Any of half-a-dozen crises could have begun that war, but none of the experts who had planned for it had accurately predicted its nature. They had expected a swift war of movement, led by cavalry and with infantry attacks across open country. What happened in reality was stalemate and attrition, as evenly matched sides failed to outflank each other and settled into trench systems. Cavalry, on the Western Front at least, was left with no useful function, and heavy artillery blasted landscape, defences and opposing armies into oblivion.

The 1914–18 conflict produced a concept that was new: total war. There had been other wars in which nations had fought to the last ditch, but there had never been one in which the entire populations of belligerent nations had been mobilized. The demand for men was so great that regular armies could not meet it, and both sides had to call up almost every available young man. Even Britain, with its traditional dislike of a standing army, introduced conscription in January 1916 for the first time in its history.

The entire economy had to be put at the disposal of the war effort. Vast loans, both from other countries and from their own citizens, were floated by governments to pay for the resources they needed. Production of consumer goods had to be suspended and industry converted entirely to manufacturing war materials. For the first time, every family in a nation at war would be somehow involved in that war, whether or not they lived near the front line. Though this conflict was not the longest in recent history, it was the worst. The weapons were deadlier, the battlefronts vaster, the casualties were more enormous than anything previously seen. To give one example: the Boer War had cost Britain 22,000 dead. That is almost the same as the number of Allied troops killed on the first day of the Battle of the Somme.

Casualties were not confined to the battlefields. The sinking of ships by submarines – most notoriously the *Lusitania* in 1915 – meant that travel was unsafe, even for neutrals. The bombing of Paris and London by aircraft and airships, the bombardment of the French capital by massive gunnery from more than 70 miles away, caused relatively few deaths but meant that civilians shared the danger. The sea blockade of Germany, with which Churchill was much involved, brought starvation to millions of people in Central Europe.

On the battlefields themselves the impasse that developed on most fronts meant that only the weight of firepower and the amount of available men could decide the contest. On that basis, Germany and her allies were doomed. Though they fought with immense skill and perseverance, without access to the oceans they could not supply their armies or feed their peoples. Nor could they hope to win when their opponents included two nations with seemingly limitless men and resources: Russia and the United States.

New technology abounded. The aircraft, already an established part of military forces by 1914, brought conflict into an entirely new element: the stratosphere. Initially used for observation, it soon developed into a weapon, capable of bombing transport, supplies, fortresses and troop concentrations. The airship, slow and vulnerable and therefore ultimately unsuccessful, was part of this revolution.

On the ground, the tank created the concept of the mobile blockhouse. Had they been launched *en masse* as Churchill had envisaged they might have ended the war more quickly. The ungainly trench-crossing vehicles of the Western Front were, however, only the first glimpse of an idea whose time had not yet come. It would require another 20 years before the tank became master of the battlefield.

War had not been a genteel pursuit in the 19th or any other century, but the Great War added significantly to its inhumanity. Poison gas, perhaps the most potent symbol of this new dimension of horror, was first used by Germany in April 1915. Fired from shells or let loose on the wind, it caused severe and immediate damage but its effects could also kill many years later. On the Western Front the Allies quickly matched this barbarity, and the Germans suffered most because the prevailing wind blew from west to east.

Static warfare, typified by the trench systems of the Western and Eastern Fronts and by a fortress such as Verdun, was the most memorable and significant feature of the war (though the impasse was broken in the West in 1918), but it was also a war of movement. In the Middle East, where the Ottoman Empire was breaking up and TE Lawrence was able to harness Arab nationalism, there were guerrilla campaigns, epic marches and running battles. Some of the most successful battles in history, in terms of territory gained and prisoners taken, were achieved by French and Commonwealth forces in this region. In East Africa, a motley collection of German colonial troops led by the brilliant von Lettow-Vorbeck tied down Allied forces many times their size for the entire duration of the conflict. At sea, though there was comparatively little action by surface fleets, the war ranged across the globe. Germany won one battle – Coronel; Britain won another – the Falklands; and both sides claimed victory in the epic struggle at Jutland.

It was on land that the issue was decided, and it was exhaustion that ended the war. After more than four years, the strain on Germany's weaker allies became too much. First Bulgaria, then Turkey and then Austria sued for peace. The German armies continued fighting, though with increasing desperation, until their government succeeded in arranging an armistice in November 1918. Unrest among the civilian population, and the refusal of the fleet to sail into action, brought down the government.

TERMS OF THE PEACE

The Great War ended not with victory and defeat but with an armistice, implying to the Germans at least that both sides had given up voluntarily. Following the end of hostilities, the Allied powers convened a conference in Paris to decide the future shape of Europe. They also decided on the punishment of Germany, and the French, in particular, were bent on revenge. The German delegates, who had believed they were signing an armistice rather than an admission of guilt, were not allowed to see the terms until they were summoned to Versailles to be presented with them in June 1919. Only when faced with this peace settlement was it fully demonstrated that Germany had lost the war, and her delegates were appalled by the punitive nature of the terms. Germany was to lose her navy and her overseas colonies. Her army was to be reduced to a token force of 100,000 men and she was permitted no air force. She was deprived of Alsace and Lorraine, which were returned to France. Worst of all, Germany was expected to pay a colossal sum of war reparations, partly in cash and partly in raw materials. Failure to agree to this would cause resumption of hostilities, and her armies could no longer defend her. The delegates signed.

The German Empire, which had been proclaimed in the Hall of Mirrors at Versailles in 1871, ended (by deliberate design of the French) in the

Visiting Cologne in August 1919, the Secretary of State for War inspects troops of the British Army on the Rhine. This was his first visit to Germany since the Kaiser's manoeuvres a decade earlier, and he was greatly struck by the change in circumstances.

same room less than 50 years later. Germany could only meet her financial obligations by grossly devaluing her currency. This brought widespread misery, huge unemployment and ruin to many millions of German citizens and a political climate vulnerable to extremism.

In addition, France, America and Britain held German territories hostage by creating 'Occupation Zones' which were run as *de facto* colonies. These were on the Rhine – Britain's was based on Cologne, the Americans' on Koblenz and the French at Wiesbaden – to ensure that this strategic river was 'de-militarized'. The presence of foreign troops lasted a decade.

The aftermath of the Great War brought such a sense of humiliation to Germany that, like the French after 1871, she looked for revenge. For a former world power to be humbled in this way was a guarantee that there would again be war as soon as Germany had sufficiently recovered. The Third Reich was to be born of this feeling of national grievance and resentment.

The war had caused the break-up of the empires that had controlled central and eastern Europe, and the emergence of independent nations: Poland, Hungary, Czechoslovakia, Yugoslavia. The biggest and by far the most important event, however, had been the Russian Revolution. In March 1917, the tsarist regime had been replaced by a provisional government. The following October, a Bolshevik seizure of power reduced the country to chaos and took it out of the war. Bolshevism was an international creed and this revolution threatened to reap a rich harvest in the chaos of postwar Europe. Though it was only after four years' fighting that Communism was fully established in Russia, there were short-lived revolutions in Budapest and Munich. The Entente nations – Britain, France, the USA and Japan – sent troops to Russia in an attempt to nip Communism in the bud.

President Woodrow Wilson sought to establish an organization that would work for international understanding. The League of Nations was born in 1925 as an attempt to settle international disputes before they led to war. It was flouted by Europe's most belligerent nation, Germany, and would fail to prevent Italy from invading Abyssinia in 1935. Its bluff had been called; its members were not willing to risk war for a principle.

The Continent drifted into political extremism during the 1930s, and when civil war broke out in Spain between Fascism and Communism both sides viewed the conflict as a testing ground for ideologies as well as for weapons.

THE WILDERNESS YEARS, 1922–1939

In December 1918, Churchill had been given a post that was exactly suited to his talents: Secretary of State for War and Minister for Air. However apt the choice of Churchill to fill this post, his unflagging energy and military aptitude would not find a worthwhile outlet in peacetime. 'What is the use of being War Secretary if there is no war?' he asked in exasperation, and received the succinct reply from his Cabinet colleague Andrew Bonar Law: 'If we thought there was going to be a war we wouldn't appoint you War Secretary.'

Given his enthusiasm for military technology and his earlier support of the development of aircraft, the Air Ministry was a gratifying responsibility, and he commemorated his tenure with a notable achievement: he successfully resisted pressure to disband the Royal Air Force as a peacetime luxury and absorb it into the other Services. As War Minister he was involved in the demobilization of the armed forces. Public opinion demanded that this be carried out as soon as possible, but the government needed to delay it as long as it could. With the ending of the war, Britain had acquired even more overseas territories which, potentially volatile, would now need to be garrisoned. Even at home there was the possibility that labour unrest would threaten the government. Most importantly, the Russian Revolution had brought into being an unpredictable and extremist new state that was ideologically opposed to democracy. The war had created a world as dangerous as the one it had replaced.

In Russia the Great War had merged with the Revolution, and a civil war had immediately followed. The counter-revolutionary 'White' armies were attempting to stifle Bolshevism and Churchill wanted to give them as much assistance as possible. Contingents of British, French, American, Italian, Czech and Japanese troops were in the country, with the British units (which had been in Russia since early 1918) in Murmansk, Archangelsk and Siberia. Apart from such token forces, these powers sent equipment, but Churchill believed they must be ready for armed intervention against the Soviet state and he lobbied for this at the Paris Conference. Lloyd George did not share this conviction, knowing that the move was widely unpopular with the war-weary British public, and with Labour Members in the House whose sympathies lay with the Soviets. The Prime Minister sent Churchill a message that said:

> Am very much alarmed at your telegram about planning a war against the Bolsheviks. The Cabinet have never authorized such a proposal. They have never contemplated anything beyond supplying the Armies in anti-Bolshevik areas in Russia with necessary equipment to enable them to hold their own. I beg you not to commit this country to what would be a purely mad enterprise out of hatred of Bolshevik principles. An expensive war of aggression against Russia is a way to strengthen Bolshevism in Russia and create it at home. We cannot afford the burden. Chamberlain (the Chancellor of the Exchequer) tells me we can hardly make both ends meet on a peace basis even at the present crushing rate of taxation and if we are committed to a war against a continent like Russia it is the direct road to bankruptcy and Bolshevism in these islands. I also want you to bear in mind the very grave labour position in this country. Were it known that you had gone over to Paris to prepare a plan of war against the Bolsheviks it would do more to incense organized labour than anything I can think of.

Both of these factors caused Parliament to withdraw support for the White armies, and the Bolsheviks consolidated power. Churchill had become notorious with left-wing voters for his determination to pursue further wars and to interfere with the internal affairs of another country.

There is no doubt that he had thoroughly studied the country and the situation there. Andrew Soutar was a correspondent for *The Times* with British forces in Russia. Returning to London, he was invited to visit Churchill:

> When I entered Winston's room he greeted me affably, placed a chair in position for me so that I should face him and began: 'Now tell me all about it.' On his writing pad he had a single sheet of paper and a lead pencil. I began to describe the situation. His stolid expression conveyed to me the idea that the names of Russian villages and trails and positions were simply blending into a mournful song that came to him from a vast distance. I said to him: 'Give me your pencil and I'll give you a rough sketch with the names of the places.'
>
> 'I have them all in my head,' he said. And to my surprise, he named village after village, point after point – villages with unpronounceable names. The area covered thousands of miles! He knew his North Russia perfectly.3

Nor was there any doubt of his abhorrence of Communism. When in 1924 the British Government officially recognized the Soviet Union and they sent an ambassador to London, Churchill refused to meet him and asked Lloyd George: 'Did you shake hands with the hairy baboon?' Though Lloyd George and many others did, Churchill was never reconciled to the new Russian state. In the Soviet Union, and among its well-wishers in the West, he became a symbol of reaction and implacable hostility. He recognized the danger from a state so immense and so hostile to democracy, writing that the great powers 'would learn to regret the fact that they had not been able to take a more decided and more united action to crush the Bolshevist peril at its heart and centre before it had grown too strong'.

Another difficulty was Ireland. The Easter Rising had failed in 1916, but the country had continued to agitate for independence. Churchill (who was appointed Colonial Secretary) and Lloyd George met a delegation of senior Irish politicians for negotiations in London, as a result of which the Irish Free State was established in 1922. This remained within the British Empire, a fact so unpalatable to many Irishmen that the treaty was followed at once by civil war. Michael Collins, one of the negotiators, who met Churchill in London and was subsequently killed fighting against his own countrymen, jotted down his impressions of him:

> Don't know quite whether he would be a crafty enemy in friendship. Outlook: political gain, nothing else. Will sacrifice all for political gain. Studies, I imagine, the detail carefully – thinks about his constituents, effect of so-and-so on them. Inclined to be bombastic. Full of ex-officer jingo or similar outlook. Don't actually trust him.

Yet as Collins left the conference he was to say: 'Tell Winston we couldn't have done it without him.'

Sinn Fein, the Republican faction in the Irish crisis, committed acts of terrorism in London and Churchill seems to have been a target. Detective-Inspector WH Thompson remembered:

> Following the assassination of Sir Henry Wilson by Sinn Feiners in London in 1922 the guarding of Churchill was intensified and he received full protection throughout the whole twenty-four hours of the day. One of my duties at that time was to arrange for his car, an armoured Rolls-Royce to travel by different routes to Whitehall to avoid possible ambush. One morning we were driving through Hyde Park, travelling parallel to Bayswater Road, when I noticed two men, who looked suspicious to me, waiting by the side of the road. One of them gave a signal to someone ahead of us while our car was travelling slowly owing to the traffic in front. I saw that Churchill had also noticed the incident and had evidently read into it the same significance that I had. He calmly suggested that the car should be stopped. 'If they want trouble they can have it,' he murmured with a smile, and I knew that he had his own Colt automatic ready. But it was not part of my duty to allow him to become involved in any affray. My job was to avoid trouble and prevent anything happening. I leant over to the chauffer and snapped, 'Step on it; drive like the Devil.' He immediately responded without question, swung the car into the middle of the road and sped on to Whitehall without incident.

He also used negotiating skills in the Middle East. As Colonial Secretary he set up and chaired a conference in March 1921 at Cairo to determine the future shape of the Arab countries in the former Ottoman Empire, and this established the Kingdoms of Iraq and Transjordan. One of his major advisers was Colonel TE Lawrence ('Lawrence of Arabia'), with whom he remained friends until Lawrence's death.

It was fortunate that both of these conferences ended successfully, for time was about to run out. In 1922 Lloyd George's government fell, and Churchill lost his seat in Dundee.

Also in 1922, after inheriting a sum of money from a distant relation, he bought a small country house called Chartwell, near Westerham, a village in Kent 25 miles from London. This was to be his principal home for the rest of his life and it became an important centre of political discussion and influence even during the years that he was out of office. Here he indulged the passion for painting that he had first developed after leaving the Admiralty in 1915. He also found pleasure in bricklaying, and built an entire garden wall himself.

Without any government post, he turned to his second career: writing. In 1923 he published the first volume of his war memoirs (there were to be another five). He made his last attempt at election as a Liberal candidate in Leicester West. He then left the party because of what he perceived as a leftward drift. He stood as an Independent in an election at Westminster, but lost to a Conservative. A few months later, he stood as a 'Constitutionalist' (a quasi-Conservative) in Epping near London and was elected. He was welcomed back into the Conservative Party by Stanley Baldwin, the new Prime Minister, and given the post of Chancellor of the Exchequer. (This had been his father's old job and he still had the ceremonial robes for it: his mother had refused to hand them back to the Government, saying 'I am keeping these for my son'.) Unfortunately he was not a very successful one. He was advised by the Bank of England to return to the Gold Standard as a way of strengthening the pound, but this measure ultimately resulted in the General Strike of 1926.

During this serious and widespread industrial action, one of the major landmarks in British labour history, newspapers ceased publication because the printing unions refused to work. With his usual energy, Churchill produced an emergency paper, the *British Gazette*, which ran for eight days and ultimately achieved a circulation of two million. He took over the printing presses of the *Morning Post* and called in members of the Royal Navy to operate them, using printing students from London University to set the type for his newspaper, while the Automobile Association provided couriers to distribute bundles of copies. As paper supplies ran out he commandeered stocks held by *The Times*, whose editor complained to the Prime Minister. When sabotage put a machine out of action, Churchill called in naval engineers to repair it; and when staff were attacked by supporters of the strike, he drafted in the Irish Guards for protection.

His tenure as Chancellor lasted the rest of the decade, but in 1931, disapproving of his party's India policy (he did not favour self-rule), he resigned from the Shadow Cabinet. In the same year he published *My Early Life*, an immensely popular memoir of his youth. The following year, horrified by the cravenness of Prime Minister Ramsay MacDonald in the face of German rearmament, he began his own campaign to warn of the danger from that quarter. In August 1933, five months after Hitler became Chancellor, he made a speech on this theme.

Out of office, he again resumed writing, churning out a huge number of well-paid articles for newspapers and magazines, and he also made a lecture tour of the United States. His great literary project now was a multi-volume biography of his ancestor, the Duke of Marlborough. The first volume appeared in 1934 and the second two years later. He was active in urging the increase of Britain's air defences and persued this theme over several years. Germany was still restricted by the terms of the Versailles peace settlement and was forbidden to have an air force. It was increasingly obvious, however, that rearmament was clandestinely going on and that, as he warned, by 1935 Germany's secret but all-too-real air force would be equal to the RAF. During 1935 itself Churchill wrote an article in *Strand* magazine that was so openly critical of Germany that there was an official protest from Berlin. Not being privy to restricted information, he nevertheless learned a great deal of what was known in Government circles through a network of friends, acquaintances and informers who shared his concern and saw him as a rallying point. He demanded a parliamentary enquiry into the state of Britain's defences, and his persistence at least gained him an official post during this time: he became a member of the Committee of Imperial Defence on Air Defence Research.

At home, the crisis caused by the decision of King Edward VIII to marry a divorced American found Churchill on the wrong side of public opinion. He supported the King long after the British people had lost sympathy with him, and this added to his reputation for bad judgement.

He continued his protests and warnings about Hitler's Germany without success. He was seen as a spent force in politics, and his views as alarmist. In 1937 Neville Chamberlain succeeded Stanley Baldwin as Prime Minister. Baldwin's slogan, 'Safety First', which meant doing nothing about the threat from a resurgent Germany, was followed with even greater zeal by his successor. Chamberlain was no fool. He was aware of the real and growing menace of Hitler, which had been demonstrated by the

Though out of office in the 1930s, Churchill retained considerable influence as a politician, writer and speaker, and his home was visited by many prominent figures and admirers. Here, the Churchills entertain the former French Premier Leon Blum (second from right).

reoccupation of the demilitarized Rhineland, the rebuilding of the German armed forces and by German participation in the Spanish Civil War. His philosophy, however, was that the last world war had been so terrible that any repeat of it was unthinkable. No matter what compromise or moral surrender was necessary, it was preferable to the alternative. Hitler clearly had no territorial designs on Britain, and if he were not provoked he might channel his aggression in other directions. His real foe was Communism, and that was Britain's enemy too ...

With hindsight it is obvious that appeasement was a doomed policy. The government responsible for it seems naïve and spineless, yet a member of this government, Quentin Hogg (later the Lord Chancellor Lord Hailsham) has pointed out that appeasement bought time to re-arm and to consolidate national opinion. Had war begun in 1938 over Czechoslovakia, Churchill would probably still have become Premier, and would have put up the same resistance to Hitler, but without an air force strong enough to defend Britain the result could have been very different. It could be argued, in other words, that without Chamberlain there could have been no 'finest hour'. Hogg commented that:

> I had absolutely no doubt that Chamberlain had an absolutely straightforward choice between starting a Second World War with all its consequences, as he did over Poland a year later, and something like Munich. I have absolutely no doubt, in the light of subsequent events, that Chamberlain made the right choice.
>
> My conviction is strengthened by the weakness of France. Fighting in 1939, and persisting after the fall of France in 1940 until Hitler's assault on Russia and the Japanese attack on Pearl Harbor, we fought as a united nation, with the Hurricanes and Spitfires to defend the Channel, with [a] radar screen in place along the south and east coasts, with our land forces brought to a certain degree of readiness. Fighting in 1938, which was the only other option, we should have entered the war a divided nation, armed with obsolete aircraft and without radar, allied with a French Republic as divided and unready as ourselves.

When Hitler demanded the right to sieze the Sudenten territory from Czechoslovakia because of its German-speaking minority, Chamberlain met Hitler and, in Munich on 30 September 1938, signed an agreement (as did France) allowing the dismemberment of the Czech state without interference by other powers. Chamberlain was feted as a hero on his return to London, though all he had done was give in to German aggression. Churchill, disgusted by this, said in the Commons:

> The utmost that [Chamberlain] has been able to gain for Czechoslovakia has been that the German dictator, instead of snatching the victuals from the table, has been content to have them served to him course by course. [He was right – Hitler soon annexed the rest of Czechoslovakia]
>
> If the House will permit me the metaphor. £1 was demanded at the pistol's point. When it was given, £2 was demanded at the pistol's point. Finally, the dictator consented to take £1 17s 6d and the rest in promises of good-will for the future.

In August 1939 the skies darkened still further. Europe's two political extremes – Nazi Germany and Soviet Russia – signed a non-aggression pact, a marriage of convenience that had seemed unthinkable. Stalin had agreed not to aid any nation with which Germany was at war, thus dashing the hopes of those who had seen Russia as a check on German ambition. A major player in the drama – a potential though unsympathetic ally – had retired from the scene. Poland was doomed and war inevitable.

Those who shared Churchill's views put their faith in the notion that he would become Premier, or at least Foreign Secretary. A press campaign with the slogan 'What price Churchill?' agitated for his return to government, but it was a forlorn hope. He was over 60 and so thoroughly out of favour that his return to government would require a miracle. He was perceived as having failed in the great offices he had previously held and he had had no recent experience of government at all. His appointment would be a direct insult to Hitler, since he was hated in Germany. His warnings about the growth of German power and ambition were well known there and, because they were obviously true, led the Führer himself to single Churchill out for savage criticism:

> If Churchill came to power in Great Britain instead of
> Chamberlain we know it would be the aim to unleash
> immediately a world war against Germany. He makes no
> secret of it . . . I naturally cannot prevent the possibility of
> this gentleman entering the Government in a couple of years,
> but I can assure you that I will prevent him from destroying
> Germany. As long as people talk about disarmament and leave
> the war-mongers to carry on, I assume that their desire is to
> steal our weapons and to bring about again our fate in 1918.
> I can tell Churchill that it happened only once and that it will
> not happen again!

An indication of how far his star had fallen is given by the actor Douglas Fairbanks Junior, who met him at the Savoy one evening in 1939. We are so accustomed to thinking of Churchill from a post-1940 perspective that it is almost shocking to discover the way he was seen by some people before the crisis came:

> One night Dickie and Con Benson included me in a theatre
> party of six or eight. After the play we all went to supper at the
> Savoy Grill. We'd been there awhile when I spied an older couple
> entering who were escorted to the back of the Grill. I turned to
> Con and asked, 'Wasn't that Winston Churchill?'

'Yes,' said Con, 'Why?'

'I have a message for him from a friend in the States. What kind of a fellow is he? Dare I write a note and introduce myself?'

Con laughed. 'Oh, he's very easy! Quite a character in fact – but a sad one. Over the years he's had practically every job there is in the Cabinet and made a flop of each one. Now he's getting old. He's switched his political party twice, but he's in Parliament still. He makes amusing speeches as one half of a 'party of two' – he and a chap called Brendan Bracken.' Con smiled in a mixture of amusement and pity, and continued, 'Keeps warning everyone about Hitler and war, and he's won over quite a few new men like Anthony Eden. But though he's witty, he's washed up. Few would trust him nowadays, poor fellow. He also used to write rousing adventure books, but nowadays he's so down on his luck that your friend [film-director Alexander] Korda felt sorry for him and commissioned him to write a script that he'll never film about the great Duke of Marlborough – one of his ancestors. His father was a brilliant M.P. married to an American. Winston is brilliant too, no doubt, but he has just missed everything. Life has passed him by.' Con then brightened, gave my arm a gentle shove, and said, 'But do go over and speak to him. He'd love it. He's one of our last eccentrics!'

So I took a chance and sent over a note of introduction to which Mr Churchill immediately replied by inviting me to his table for a drink. I went over, shook hands with both Churchill and his wife, and explained that I was acting as 'confidential postman' for [a mutual friend]. Mr Churchill mumbled affection for Herbert and gave instructions about where to bring the envelope next day. He then began a long and amusing monologue that touched on a dozen now forgotten subjects. I do remember, though, that he was fascinating – and Mrs Churchill was charming. He would have gone on and on had I not felt it tactful to return to my hosts, the Bensons. I thanked him, bade them both good night, and thought to myself what a shame that this brilliant old guy had missed the bus with every chance he'd had. I now agreed he seemed too old and politically 'done for', with hardly any useful future in sight. Even so, I was immensely glad to have met him.

Later I had reason to check the date. It was just ten months before World War II began in England.

10
COMMAND, 1940–1945

Britain declared war on Germany on 3 September 1939. Having abandoned Czechoslovakia to Hitler through the Munich Agreement the previous year, Chamberlain's government had been obliged to make a guarantee to assist Poland, which was clearly next on Germany's shopping list. When Poland was invaded on 1 September, there could be no further doubting Hitler's cynicism. On the day that war began, Churchill rejoined the Cabinet. He returned to his old job as First Lord of the Admiralty (the Royal Navy immediately received a signal: 'Winston is Back'). He was delighted, and reinvigorated, to resume an active role. Now he could fight Hitler at last.

Churchill's first task was to assess the naval situation. As an island, Britain would depend on imports, and the sea lanes must be protected. He therefore immediately set the convoy system in operation. Introduced in the previous war, this meant that merchant ships, with an escort of warships, sailed in tightly packed groups and were much more difficult for U-boats to attack.

Prime Minister Neville Chamberlain had no military knowledge or experience and certainly did not have the personality necessary for a wartime leader. Churchill was, from the beginning, the chief military influence in the government. He was made President of the Military Co-ordination Committee of Service Ministers, which meant that he was, *de facto*, running the country's war effort. Although this kept him fully occupied, there was little sign of aggression from across the North Sea. Nevertheless, British children were evacuated from cities, gas masks were issued to every citizen (this was a threat that was never to materialize) and men of military age were conscripted, yet the expected air raids did not come. On the Continent, French troops waited confidently behind the concrete ramparts of the Maginot Line, and the British Expeditionary Force crossed the Channel just as they had done in 1914. Winter came, and then spring 1940, and still the German armies made no move. The British called this the Phoney War, their opponents the 'Sitzkrieg', or 'sitting war'.

It was not quiet everywhere. U-boats were highly active in the Atlantic and the war at sea was gaining momentum. In April, Germany struck at Scandinavia, overrunning Denmark and Norway in order to secure the country's iron ore. Churchill at once dispatched an expeditionary force to seize the vital Norwegian port of Narvik before the Germans reached it. A combined operation by Navy and Army, the force succeeded in landing but was driven off by skilled German mountain troops, and vessels were lost in the withdrawal. The operation was a disaster.

Yet Churchill escaped blame. Though this had been an expensive mistake, the public immediately forgave him. He had, after all, been vindicated by events. While others had sought to ignore the danger of Hitler, he had seen it all along and had alone been prepared. He was aggressive and his action in sending troops to Narvik had shown that Hitler was not to have things all his own way. Chamberlain, who had done no more than approve the venture, got the blame for its failure.

The Prime Minister, greeted as a hero on his return from Munich the previous year, was now a virtual outcast. He was, in any case, dying from cancer and did not have the strength to lead the country, even had he not been entirely overshadowed by the aggressive First Lord. The author Philip Paneth described the environment in which Churchill directed the naval war:

> . . . when war came and anchored him to his big room in the Admiralty whose two large windows overlooked the Horse Guards Parade. It was a warm and cheerful room, with historic associations that could not fail to inspire the man working in it. A coal fire would blaze in the grate, two arm-chairs, upholstered in red leather, gave comfort to the visitor. No creature comfort was needed by the man who assumed office as shipping losses were rising in a grim upward curve. His chair had no upholstery, only a carved wooden back. The desk had a telephone on it, some papers, tidy and in order; it did not look like the desk of a poet or artist, and certainly not like that of a hard-working journalist. A table stood nearby, bearing a set of glasses, a soda-syphon and a biscuit tin. On the walls were signed photographs of Jellicoe, Beatty and other Sea Lords of the last war . . . There was also a chart, presented to Churchill during the last war when he was Minister of Production, showing a graph of gun production, of which he is still proud. But the room was, of course, dominated by pictures of the sea. A picture of the Victory

of Camperdown hung over the mantelpiece, over a clock and a plain little mirror.

From this room he would go home for lunch and dinner. Here he would dictate his memoranda, letters, articles and books. He would walk up and down, dictating easily and hardly ever halting or correcting what had been taken down. His work would be interrupted by occasional callers, or by a conference with the Admiralty chiefs. Those conferences were held at the five-sided table, covered with blue baize, which took up the centre of the room. The maps hanging on the wall near the fireplace were consulted; others could be let down from near the ceiling by an arrangement of ropes over pulleys, and there was a large globe standing on the floor.

From this room he waged his great battle for keeping open the Atlantic life-line, his fight for the freedom of the seas, and the final struggle that was to bring him to No. 10, Downing Street. During the Battle of Narvik he was often called to his room after only a few hours of sleep at home, when he was not using a truckle bed in the Admiralty itself. When staying at home, he would rise at 7.30 a.m., when a dispatch case full of urgent papers would already await him. He studied them for an hour, called for his secretary to whom he dictated notes and replies to be typed on the spot, and then he would dress for the Cabinet meeting at 10.30 a.m.

In May 1940 a debate in the Commons brought the end of Chamberlain's government. The Prime Minister saw it as his duty to stay in office, but was assailed by Leo Amery, Churchill's old schoolfellow, who quoted at the government front bench the words used by Oliver Cromwell nearly three centuries earlier to dismiss the Rump of the Long Parliament: 'You have sat here too long for any good you have been doing. Depart, I say, and let us have done with you. In the name of God, go.'

Churchill remained loyal to the Prime Minister with whose policy he had heartily disagreed, and in the debate defended Chamberlain against criticism. Duff Cooper, who was opposed to the government, had expected this:

I warned members against being too much affected by [Churchill's] brilliant oratory. 'He will be defending,' I said, 'with his eloquence, those who have so long refused to listen to his counsel, who treated his warnings with contempt and refused to take him into their confidence. Those who so often trembled before his sword will be only too glad to shrink behind his buckler.

The following morning, 10 May 1940, Germany launched its invasion of The Netherlands, Belgium, Luxembourg and France. The 'Phoney War' had ended with a bang. Chamberlain had resigned the evening before, but his successor had not yet been formally chosen. Lord Halifax had been seen by many as the front runner, and this view had been shared by the king. For all his dash and fire, his oratorical skill and his commitment to victory, Churchill was still perceived as both elderly and unstable. Halifax, however, knew that he himself lacked the necessary qualities. As Prime Minister he would be as overshadowed by Churchill as Chamberlain had been. A natural diplomat, he lacked the blunt aggression that would be necessary, and he felt his health would not stand up to the stress. He had offered the excuse that, as a peer, he was not able to sit in the House of Commons and that the war effort should be directed from there.

PRIME MINISTER

And so it was Churchill. On the afternoon of the 10th he was summoned to Buckingham Palace, as is the British custom, to be invited by the sovereign to form a government. In a moment of light-heartedness King George VI asked Churchill if he knew why he had been sent for, and Churchill replied that he really could not imagine. Then he accepted the King's request and became Prime Minister. His appointment would raise both cheers and eyebrows. He was still considered reckless, mercurial, emotional and self-interested. 'Are we going to be ruled by that Yankee careerist?' asked the writer Hilaire Belloc. The British people, including many who had known him well, seriously doubted whether Winston Churchill had the stability to lead the country at such a moment.

His bodyguard, Detective Inspector Walter Thompson, remembered the occasion:

I recall the day he became Prime Minister. After visiting King George VI he said to me, 'You know why I have been to Buckingham Palace, Thompson?' 'Yes, sir,' I replied, and I congratulated him on his appointment. He looked pleased but was obviously tense and strained. So I went on: 'I am very pleased that at last you have become Prime Minister, sir, but I only wish that the position had come your way in better times, for you have taken on an enormous task.' He replied grimly: 'God alone knows how great it is. I hope that it is not too late. I am very much afraid it is.' It seemed to me that tears came into his eyes as he turned away, muttering something to himself. Then, I thought, he appeared to set his jaw and, with a look of determination, mastered all his emotion . . .

But he knew what he was doing, and he felt qualified for the job. He later recorded his feelings at the end of that day:

> As I went to bed at about 3a.m., I was conscious of a profound sense of relief. At last I had the authority to give directions over the whole scene. I felt as if I were walking with destiny, and that all my past life had been but a preparation for this hour and for this trial.

He had deep personal acquaintance with failure and frustration – things that the whole nation would experience in large measure over the coming years. He understood the dogged, unflinching determination that would be needed to see Britain through the years ahead. Though nobody would now dream of trusting a promise of Hitler's, Churchill fully recognized that there could be no possible reconsidering, parleying, negotiating. While others, including Halifax, were prepared at least to suspend hostilities while talking to the German leader, Churchill knew that Britain must slam the door on these proposals and make it clear that the country was committed, body and soul, to opposing him – regardless of the lack of allies or the prospects of success. The public realized that he was right, and they supported him.

The diary of Miss Nellie Carver, who lived in London, gives some idea of how his appointment as Premier was seen by a faithful Conservative, though her reaction was probably typical of other members of the public:

> 5–10 May 1940
> News not good, listened into angry scene in Commons described . . . the withdrawal of our troops from Norway earlier in the month. Poor Mr Chamberlain hopelessly out of favour now. Government falls & Winston Churchill is Prime Minister. Feel a little relieved as he is a real fighter, but am also very sorry for Neville. It has been too much for him to tackle & we were

all to blame together. Nevertheless am sure worse is coming, but now perhaps [something] will be done about our sickening reverses.

At this time Churchill began his radio broadcasts to the nation. The first of them contained these immortal lines:

I should say to the House, as I said to those who have joined the Government, 'I have nothing to offer but blood, toil, tears and sweat.'

We have before us an ordeal of the most grievous kind. We have before us many, many long months of struggle and suffering. You ask, what is our policy? I will say: It is to wage war, by sea, land and air, with all our might and with all the strength God can give us: to wage war against a monstrous tyranny, never surpassed in the dark, lamentable catalogue of human crime.

That is our policy. You ask, what is our aim? I can answer in one word: Victory – victory at all costs, victory in spite of all terror, victory, however long and hard the road may be; for without victory there is no survival . . . But I take up my task with bouyancy and hope. I feel sure that our cause will not be suffered to fail among men. At this time I feel entitled to claim the aid of all, and I say, 'Come, then, let us go forward together with our united strength.'

These words bring goose pimples even now, yet for all his undoubted skill as an orator and his even greater ability as a writer, his famous speeches often sound disappointing when recordings of him are heard today. The words are inspiring, the growling voice full of authority, yet the cadence can sound weary and wooden, as if he were reading something aloud from a book. It is necessary to remember that he was often re-reading for the wireless, speeches he had given hours earlier in the House of Commons, and that at the end of a long day he was indeed weary. It is also necessary to bear in mind the circumstances in which they were first heard to appreciate their impact. The listening public was interested in his words, not their delivery. They made a tigress, for instance, of Miss Carver:

13 May
News not good, our men being pushed back in Flanders after going to the aid of the Belgians & Dutch. Everywhere talk of

invasion, if the Huns can get to the channel Ports they may try it.

Winston Churchill is getting into his stride – we now feel a strong hand guiding the country – someone who knows and understands us. He warns of possible horrors quite openly, but this has a strong effect on me at any rate. Whereas before the war & all this last year I've been scared of what MIGHT happen, now it is possible at any moment, am getting mentally ready for the fray, Winston's speeches send all sorts of thrills racing up and down my veins and I feel fit to tackle the largest Hun! Probably that is as it may be! The fact is that I am not the only Briton to be strengthened & inspired by our P.M. He is so supremely the Fighting Bulldog & in his right place at last.

One great strength of Churchill's position was that he never promised an easy war. This was the thrust of the 'blood, toil, tears and sweat' speech with which his premiership began. His old-fashioned rhetoric was genuinely inspiring and put fight into a nation that expected invasion at any moment. While fighting continued in France, he frequently crossed the Channel to bolster the commanders of the French armies, and even offered to create a sort of federal union between Britain and France – a joint citizenship and a sharing of resources. This bribe to keep France in the war seems astonishing, considering the two countries' mutual incompatibility, and was immediately rejected by France. It was, in any case, too late. On 18 June the French armies capitulated and sued for peace. The British Expeditionary Force fought an increasingly desperate rearguard action that ended at Dunkirk with the evacuation of over 500,000 troops in the early days of June. While the army had been saved, almost all of its equipment had been lost. Though there was a feeling of relief, there was also an acute sense of imminent danger. Churchill seized the moment, and the national mood, with rhetoric that rings like a pistol shot, in another of his speeches on 18 June:

> The Battle of France is over. I expect that the Battle of Britain is about to begin. Upon this battle depends the survival of Christian civilization. Upon it depends our own British life, and the long continuity of our institutions and our Empire. The whole fury and might of the enemy must very soon be turned on us.
>
> Hitler knows that he will have to break us in this island or lose the war. If we can stand up to him, all Europe may be free and the life of the world may move forward into broad, sunlit uplands.

But if we fail, then the whole world, including the United States, including all that we have known and cared for, will sink into the abyss of a new Dark Age made more sinister, and perhaps more protracted, by the lights of perverted science.

Let us therefore brace ourselves to our tasks, and so bear ourselves that, if the British Empire and its Commonwealth last for a thousand years, men will still say: 'This was their finest hour.'

Philip Paneth, an author who had met Hitler and assessed his rhetoric, examined Churchill's speaking style:

His speeches have always the appearance of felicitous improvisations – which is explained by the fact that they are the result of very thorough and careful preparation. He usually puts down only a short key sentence or two which are then worked up into a speech. When he delivers it he lifts his head, giving a convincing impression of speaking extempore, although he never departs from the written text. His typical stance is well known: arms hanging down by his side, palms forward, his face thrust forward aggressively while his eyes search the faces of his listeners. Sometimes he waves his pencil in a sweeping gesture as though to underline a point, or he readjusts his glasses which keep slipping down. When a friend commended him for his outstanding oratory he said: 'Oh, I don't need to prepare anything. I always just get up and speak.' In this he shares a characteristic of all Englishmen who disclaim oratory and profess to dislike it, while in fact they are a nation of born speakers . . .

And Jean Crossley, a schoolmaster's wife, remembered the effect of another classic address:

That evening we heard the broadcast of the speech Churchill had delivered earlier in the day in the House of Commons: 'We shall fight on the beaches, we shall fight on the landing grounds, we shall fight in the fields and in the streets, we shall fight in the hills, we shall never surrender . . .'

This speech was not an order, nor even an exhortation. Churchill was putting into words what the majority of us instinctively assumed – that, being British, we could not be defeated. Our so-called allies had crumbled, but what could one expect of bloody foreigners, he implied, and made Hitler into a joke without ever playing down the 'blood, toil, tears and sweat' that would face us before he was beaten. Those speeches and the propaganda made out of Dunkirk certainly boosted our morale and impressed the rest of the free world, but my main recollection of that time is that everybody just got on with what had to be done day by day, worrying, of course, and facing each sorrow and disaster as it came.

Not everyone was inspired, or continued to be inspired by Churchillian oratory. Christopher Gould of the Royal Navy wrote home of a radio broadcast in 1942:

I was on watch last night for Churchill's speech but he gives me the pip anyway so I didn't miss much. I don't need him to give me moral support and if a vote was cast in the Services for him he would not be there anyway, the navy has a special dislike for him as we do all his dirty work for him.

France as an ally was lost, and apart from the small group of followers that assembled around an unknown general, Charles de Gaulle, French forces became the enemy. France's overseas territories followed orders from Paris, as did her fleet. Britain had demanded that French ships anchored in the harbour at Oran, in French North Africa, be surrendered to the Royal Navy to keep them from falling into enemy hands. When this was refused, Churchill ordered the Royal Navy (for Britain had control of the Mediterranean) to attack and sink the French warships. They did so, on 4 July 1940, with considerable loss of life among the crews.

This was one of the most controversial Allied actions of the war and was vociferously criticized. Yet it showed the world that Churchill was willing to be as ruthless as necessary to win against Hitler. One important consequence was to impress on Franklin Roosevelt that Britain would continue the fight and that she was led by a man who deserved support. Another – disastrous – result was that the consequent hostility of Vichy France enabled Japan to use bases in French Indochina to attack British territories. The loss of Malaya and Singapore followed.

On hearing the news, Roosevelt turned to his aide, Harry Hopkins, and said: 'Well, Harry, if we give aid to England, it's not like the French – money down the rat hole. As long as that old bastard's in charge, Britain will never surrender.'

With invasion an immediate possibility, he was naturally preoccupied with defence of the United Kingdom. Britain was not 'alone' as the mythology of 1940 usually suggests. The entire empire had come to her aid. This was not a reflex action; the self-governing dominions had debated the issue in their own parliaments before declaring war. Once hostilities began, they started sending troops, aircraft and supplies. Their contribution was, needless to say, invaluable, but it could not remotely match the resources of the United States. Before the end of the year, Churchill's determination over Oran had paid dividends: Roosevelt had signed a 'Lend-Lease' agreement with Britain, allowing the loan of 50 warships and a great deal of military equipment in exchange for American use of British bases in the Caribbean.

This arrangement was not made without difficulty. The necessary legislation was passed by Congress only after bitter debate. While Roosevelt saw the danger and wanted to join the crusade against Hitler, much influential opinion rejected any involvement in a European quarrel that posed no threat to American territory or interests. Some prominent Americans – including the aviator Charles Lindbergh and the Ambassador to Britain, Joseph Kennedy – were even admirers of the Nazi regime.

Isolationist views lost ground as Germany's military gains increased and Britain's resistance continued. When Germany invaded the Soviet Union there was to be another bitter pill to swallow: the extension of 'Lend-Lease' to Communist Russia. Nevertheless, opinion had so shifted by then that this, too, was agreed.

Following his victories on the Continent, Hitler had made an address to the British people. Entitled 'A Last Appeal to Reason', broadcast on German radio and air-dropped as leaflets by the Luftwaffe, it called on them to demand that their government make peace. To his intense annoyance there was no official reply, and the war carried on as before. When asked whether he did not wish to make some response, the Prime Minister had answered, 'I have nothing to say to Herr Hitler, not being on speaking-terms with him.' It was noticed that, when talking about the German leader, he almost invariably referred to him as either 'Corporal Hitler' or 'Herr Schickelgruber' (Hitler's family's real name), while another trademark was his pronunciation of the word Nazis ('Naarzis'), which became almost a symbol of defiance.

To Hitler, Britain had shown that she was an implacable opponent and would therefore have to be destroyed. The island must be invaded, and he made plans that set this operation in motion. First, the Luftwaffe must defeat the RAF and establish air superiority over Britain, then the Royal Navy must be driven out of the Channel, and finally the invasion would proceed. Hitler expected this to happen during August 1940. His opponents expected it too.

All over the country, measures were taken to defend the coastline against a naval assault and the inland areas against landings by parachutists. All beaches were declared out of bounds to civilians and heavily guarded. Road-signs throughout the entire country were removed to deprive invaders of directions. Obstacles such as old cars were placed in the middle of fields to prevent planes or gliders landing, and over a million men were enrolled in the Local Defence Volunteers. The determination inspired in ordinary citizens is suggested by this diary entry of Jean Crossley:

> So utterly glad Winston is in command, am certain he will not surrender to those devils of Huns – not one inch. The LDV is assuming large proportions now & is to be seen everywhere. The P.M. has renamed them the 'Home Guard' – which is much more appropriate.

Churchill devoted a great deal of thought to the measures that would have to be taken in the event of German landings. He had always had a schoolboyish delight in gadgets, and he had experts examine the possibilities for, among other things, spreading vast oil-slicks in the path of an invading force and setting the sea on fire. Colonel Stuart McRae, who was one of those recruited to test the possibilities for unconventional weapons, remembered a prime ministerial inspection at which a 'sticky bomb', which could be stuck on to the sides of passing tanks, was tested:

> A note in my diary for July 28th, 1940, reads: 'Successful trial of S.T. (Sticky) Bombs at Farnborough P.M. very satisfied.' For Sunday August 18th, 1940 part of the entry reads: 'gave demonstration of Blacker Bombard at Chequers. Used 23lb. Bomb. P.M. most impressed and gave the all clear to go ahead with this project. As First Lord of the Treasury, authorized us to spend £5,000 for a start.
>
> This, our first demonstration at Chequers, was rather fun. The threat of invasion was still hanging over and causing the P.M. intense worry. His main cause for concern was that although we had the Home Forces and the Home Guard very ready and

willing to repel an invader, they had nothing to do it with. Tanks could just walk through them without hindrance. The accepted weapon for tank attack had been the Boyes rifle, but against the German tanks it was no more than its name suggested. Molotov cocktails or phosphorus incendiary bombs were then supposed to be the thing, but they proved to be completely ineffective. The P.M. had been present at a demonstration at Hangmore Ranges, near Farnborough, where they had been tried out. They caught alight well enough, but caused the occupants of the tanks no inconvenience whatever. It says something for the sticky bomb that at this same demonstration we dare not try it out against inhabited tanks and had to content ourselves with blowing holes in scrapped ones.'

BRITAIN UNDER FIRE

Though Goering had absolute confidence in his pilots' ability to destroy the numerically inferior RAF, there were difficulties from the beginning. Britain's development of radar (Radio Detection and Ranging) had outstripped that of Germany. A string of radar stations across the south-east coast of England enabled the defenders to assess the speed, the number, position and direction of approaching aircraft and to wait in ambush. An accelerated programme to train pilots and build fighters meant that there were always more Spitfires and Hurricanes than the attackers had expected, and they could not, throughout the summer and autumn of 1940, gain the advantage. Not even the first phase of Hitler's plan was ever completed. The summer ended, the weather was no longer suitable, and the Führer lost heart (he had other preoccupations, for he was planning the invasion of the Soviet Union the following year). Miss Carver wrote:

> Winston made a fine speech re what we owe to the Air Force. He calls it the 'Battle of Britain' & says we are slowly but surely gaining the mastery over the Huns, who outnumber us 5–1.

The Luftwaffe did not give up. They attacked relentlessly the RAF stations of southern England and very nearly succeeded in destroying them. They had not yet bombed cities, on Hitler's direct orders, but when an aircraft accidentally dropped bombs on London and Churchill ordered instant retaliation, Hitler in turn was provoked to fury. He at once unleashed on Britain an intensive bombing campaign.

Curiously enough, this was what Churchill had hoped would happen. He realized how near the RAF was to collapse, and knew that a shifting of targets would give the pilots a vital pause in which to replenish their numbers and their equipment. This is precisely what happened during the Blitz. Waves of bombers began to hit London, and other British cities, with unrelenting ferocity. The raids were worst during September and October 1940. The bombers were attacking military and industrial targets, but naturally could not avoid causing serious damage to nearby residential areas. The docks in London's East End were especially badly hit, night after night.

The Prime Minister, as well as the king and queen, made a point of visiting bombed districts to meet survivors. Major-General Hastings Ismay, who served on Churchill's staff, described Churchill's reaction to the Blitz and remembered the aftermath of an air-raid:

> The Blitz started in earnest on 7 September. At first we could do little but take our punishment, and it was not long before the Prime minister set up the Night Air Defence Committee under his own chairmanship. Ministers and airmen, A-A gunners and scientists sat together regularly to thrash out ways and means of combating the danger. Within a few months, the most promising solutions had been identified and pressed forward with the utmost vigour. Soon there was a progressive increase in the number of enemy aircraft destroyed, and those that survived were kept at a respectful height by the improved efficiency of the A-A guns. The situation improved out of recognition.
>
> Churchill lost no opportunity of visiting the stricken areas, and I had my first experience of the effects of air bombardment on a big scale when I accompanied him to the London docks immediately after the first heavy attack. The destruction was much more devastating than I had imagined it would be. Fires were still raging all over the place; some of the larger buildings were mere skeletons, and many of the houses had been reduced to piles of rubble. The sight of tiny paper Union Jacks which had already been planted on two or three of these pathetic heaps brought a lump to one's throat.
>
> Our first stop was at an air-raid shelter in which about forty persons had been killed and many more wounded by a direct hit, and we found a big crowd, male and female, young and old, but all seemingly very poor. One might have expected them to be resentful against the authorities responsible for their protection; but, as Churchill got out of his car, they literally mobbed him.

'Good old Winnie,' they cried. 'We thought you'd come and see us. We can take it. Give it 'em back.' Churchill broke down, and as I was struggling to get him through the crowd, I heard an old woman say, 'You see, he really cares; he's crying.' Having pulled himself together, he proceeded to march through dockland at breakneck speed. I could never understand how he managed it. He was no longer a young man, and normally never took any exercise at all. If he had been asked to walk from Downing Street to the House of Commons, he would have refused indignantly. And yet, on his inspection visits, he would cover miles of ground at a remarkable pace.

On and on we went until darkness began to fall. The dock authorities were anxious that Churchill should leave for home at once, but he was in one of his most obstinate moods and insisted that he wanted to see everything. Consequently, we were still within the brightly lit target when the Luftwaffe arrived on the scene and the fireworks started. It was difficult to get a large car out of the area, owing to many of the streets being completely blocked by fallen houses, and as we were trying to turn in a very narrow space, a shower of incendiary bombs fell just in front of us. Churchill, feigning innocence, asked what they were. I replied that they were incendiaries, and that we were evidently in the middle of the bull's-eye!

It was very late by the time we got back to No 10 Downing Street, and Cabinet Ministers, secretaries, policemen and orderlies were waiting in the long passage in great anxiety. Churchill strode through them without a word, leaving me to be rebuked by all and sundry for having allowed the Prime minister to take such risks. Fatigue and fright are not conducive to patience, and I am alleged to have told the assembled company, in the language of the barrack room, that anybody who imagined that he could control the Prime Minister on jaunts of this kind was welcome to try his hand on the next occasion.

As well as displaying notable courage himself, Churchill was very aware of this quality in others. In September 1940 he conceived the idea of a gallantry award for civilians, noting that this new conflict produced casualties – and acts of bravery – at home as well as in the front lines. Citizens who risked their lives in air raids were not eligible for military medals. He therefore proposed:

Despite his traditional military background, Churchill brilliantly understood the potential for unconventional actions by small teams of specialist troops. The commandos, established at his instigation, made an important contribution to victory.

Now that the country is under sporadic Air bombardment, many brave actions are being performed by the A.R.P. Services and also by civilians of all kinds. In particular the workmen in all factories engaged on war work must be encouraged to stand to their work under air raid warnings. I am anxious that a considerable number of recommendations for gallantry and good conduct shall be made every month, from all parts of the country affected, and that these shall be rapidly sifted, promptly decided, the awards made, and the decorations bestowed. At present the difficulty is not so much approval at the summit as getting the recommendations started on the spot. We need therefore someone to stimulate and standardize this process.

The result of this scheme was the creation of the George Medal and George Cross. Churchill was very interested in ensuring that awards were given promptly to those who deserved them. 'We must never forget that these medals are the poor man's escutcheon,' he said.

Though the RAF held on in the air, there were no other successes to boast of in 1940 and the first half of the following year. Churchill continued to study and adapt to the conditions of this new war. In order to get back at the enemy, he established special forces, 'commandos', whose task was to land in enemy-occupied territory and cause chaos and destruction. On 3 June 1940 he sent a minute to the Chiefs of Staff:

> The completely defensive habit of mind, which has ruined the French, must not be allowed to ruin our initiative. It is of the highest consequence to keep the largest numbers of German forces all along the coasts of the countries that they have conquered, and we should immediately set to work to organise raiding forces on these coasts where the populations are friendly. Such forces might be composed by self-contained, thoroughly equipped units of, say, 1,000 up to not less than 10,000 when combined.

He added two days later a phrase that became famous: 'Enterprises must be prepared with specially trained troops, who can develop a reign of terror on the *butcher and bolt* policy.'

He is credited with coining the term 'commando', with reference to his South African experiences. In fact it was an army officer, Lieutenant Colonel Dudley Clarke, who suggested it. Clarke realized that:

> I was Military Assistant to the Chief of the Imperial General Staff [Sir John Dill] and he spoke to me one day on the subject. I told him I had some ideas . . . based upon experiences gained in Palestine at the time of the Arab rebellion. I think [I] suggested the name 'commando' from the very start. At least it was arrived at without much effort and I don't remember any rival titles having been seriously considered.
>
> It did seem to suggest exactly what was wanted. After the victories of Roberts and Kitchener had scattered the Boer Army, guerilla tactics by the Commandos snatched victory for many months from an enemy vastly superior in numbers and arms. I had myself seen the Arab armed bands in Palestine do much the same against a whole Army Corps. Guerilla warfare was always the answer of the ill-equipped patriot in the face of a vaster

though ponderous military machine, and that seemed to be precisely the position in which the British Army found itself in 1940. And, since the Commando seemed the best exponent of guerilla warfare which history could produce, it was presumed the best model we could adapt.

The Commandos initiated a parallel, covert war in which the Germans were to suffer continuous nuisance and damage. Despite Hitler's sarcastic boast that:

[Churchill finds it] 'encouraging' (e.g. evidence of victory) when some twenty or thirty Englishmen with blackened faces, rubber-soled shoes and floating kit-bags succeed in landing somewhere on the coast we occupy, only to make off again when German patrols appear . . .

They were increasingly effective. As the war went on, their triumphs included a raid on Bruneval in February 1942 that captured vital radar equipment from under the Germans' noses. The following month they crippled a massive dry dock and submarine pens at St Nazaire by ramming the dock gate with a ship filled with explosives, and in December they sank German shipping in Bordeaux harbour after paddling in in kayaks. They made a mockery of Hitler's disdain.

Special forces were not a new idea – the Germans themselves had usedsurreptitious combat teams – but the enemy regarded these as gangsters or terrorists and treated them accordingly when captured. Churchill's other contribution in this area was to order the formation of a Parachute Regiment.

On 22nd June, 1940, when the Empire was more on the defensive than it had ever been in its history, Mr. Winston Churchill directed the War Office to investigate the possibility of forming a Corps of at least 3,000 parachute troops, including a proportion of Canadians, Australians and New Zealanders, together with some trusty men from France and Norway. He was anxious that advantage should be taken of the summer to train these troops which would, if required, still be available for home defence.

The function of airborne troops is, by definition, offensive, not defensive. The creation of this unit – which became the Parachute Regiment – was a magnificent expression, during the war's darkest hours, of Churchill's faith in ultimate victory. Formed and trained while the war was going badly for Britain, the regiment achieved lasting glory as the tide turned – in Normandy, at Arnhem, and on the Rhine.

NO 10 AT WAR

The Prime Minister had, of course, an official residence at 10 Downing Street, but owing to London's vulnerability to bombs he was discouraged from spending nights there. An elaborate complex of bunkers, not unlike those in which his opponent Hitler would end the war, was built underneath a side street off Whitehall. Elizabeth Layton, a young Canadian who arrived in Britain to work at Number 10 as a typist, described this environment:

> It was explained to me that No 10 was not at present being used as the official residence of the Prime Minister. Another building, the Annexe, had therefore been prepared for him, and . . . here were also housed the offices of the War Cabinet and the Service Planning Staffs. For Mr and Mrs Churchill and the household there was a flat more or less at ground level, where they lived and slept. The location of the flat was not ideal, as it was situated between the main door and the offices of the Prime Minister's official staff, and the traffic along the carpeted passage (which incidentally was flanked by Mr Churchill's own paintings) and through the swing door was constant, almost embarrassingly so.
>
> Below it there stretched two whole floors of 'safety' accommodation. Beneath a vast concrete block which had been set in at ground level there was . . . General Headquarters, known as the Cabinet War Room or C.W.R. where the Prime Minister, all Cabinet Ministers and the Chiefs of Staff had rooms as well as the Service Planning staffs. Here some of the most brilliant British officers spent their days breathing conditioned air and working by daylight lamps, to emerge white-faced and blinking for a few hours in the evening. The C.W.R. was reached by a spiral staircase and was supposed to be safe from bombing attack. Below it, at a still lower level, had been constructed a whole floor of tiny bedrooms for the lesser lights, each with its allocated owner, and it was here that those on late duty would retire when bedtime came.
>
> Mr Churchill could hardly ever be persuaded to descend to the

C.W.R. merely for 'sheltering' purposes. He often held Cabinet meetings there in the evenings, after which he would return to the ground-level flat to finish off the evening in his study. I never knew him use his bedroom below stairs – thick steel shutters guarded the window of his bedroom in the flat, and these he felt were sufficient protection.

His working habits were as individual as everything else about him. Miss Layton remembered how his day was set out:

The hours worked by the Prime Minister were rather unusual. Mr Churchill would usually waken about 8 o'clock, and would have breakfast in bed on a tray. During this meal he would read through all the morning papers – perhaps he didn't read every word, but he always had a good idea of what each contained, and noticed if one was missing. Thereafter, having lighted his first cigar, he would recline in bed propped up with pillows, dressed in his favourite dressing-gown, which was green and gold with red dragons on it, and work on his Box, the key of which, on a long silver chain, never left him. This was a rectangular black box which locked automatically on closing – there were a good number of such about the office – and 'Gimme my Box' was a phrase we all knew well. Inside were various folders, always in their prescribed order. The first contained particularly urgent papers, such as telegrams from President Roosevelt or Marshal Stalin, or from the Generals in the field; the second, Foreign Office telegrams; then Service telegrams, Cabinet papers etc. It was always prepared by the Private Secretaries and placed on a stool next to his bed, so that as soon as he awoke in the morning he could open it if he wished.

It was necessary to understand that Churchill had some unusual habits:

Mr Churchill found it more restful to work in bed, and because of the great calls upon his strength he was urged by his medical advisors to do so as often as possible. He would remain there until half an hour before his first appointment, sometimes receiving visitors but often working the entire morning at his Box. Half an hour was always allowed for bathing and dressing, and the day would vary according to the business written on

the Card, a large white square with a space for each day of the
month, on which all appointments were recorded. Luncheon
was invariably at 1.30, and every day at some time before dinner,
which was at 8.30, he would have a sleep of at least half an
hour, from which he would awake refreshed and ready – which
perhaps his staff were not – for another normal day's work before
bedtime. This was very seldom before 2 o'clock and might be
anything up to 4.30. 'It's amazing,' they told me, 'how quickly
you can get used to going to bed at 2.30.'

She quickly became used to Churchill's moods:

The Prime Minister always seemed at his most approachable and
considerate and easiest to work for when there was a crisis on,
and one would have a feeling of sharing a tremendous experience
with him. In calmer times, when there was less to worry about, he
would sometimes be irritable and easily upset . . .

When there was news of a calamity, Mr Churchill was always
the fountain of strength from which emanated comfort and
reassurance. But within himself he minded – terribly. He is a
patriot to his last ounce, he loves the British nation; and when
lives or prestige were lost it hurt him deeply. One of the most
terrible blows of the war for him was no doubt the sinking of the
battleship *Prince of Wales* (in which he had gone to the Atlantic
Meeting) and the battlecruiser *Repulse* by the Japanese in December
1941. Always a lover of things naval, that was to him a personal loss
as well as a loss to our naval forces and prestige. When a city had
received a bad bombing, he would try whenever possible to pay it
a visit, to cheer up the inhabitants, but his grief at the sight of the
devastation was moving to see. However, he was always on top of
his feelings, and the people, revitalized, would show their delight
at the sight of him. Once or twice I went with him in London to
see bomb scars, sometimes only a short time after the bombs had
fallen. On one occasion I remember him speaking to the shaken
occupants of a recently shattered small home. As he left, some
papers blew about, so he turned to say quickly 'Hope that's the
Income Tax form,' which left them smiling . . .

The P.M. made me smile one day. I was so bold as to point out
a slight error in a direction he had given me, and he turned to me
in surprise. 'Quite right, quite right; take a good mark. Or rather,

cancel the last bad one I gave you.' I suppose he thought too much congratulations might produce too much self-confidence.

His temper could be ferocious and his ruthless perfectionism could be upsetting:

> Let me say at once that neither I nor anyone else considered this treatment unfair. The Prime Minister carried a terrific load; he was the spear-head of our stand against Nazism. The war was hard and heavy and he had a right to expect perfect service from those given the honour of being attached to him.

THE WIDER WAR

Mussolini had attempted to conquer Albania and Greece, had been defeated and had been assisted by Germany. Churchill sent troops to Greece to bolster the defence, but first the mainland and then the island of Crete had to be evacuated with losses. With invasion of Britain clearly not feasible, he had decided that the Middle East was the most vital theatre of war. Britain's Mediterranean colonies – Gibraltar, Malta, Cyprus, Egypt – and the Suez Canal with its strategic importance must be defended. For this reason, he sent British forces to the Middle East, and North Africa became the scene of extensive fighting against Italian and German troops. The Italians were defeated within a short time and their African colonies liberated. The Germans were a much tougher opponent and fighting was to continue against the Afrika Korps and its able commander, Field Marshal Rommel, throughout 1942.

Two crucial events during 1941 changed the entire conflict. The first was Hitler's invasion of the Soviet Union in June 1941. Hitler completely disregarded the pact he had made with Stalin, and from that moment on, the 'fury and might' of the Nazis was turned on Russia. Britain had an ally which, though suffering grievously, had immense resources of manpower and materials. Churchill was no longer in sole charge of the war against Hitler.

That December, Japan entered the war with a surprise attack on the US fleet at Pearl Harbor. Again, Churchill rejoiced at the news. Although this introduced a formidable new enemy into the conflict, and led to the rapid destruction of Britain's Far Eastern empire, it meant that the eventual defeat of the Axis powers was assured. Hitler declared war on America. As in 1914, Germany had made the mistake of provoking war with immensely powerful countries to east and west, but this time, unlike the last war, she would be fighting them simultaneously.

The film actor David Niven, now serving in the Rifle Brigade, met Churchill on several occasions at Ditchley Park, the Premier's weekend retreat, which was owned by mutual friends. They habitually talked while strolling in the house's walled garden. Niven remembered:

> In the autumn of '41, Churchill bade me take another walk in the walled garden. Things were looking grim – the war in the desert was at its lowest ebb with Rommel snapping at the gates of Alexandria. Food was getting more scarce and a glance at the map sent cold shivers down one's back
>
> 'Do you think, sir,' I asked, 'that the Americans will ever come into the war?'
>
> He fixed me with that rather intimidating gaze and unloosed the famous jaw-jutting bulldog growl. 'Mark my words – something cataclysmic will occur!'
>
> Four weeks later the Japanese attacked Pearl Harbor.
>
> Months after, when we were once again enjoying the delights of Ditchey, I asked if the Prime Minister remembered what he had said so long ago. His reply gave me goose pimples.
>
> 'Certainly I remember.'
>
> 'What made you say it, sir?'
>
> 'Because, young man, I study history.'

During that year, Churchill twice met with Franklin Roosevelt. The two had had a previous encounter 20 years earlier and Roosevelt was nettled that Churchill had no memory of it, but they nevertheless found a personal chemistry that was to create the most important friendship of the 20th century. Churchill, representing a less powerful country but more seasoned in war, persuaded Roosevelt that the war against Hitler had to be won before Japan could be dealt with.

The first and most significant meeting had taken place at Placentia Bay off the Newfoundland coast, and both Churchill and Roosevelt had arrived aboard naval vessels. Their meetings took place in Churchill's ship, HMS *Prince of Wales*, which tragically was to be sunk only a few months later by Japanese aircraft off the coast of Malaya. An account of Churchill's voyage across the Atlantic was later 'published' in *Clink Chronicle*, a typewritten periodical produced by inmates of Changi Prison in Singapore. The anonymous author was a radio operator on board:

Early in August, 1941, HMS *Prince of Wales* sailed from Scapa with

Winston Churchill aboard, bound for an unknown destination.
At the same time we also had aboard Harry Hopkins, the First
Sea Lord, the Air Chief Marshal, and the war chief, together
with their Aids, secretaries, valets detectives, pressmen, yes-men,
and cameramen. I doubt if any warship had ever carried such an
important human cargo before in the history of the world. We
were escorted by about six destroyers most of the way over, and
the journey took roughly five days through a moderate Atlantic
swell.

Churchill was a queer-looking little man who wore his peaked
yachting cap stuck jauntily over his left ear (like the kids in the
'Our Gang' comedies) and masticated massive cigars throughout
the whole of the twenty-four hours. He was a glutton for news,
and we wireless-operators scarcely had a spell [of relaxation] from
the time we left Scapa to the time we got back in. Modern as the
Prince of Wales was, we were obliged to run every set in the ship
and a half-dozen portable as well. In addition to this constant
watchkeeping we managed to show Winston one of the latest
'talkies' each night in his spacious cabin right astern, rigging all
the heavy apparatus in the process. I remember *Lady Hamilton*
was one of those films, portraying the life of Lord Nelson and
the glorious victory of Trafalgar. When the final reel had run
through and the lights were switched on Churchill clamped the
inevitable cigar in his mouth and turned to the officers who had
shared his evening's entertainment. 'There gentlemen,' he said,
with a bland smile, 'is a fine example for us to follow.'

I cannot deal justly with Roosevelt in so limited a space;
his personality is too great to be dismissed with a few words.
He took Churchill back via Iceland, where he (WSC) paid a
lightning surprise visit to the troops, and before disembarking
at Scapa he made a characteristically Churchillian speech on our
quarterdeck. He mentioned the history the *Prince of Wales* had
already made, and the history it would undoubtedly make in the
future prosecution of the war (how prophetic he was!). Then he
left for the mainland in a destroyer, a sturdy little figure with a
peaked cap over one ear, a cigar in his mouth, and a hand raised
in farewell with the fingers representing a confident 'Victory-V'
sign . . .

Churchill, with his love of dressing up, liked to wear the uniform of the

Royal Yacht Squadron, the most exclusive British sailing club, when with the Navy, but in this dark-blue, brass-buttoned uniform he may have looked too much the part. An uncorroborated story told by an American sailor, TM Allison, describes an incident when the two vessels met at sea:

> The American President was host to the Prime Minister on the 9th of August 1941 and because of the spacious compartments aboard the *Prince of Wales* and the President's infirmity, it was decided to transport all the American contingent via destroyer to the British battleship. *McDougal* (an American destroyer) was underway from the USS *Augusta* at 1015, 10 August and approached the man-of-war for a 'Chinese landing': that is, to have the bow of the destroyer secured to the stern of the battleship.
>
> That Sunday, at about 1100, while *McDougal* was near her landing, a Chief Petty Officer on the destroyer noticed a sailor dressed in pea jacket and blue rain hat standing by idly. The Chief yelled, 'Ahoy on the deck of the *Prince of Wales*, bear a hand and secure this line!' The Chief then ordered one of the men to throw a line to the deck of the battleship. Seeing this, the idler hurried to the line and made it fast. This idler was Winston Churchill.

There were to be several meetings between the two leaders, as well as a ceaseless flow of letters, telegrams and phone conversations. Churchill visited the United States several times, most significantly, perhaps, during Christmas 1941 when America had just entered the war. He found himself fêted by the American press (he was asked to model his siren-suit for photographers) and by Congress. Churchill's oft-described vision of a common purpose for the English-speaking democracies was greeted with scepticism by many Americans, who saw it as an attempt to enlist their country's help in saving the British Empire. However, his resolute defence of democracy in the face of apparent German victory had won him many admirers, from the President downwards. Eleanor Roosevelt wrote:

> The friendship and affection between my husband and the Prime Minister grew with every visit, and was something quite apart from the official intercourse. It was evident that Great Britain and the United States would have to co-operate in any case, but the war could be carried on to better advantage with

the two nations closely united through the personal friendship of Churchill and my husband. The two men had many interests in common in addition to the paramount issue of the war. They were men who loved the sea and the navy. They both knew a great deal of history and they had somewhat similar tastes in literature. It always gave my husband great joy when Churchill quoted aptly from Lear's 'Nonsense Rhymes', which were among Franklin's favourites. Both of them had read much biography. My husband did not have the same interest in art, but both of them loved the out-of-doors and could enjoy themselves either in the country or in the city. Their companionship grew, I think, with their respect for each other's ability. They did not agree on all things; I heard my husband make remarks which were sometimes inspired by annoyance and occasionally by a realistic facing of facts . . .

For his Atlantic crossings, Churchill did not always have a battleship for personal use. He often travelled on requisitioned liners along with troops proceeding overseas, but he did not mingle with these. A young West Indian servicewoman, Louise Osbourne, who travelled to England aboard ship with him, remembered the arrangements:

We went across on the same ship as Mr Churchill, his secretary and others – we never saw them. When he had to come out of his cabin, we the soldiers (lots of Americans, lots of British, British who were working on the ship) and everybody had to go to their cabins. [At] first we didn't know why and said 'What is all this?'

We were called in numbers (number one, number two, number three, number four . . .) to our meals, and we didn't all meet up [with] each other. We were called out at different times. When Mr Churchill was to come out of his cabin (and we didn't know then that he was on board) we would be told to go to our cabins. We had to obey orders at all times, nobody's going to stay out as they like. And then we were told we could come out, that's when he's gone back inside. So we were not to know he was there.

As well as travelling by sea Churchill liked to fly, and the Royal Air Force put a personal aircraft at his disposal. Though there were to be several aeroplanes, the crew remained essentially the same. One of them, JL Mitchell, navigator of the RAF crew between 1939 and 1945, recalled that:

Churchill had enjoyed flying since 1911, and during World War II he flew extensively.
Wartime passenger air travel was often highly dangerous; General Sikorski, Admiral Ramsay
and the actor Leslie Howard all perished in the air.

Mr Churchill was the first Prime Minister to genuinely exploit
the flexibility of air travel. The requirement of a long range
aircraft arose in August 1942, when the P.M. made the first of
his war-time long-distance flights to an overseas theatre. These
had been made in a Liberator B24X-bomber. The passenger
accommodation was most rudimentary.

Churchill had, of course, a long-standing interest in flying, and this could
give his crew some anxious moments:

> The PM came forward on the return journey and enjoyed
> sitting in the sunshine in the co-pilot's seat. He announced
> that he would like to try the controls. He did so, and when
> Collins attempted to smooth out some of the resulting
> attitudes of the aircraft with discreet use of the tail trimmer,
> the Owner admonished him. He soon conceded that he would

share the controls: Collins to work the rudder he, the PM would try climbing and diving. He clearly enjoyed himself much to the consternation of the passengers who were thrown about in the back, and to the astonishment of the USAAF fighter escort of P.38 Lightnings which were then keeping a more sensible distance from us. On landing at Maison Blanche, Collins explained to our escort commander who was doing the driving.

As the war progressed and Churchill's travels increased, his requirements expanded. A new aircraft was designed with all 'mod cons'.

It quickly became clear to us that apart from getting from A to B on time and in comfort, the Prime Minister expected a high standard of catering wherever we were. Once out of the UK we should have to rely on a local Commander in Chief's Mess, a Colonial Governor's Palace or an Ambassador's Residence for top-class re-victualling. Fresh, clean water was of course a must. The emptying and cleaning of three lavatory cans was a problem. The RAF even at home base was ill-equipped to store the cutlery and china, the linen and blankets clean and dry – in a Spitfire hanger. In these early days, too, a 2,000 gallon petrol bowser had to be specially despatched from Hendon for our use. But the provision of food – in rationed U.K., was to remain a problem and its solution overseas was often unorthodox – but our provisions usually satisfied the Owner. Drink – well, the NAAFI could supply whisky and gin but more exotic drinks and favourite wines had to be found from No. 10 resources.

Emergency arrangements were theoretically in place so the Prime Minister could escape in the event of disaster:

On the Skymaster, one parachute harness and pack was provided for the PM and stowed beneath his bed, accessible only by providing the mattress (for the designers had not given us sideways access to the space under it). The PM said he would only make a parachute descent in company with Sawyers, his valet, to look after his comforts on the way down. Quite apart from the matter of launching the PM into space through an outward-facing cabin door – which had never been tested for evacuation

safety in the wind tunnel, one can imagine the problems of
persuading the PM to leave his bed, on which he spent a lot
of every journey either sleeping, reading or dictating, in an
emergency!

There was not a great deal of space in his cabin in which to
assist him into the parachute harness and to adjust the straps,
etc. The whole situation could only be described as a certain
farce, but nevertheless, we were ordered to carry this unnecessary
bulk and weight – out of sight – and pretty well out of mind.

Much of this air travel involved meetings with Stalin. This highly critical ally
of the Western democracies had to be courted and, if possible, befriended.
For this it was necessary to put aside 20 years of ideological differences as
well as the dictator's well-documented atrocities and his recent alliance
with Hitler. Stalin would not leave the Soviet Union, so Churchill had to
go to Moscow. A less likely relationship would be difficult to imagine, yet
both men were realists who knew that without co-operation they could not
defeat Germany. Stalin, like Hitler, used violent tantrums to intimidate
others. This failed to work with Churchill, who simply shouted back, and
thus won a good deal of respect.

Stalin demanded the opening of a 'Second Front' in the West to take
the pressure off his own armies. Churchill had to tell him that no such
development could take place in 1942 – the time was not ripe – and that all
he could offer was to pin down German troops in North Africa. It was no
small tribute to Churchill's skill that, in spite of this, he formed an alliance
(friendship is perhaps too strong a word) and won a good deal of trust.

Churchill may have seemed a superman but he made huge mistakes, and
these caused his popularity to sag dangerously during the middle period of
the war. He sent tanks and aircraft to Russian that were needed in Malaya.
The resulting loss of Singapore proved the greatest humiliation in modern
British history. Only once Allied successes became more evident did his
stock rise again.

The year 1942 began badly as the Japanese, continuing their advance
through Burma and Malaya, captured Singapore and the Philippines. Yet
within months their expansion had been halted. In May, Japanese sea-
power was checked by a US fleet at the Battle of the Coral Sea, and in the
following month suffered a decisive, humiliating defeat at Midway. Japan
had lost the initiative for good. Though it would take three more years to
defeat her, she was on the defensive from now on.

Nearer home, there was better news. In North Africa, General Montgomery (who had replaced the earlier commanders, Wavell and Auchinleck, sacked by Churchill) defeated Rommel at El Alamein and drove the Axis out of Africa. Major AF Flatow of 45th Royal Tank Regiment, who was present at El Alamein, recalled a visit by the Prime Minister:

Of the war proper we saw or heard little. Apart from an occasional bomb dropped in the distance and once a Hun aeroplane brought down within a few miles of the camp life was peaceful enough. The authorities were not fussy about blackout – we were nearer the enemy when we were stationed in Hove. The Italian P.O.W.'s at Qassassin who repaired our boots and where I tried in vain to get medals were the only enemy we saw. Towards the end of August however something was 'in the air'. Fantastic rumours as usual rushed round until the most fantastic of all came true. The P.M. – Winston Churchill – was here in the MEF (Middle East Forces) and was going to visit the Brigade. The news came during a Brigade scheme which was happily cut short so everyone could dash back to camp bouncing over the desert in all our weird vehicles in order to get everything ready. All kinds of preparations were made – most of them of course were unnecessary but you could never be sure what he'd want to see – the Brigadier and C.O.'s remembered he had been a soldier once himself and in Egypt too. However no one minded for we all were keen to see him and secretly every one of us were hoping that the P.M. 'would have a word with me'. The next day Officers of the Regiment above the rank of lieutenant were summoned to Brigade Mess where the rest of the officers of the Brigade were gathered. We waited there for him with quiet trepidation. Suddenly we heard distant shouting which got nearer and then heard cars draw up on the gravel outside the Mess. The Great Man himself walked in. He was wearing a lilac coloured suit with waistcoat and carrying a topee (sun helmet). He was perspiring profusely and dropped into a chair which had been prepared for him and mopped his brow furiously. The first thing we heard his well known voice – we had all heard it so often on the radio – croak was – 'Have you a glass of iced water?' Cpl. Rowlands produced this from somewhere. Mr Churchill seemed very tired and very ill – we heard later that he had been suffering from 'Gyppy Tummy' – but he had far too many clothes on. He was accompanied by Sir Alan Brooke, Averil Harriman (the U.S.

Trade bloke) and others. All three – including the PM – spoke to us. Mr Churchill told us how he had spoken to Mr Roosevelt a few weeks before about tanks and armaments in general and how the President of the USA was at this moment sending Sherman (Mr Churchill did not call them Swallow) tanks to us although they had been destined for a U.S. Armed Div. The PM also hinted that something was going to happen soon. It was all very inspiring. When he had finished he got into his car – sat up in the back – was passed down the cheering ranks of the Brigade. All the men in the Regiment saw him – waving his hat and giving the V sign.

Churchill described this as 'not the end, not even the beginning of the end but perhaps the end of the beginning', but in Britain church bells were rung in celebration for the first time since the war began. At the end of the year came an event that really was the beginning of the end. The German Sixth Army, which had driven through Russia as far as the Volga, was surrounded at Stalingrad and decimated. Though the survivors hung on miserably until the first weeks of the following January, this unambiguous defeat showed that Germany was not invulnerable and that Hitler could after all be overcome. At the same time, a massive and growing bombing campaign against German cities and industry was systematically destroying much of the country's infrastructure. From 1943 there could no longer be any doubt that Germany would lose the war; it was only a matter of how long her people could hold out. By the end of that year, too, Churchill had attended the Quebec conference, and plans for the postwar shape of Europe were well advanced. Having conquered North Africa, Anglo-American forces carried out Operation Husky – landings that captured Sicily and then moved the war to the Italian mainland. As Allied armies moved steadily northwards up the leg of Italy, King Victor Emmanuel dismissed Mussolini from his post as prime minister. Fascist government ended and Italy changed sides. The Germans, who occupied the north of the country, held out stubbornly, while Mussolini resumed control of a Nazi puppet state protected by his allies.

In North Africa for the Casablanca Conference, Churchill had developed pneumonia and almost died, remarking sardonically that the ruins of Carthage were a suitable place in which to do so. Although he made a full recovery, his age and his health were a cause of some concern. Lady Diana Cooper, the wife of an eminent Cabinet Minister, had a conversation with Clementine in which this became apparent:

I had a curious calm and sad conversation with her before dinner that I have thought of ever since. I was talking about post-war days and proposed that instead of a grateful country building Winston another Blenheim, they should give him an endowed manor house with acres for a farm and gardens to build and paint in. Clemmie very calmly said: 'I never think of after the war. You see, I think Winston will die when it's over.' She said this so objectively that I could not bring myself to say the usual 'What nonsense!' but tried something about it was no use relying on death: people lived to ninety or might easily, in our lives, die that day. But she seemed quite certain and quite resigned to his not surviving long into peace. 'You see, he's seventy and I'm sixty and we're putting all we have into this war, and it will take all we have.' It was touching and noble.

As well as his health, his popularity was not what it had been. Though his rhetoric had inspired in 1940, it no longer seemed appropriate, for the moment had passed. Many people had come to find the cult of 1940 overblown and slightly embarrassing. The Labour MP Aneurin Bevan said:

> We see the personality of Winston Churchill paraded on the radio, in the Press, built up to gigantic dimensions until everybody around him looks like Lilliputians. When a man is in a very big position the bigness of the position comes to be described as the bigness of the man. Because water comes through a tap it doesn't follow that it comes from it and many of the merits of the Prime Minister belong to the office and not to the man . . .

Churchill was deeply involved in the planning of Operation Husky. The extent to which he shaped decisions and dominated military commanders is illustrated by an account of a conference that was chaired by him to discuss the feasibility of the operation. Admiral Sir Algernon Willis, who was present, recalled:

> Churchill called a meeting of the Supreme Commander Italy (Eisenhower) and the three Cs-in-C to discuss the projected Anzio operation, which was intended to get behind the German lines and open the way to Rome. The decision whether to carry

out this landing or not depended on the sufficiency of landing craft available.

John Cunningham told me after the war about this conference. He took his Staff Officer (Plans), Acting Captain Manley Power with him and before the conference started Churchill looked round the room and his eye resting on Power, said 'I didn't invite midshipmen to this party.' Cunningham told him he had brought his Staff Officer because he knew all about the landing situation, at which Churchill just grunted.

As the meeting progressed Power sent a note to his C-in-C, who was sitting on the Prime Minister's left, on which he had written 'The soldiers are talking tripe.' This referred to the fact that the Army were suggesting that the Anzio operation couldn't be done because of shortage of landing craft.

Churchill saw the note handed to Cunningham and said 'Give it to me,' and having read it, beckoned to Captain Power to come and sit next to him, and asked him to tell the meeting about the landing craft situation. Power then gave a masterly statement on the subject, which showed that there were enough landing craft to do the job, and on this the Conference decided to mount the operation.

The year 1944 might have seen the end of the war. It was certainly the year that sealed Hitler's fate. The Allies prepared to invade Europe in the biggest seaborne landing in history: Operation Overlord. Hitler, expecting such an invasion, had boasted of creating an 'Atlantic Wall' – a series of coastal fortifications stretching from Norway's North Cape to the Pyrenees. Allied planners decided to launch the invasion, from ports in south-west England, toward the Bay of the Seine. Immense trouble was taken to convince German intelligence that this attack was merely a feint and that the main thrust was coming in the place where Hitler expected it: the Pas de Calais. This ruse succeeded and enemy forces were not committed to the Normandy invasion front quickly enough to prevent an Allied breakout. Churchill was intent on sailing with the invasion fleet on D-Day, the 5th of June (it was in fact postponed to the 6th), and was only prevented from doing so – on the grounds that his life was too valuable – by a direct order from the king, who said that since he was not able to go himself, his Prime Minister should not either. Both were to visit the beaches a few days after the landings. A young naval officer, Eric Bertrand Rhead, was serving aboard a vessel moored off the Normandy coast:

. . . our instructions were to proceed to Arromanches and act as floating hotel for the Prime Minister – Winston Churchill. Frantic preparations – Captain moved out of his quarters to his sea cabin on the bridge, cabins for staff had to be arranged and not least we had to get to Arromanches. By this time it was well organised with a Harbour Master and some anti-aircraft defences. We duly arrived and moored stern on to the concrete breakwaters and anchors too. The great man duly arrived late afternoon, again with Peter Scott in his MTB and fortunately only two staff – a secretary – male and Commander Thompson RN who was his naval ADC and the one man who had most influence with Churchill. We made him an honorary member of the wardroom mess, knowing his strict adherence to naval etiquette he was certain to come to dinner. The first night was uneventful and he stayed and dined in his cabin. There was an air raid that night and we were at action stations. There was a plaintive cry over the telephone from a sub-lieutenant on duty on the quarter deck saying Churchill was on deck without a tin hat and would not go below but just commandeered sub-lieutenant's tin hat and announced he was staying to see the fun. Commander Thompson eventually persuaded him to go below, but the raid ended anyway.

He went ashore the next day and returned in the late afternoon again in Peter Scott's MTB. Our Captain sent a young sub-lieutenant to the bottom of the gangway to give Churchill a hand jumping from the MTB to gangway. The young man trying to be helpful put out a hand and got a blast of language – 'to get out of my way'. Churchill announced he would join us for dinner in the Wardroom that evening and duly arrived. After dinner he made a major political speech on the overall situation as he saw it. Not only on Europe but the world and said things he probably would not have said with press present.

WARTIME TRAVELLER

Since the beginning of the war Churchill had been required to travel extensively around Britain, visiting camps, units, bombed cities and a host of other sites. The problems of moving his entourage and their equipment necessitated an unusual method of transport. Gerald Pawle described it:

Soon after becoming Prime Minister he had found that war-time travel created awkward problems. Often he had to be away from

London over-night – at times for several days on end – and to stay
in hotels involved complex security arrangements, embracing
not only his own personal protection but the safeguarding of
secret documents and telephone communications. Commander
Thompson was therefore sent to discuss the difficulty with Sir
Harold Hartley, and after he had outlined what was needed
a special composite train was built up from rolling-stock not
required for normal passenger services.

The key coaches were two 'semi-Royal' saloons, which had
a small compartment at each end and a large open lounge in
the centre. In the Prime Minister's personal coach a bedroom
and bathroom occupied one end; at the other was an office for
his Private Secretary and a typist, with a scrambler telephone
connected to Mr Churchill's bedroom. The other large coach was
unaltered, the lounge being used by the staff and official visitors,
while the small compartments were available for V.I.P.s who
wanted to work undisturbed.

In the rear of Mr Churchill's coach was a sleeper coach, fitted
with a shower, and following this came a passenger coach and
a van carrying a diesel generator. In front of the second 'Royal'
coach was a dining-car. Its rear compartment had a long table
with seats for a dozen people: the front half of the coach was
used by the detectives, photographers, telephone engineers,
and others who usually accompanied the Prime Minister on
his journeys. The rolling-stock was completed by a kitchen car,
a sleeper coach for the retinue and the crew of the train, and
another corridor coach and luggage van.

This immediately solved the communication problem, for
whenever the train stopped the engineers merely had to plug in
one end of a length of wire to a socket on the side of the Prime
Minister's coach and unreel the rest of the wire until they reached
the nearest telephone line. Number 10 Downing Street, had a
Top Priority number, known to every exchange throughout the
country. Once contact had been made with the nearest trunks
supervisor it was only necessary to ask for 'Rapid Falls 8833',
and within a few moments of the train coming to a halt the staff would
be speaking to Whitehall. Even on arrival at some remote Scottish
moorland siding the system worked with astonishing efficiency.

On overnight stops the train would generally be shunted into
some quiet siding in the depth of the country where the Prime

Minister could sleep undisturbed. When close to big cities it was usually placed near some tunnel which could provide refuge in the event of an air raid. Using the train allowed Mr Churchill to carry out a morning inspection and then travel on to his next rendezvous, lunching on the journey and continuing discussions with his advisers. In this way much time was saved, and he could snatch an occasional rest.

Elizabeth Layton added further to this picture of the prime ministerial train, and intriguingly she gives a different 'Rapid Falls' number:

Our special train would usually leave one of the main London stations between 12 and 1 o'clock in the morning (giving us all, according to Mr Churchill, the chance of a nice early night). It consisted of the Prime Minister's special coach, which contained his bedroom, bathroom and lounge, and the office; a dining-car divided into two sections, for the main party and for the staff; and a first-class sleeping-coach with twelve compartments, on whose doors would be tickets denoting the allotted occupant.

The routine for me would be that on arising I would telephone through to the Annexe for the morning news. The Scrambling telephone would have been connected to the nearest exchange as soon as we arrived at the outlying station where we were 'stabling' for the rest of the night, and by mentioning the magic number Rapid Falls 4466 one would be put through to the No. 10 exchange, from any part of the England, usually within a minute or so. Then perhaps the Prime Minister would work on his Box, after which the train would be drawn into the main station at the arranged time, and the party would go off about its business, the Prime Minister in the van and the photographers in the rear, leaving Sawyers and me to mind the train and have all in readiness for their return, including any news or information from London.

An impression of Churchill's wartime travel in Britain is given by a young officer, Captain TL Cook, who unexpectedly spent a day with him:

On the afternoon of Thursday 29th June 1944 I heard that some distinguished visitors, including the Prime Minister himself, were going to visit certain of our Anti-Aircraft sites the following day and that a guide was wanted to show them the way round. It was a humble task, and one that only required a certain amount of knowledge of map-reading, but I thought on the spur of the moment that it might be quite interesting to see the Great Man and whoever it was who was accompanying him, so I said 'I'll do it' without giving it another thought . . .

I got the numbers and map-references of the sites to be visited and forthwith set out to plan the route I would lead the exalted column. It was no little distance, as it turned out, and it took me an hour or two just to go round and decide on the best roads, and try to remember which way to turn at each corner. The thought of leading the Prime Minister along the wrong road was too much, and I couldn't afford to make any mistakes. It had been decreed that 'an officer in a car' should act as guide to the party, but as we only have what they call 'utility vehicles' on the establishment, that rather humble type of transport had to suffice. It was in such a vehicle, with my driver at the wheel, that I went round the country roads of Kent and Sussex that evening preparing for the great occasion next day . . .

And so to the great day itself – Friday 30th June 1944.

The appointed hour for my arrival at the railway station to which the special train was scheduled was 10.45 . . . The place was pretty full of all sorts and conditions of men ranging from Generals, Brigadiers down to sergeants in the Army Press Service. No one knew who was going to be there apart from Mr. Churchill and the General Officer Commanding-in-Chief. There was a total of nine vehicles . . . We had to get some idea of how this alarming convoy was to be formed and who was to go in which car. The thought of my leading this galaxy of staff cars in my decrepit little utility made me feel very humble and out of place, but there we were and it had to be done.

Twenty minutes late, at 11.20, the train arrived at the platform and there was a flutter of excitement. The only thing that happened to begin with, however, was the immediate appearance of some mechanic with an enormous spool of cable, which he proceeded to unwind all along the platform. There was no other sign of life. (The cable turned out to be telephone, which is naturally of primary importance.)

After some five or ten minutes things began to happen, and the train began to open up its gates and deliver the occupants. Among the first was the Prime Minister himself, in fact only preceded by his personal bodyguard, wearing the uniform of a full colonel in some curious regiment. With him was Mrs. Churchill, bright and charming as I always imagine from her photographs, and a host of Generals, Brigadiers and what have you.

The train was the P.M.'s own private one consisting of eight coaches and I wasn't surprised any longer when I saw the number of people he carries around with him. After all the hand-shaking and general greetings the party began to move towards the exit from where I had been watching. My cue for action had arrived, and I fled to my car and prepared to lead the procession. In a very short time all the bodies were in one car or another, and I felt justified in setting out . . .

In the afternoon all went well, and I eventually deposited them at the last of the four sites, where my job was officially done. There seemed to be some doubt as to what was going to happen after that, and I was instructed to wait and see if my services were required any further before departing. This site was the one on which the Prime Minister's daughter Mary's battery is deployed, so there were some very domestic scenes to be witnessed in the course of the hour or more spent there. For the first and only time in the course of the day the guns went into action during the party's tour on a site, and I think the P.M. was secretly rather pleased that it happened to be that particular one.

The next stage was to be an unofficial visit to Chartwell, one of the Prime Minister's private residences, and only two cars followed the captain's:

It wasn't far to Chartwell, but the actual entrance to the drive from the main road was a little difficult to find. However, with the aid of a little dumb crambo (surreptitious mimed communication) between myself and the detective in the front seat of the P.M.'s car, we arrived in the back yard of the cottage at Chartwell.

I leapt out of my car to open the door for Mr Churchill. Of course he was half out by the time I got there – he never wastes much time – and he started to speak first before I got a chance to open my mouth. 'Where did you come from?' he said. 'I've been leading you about the countryside all day, sir,' said I, hoping he wouldn't think me impertinent for suggesting that it was a pretty poor show that he hadn't even noticed me! 'Oh, thank you very much indeed,' shaking me warmly by the hand, 'You'd better come in and feed the goldfish with me. Would you like to do that?'

Well, you couldn't have surprised me more. To be spoken to at all was, to me, a most fitting climax to the day, but to be asked in on the spur of the moment by the Prime Minister of England was more than my wildest dreams. And when I discovered that the second car contained only his two secretaries (one male and the other the stenographer) and the other detective, it was almost too good to be true. I was the only guest!

I followed him into the house . . . and was immediately told to sit down, and offered a whisky and soda . . . So there I sat drinking with Mr Churchill. The next excitement was the opening of a dispatch case by his private secretary and the production of a long message. 'Who is it from?' says the P.M. 'Stalin,' says the secretary. The P.M. reads it quietly to himself and then, when Mrs Churchill enters the room, 'Very nice message here from Joe, dear,' and proceeds to read it out. It was a very encouraging one too, I thought, but I was completely overcome by this time.

After Cook had accompanied Churchill, his ADC and a detective to wander through the garden and feed the fish, the tour continued:

Chartwell itself is delightful. Shrouded though it was amidst dust sheets etc., one could see enough to know how lovely it must have looked in the good old days. He showed me his most precious books, which he was arranging to be put down in the cellar for safekeeping, among which was a magnificent copy of Lawrence's Seven Pillars of Wisdom. In it was an inscription by Lawrence himself, and another dated ten years later, both appropriately worded, but I'm afraid I can't remember what exactly was written.

Then . . . preparations for departure. I had to lead him on to another railway station where the train had since arrived . . . This time he shook hands, and thanked me for this and that, bidding me goodbye . . .

After farewells from all the retinue and, I'm glad to say, a pat on the back for my driver for his driving, they all embarked on the train. I stood smartly to attention on the platform as the train pulled out, Mr Churchill puffing on a cigar, as he had been every minute of the day.

Although the Allied forces were commanded by the American General Dwight Eisenhower, Churchill took a great deal of personal interest in the operation. He it was who seized on the idea of the 'mulberry', an artificial harbour of concrete sections that were towed across the Channel and placed off the Normandy landing beaches (though he did not invent this, as is sometimes claimed). During that year he visited the different front lines in France and Italy. He also ordered British troops to intervene in newly liberated Greece, where Communist guerrillas were intent on taking over the government. He even visited the country himself, by warship, just before Christmas. He flew to the Greek capital, setting up headquarters aboard the warship HMS *Ajax*. There was fighting in the streets and in the surrounding hills. At one point, while Churchill was dictating to his secretary, shells landed nearby. As usual, the old warrior was unfazed by danger. He shouted: 'There – you bloody well missed us! Come on – try again!' Packing a revolver and travelling in an armoured car, he attended talks with the numerous political factions and achieved at least the semblance of a working consensus. His intervention saved one eastern European country, at least, from being included in the postwar Communist block.

The war's final year began with the Yalta Conference. By this stage in the war, Churchill's reputation notwithstanding, Britain was a less influential power and was increasingly ignored by the other two of the Big Three. He nevertheless remained firmly in touch with Britain's own war effort, and was present to watch British troops cross the Rhine in March. Major DR Vernon was there and recalled:

The morning of 24 March was one of din and action, the supporting barrage of the guns was intense, RAF rocket firing Typhoons flew constant sorties overhead to eliminate strong points. Suddenly all was quiet, as the Airborne Division swamped the opposition. Ever anxious to be quickly on the scene of historic events – as he was in Normandy – and the crossing of the Rhine was an historic event, Mr. Winston Churchill, accompanied by Field Marshal Sir Alan Brooke, Field Marshal Sir Bernard Montgomery and General Sir Miles Dempsey, arrived on the Rhine not a hundred yards from our rafts and watched

An archetypal image of Churchill as war leader: wearing army uniform he visits British troops within sound of enemy guns on the Rhine in March 1945. The Prime Minister, who had been shot at on battlefields for 50 years, positively relished coming under enemy fire.

the construction of a 9 ton folding boat bridge intended to replace the rafting operation. An orderly laid afternoon tea on a white tablecloth for these distinguished visitors; our men muttered about camouflage and helped themselves to a few cakes left behind!

At the same time one of his chief opponents, Goebbels, fulminated in his diary:

During his drive through the occupied areas Churchill addressed the troops. His speech was larded with the old monotonous tirades of hatred against the Huns. This gentleman, who can truly be called the grave-digger of Europe, had nothing new to say on the war situation.

From the twisted Nazi perspective, the triumph of the Allied armies represented the destruction of European culture. Churchill was, therefore, an arch criminal, personally responsible for obliterating German cities, and the victims of bombing referred to Allied fliers as 'Churchill Gangsters'. It was ironic that, until Dresden was destroyed in February 1945 in the most controversial Allied air raid of the war, rumour had it that the city was left untouched because Churchill's cousin was secretly living there.

Despite his venomous view of Churchill, a distinct admiration for his galvanizing leadership can be seen in another entry written by Goebbels:

> **26 March 1945**
> In the hour of Britain's war crisis Churchill addressed himself to the nation in a magnificent speech and put it on its feet again. The same was the case with the Soviet people when Stalin successfully appealed to them with the slogan 'Better to die standing than live kneeling'. Now that we are in a similar, though not much worse situation, we must do the same . . .

But there was to be no Finest Hour for Nazi Germany. The war in Europe ended on 8 May. While the Western Allies – against Churchill's better judgement – did not advance on Berlin, massive Russian forces bombarded the city and then captured it in days of heavy street-by-street fighting. Berlin fell on 1 May. The previous day, Hitler and Goebbels had both committed suicide. Unlike 1918, this time victory had been expected by the British people, and the end of hostilities did not come as a surprise. Miss Nellie Carver recorded in her diary:

> **May 7th, 1945**
> As we returned home, were told that tomorrow – 8th – was to be celebrated as VE Day, & Winston was to make a speech at 3p.m. Bombers roaring overhead taking food to Holland – a lovely sound – now!

Elizabeth Layton gives the perspective from Number 10:

> It so happened that Monday, 7th May, was my night on late duty. There was an atmosphere of great excitement in the office; we knew that the unconditional surrender terms had been signed. The war in Europe was not yet officially over, but everyone seemed to know that it would be by tomorrow, and as I walked around St. James' Park during the dinner hour there was a good

deal of shouting, cheering and singing going on. Crowds were gathering, wearing silly paper hats and blowing whistles and waving flags – throwing confetti, playing banjos and mouth-organs, banging cymbals, whirling crackly things round and round – anything to make one feel joyous and carefree. Later that night, when I went into the study for dictation, Mr Churchill looked up and said, 'Hullo, Miss Layton . . . well, the war's over, you've played your part.' As the evening progressed, a terrific thunderstorm broke – flashes, bangs and crashes. Once or twice he looked up and said, with a twinkle, 'What was that? – Oh. Only thunder.' Or, 'Was that an explosion?' or 'Might as well have another war.' It was 3.45 before he went to bed, and 4.30 by the time I had finished off the typing.

Harold Nicolson, who served in the government as Parliamentary Under-Secretary for Information, made his way to Parliament to hear the Prime Minister's speech:

The whole of Trafalgar Square and Whitehall was packed with people. Somebody had made a corner in rosettes, flags, streamers, paper whisks and, above all, paper caps. The latter were horrible, being of the comic variety. I also regret to say that I observed three guardsmen in full uniform wearing such hats. And through this cheerful but not exuberant crowd I pushed my way to the House of Commons. The last few yards were very difficult, as the crowd was packed against the railings. I tore my trousers in trying to squeeze past a stranded car. But at length the police saw me and backed a horse into the crowd, making a gap through which, amid cheers, I was squirted into Palace Yard. There I paused to recover myself, and seeing that it was approaching the hour of 3 p.m., I decided to remain there and hear Winston's broadcast which was to be relayed through loud-speakers. As Big Ben struck three, there was an extraordinary hush over the assembled multitude, and then came Winston's voice. He was short and effective, merely announcing that unconditional surrender had been signed, and naming the signatories. 'The evil-doers' he intoned, 'now lie prostrate before us.' The crowd gasped at this phrase. 'Advance Britannia!' he shouted at the end, and there followed the Last Post and God Save the King which we all sang very loud indeed. And then cheer upon cheer.

The clock reached 3.15, which is the moment when Questions in the House of Commons automatically close. We knew that it would take Winston some time to get to the House from Downing Street in such a crowd. We therefore made conversation by asking supplementary questions until 3.23. Then a slight stir was observed behind the Speaker's chair, and Winston, looking coy and cheerful, came in. The House rose as a man, and yelled and yelled and waved their Order Papers. He responded, not with a bow exactly but with an odd shy jerk of the head and with a wide grin. Then he started to read to us the statement that he had just made on the wireless. When he had finished reading, he put his manuscript aside and with wide gestures thanked and blessed the House for all its noble support of him throughout these years.

Then he proposed that 'this House do now attend at the Church of St. Margaret's, Westminster, to give humble and reverend thanks to Almighty God for our deliverance from the threat of German domination.' The motion was carried and the Serjeant at Arms put the mace on his shoulder and, following the Speaker, we all strode out. Through the Central Lobby we streamed, through St Stephen's Chapel, and out into the sunshine of Parliament Square . . .

Outside the celebrations continued. WW Mitchell, an RAF officer, remembered:

At Piccadilly tube station there was a terrific crowd jamming one exit to the street while the others were comparatively free. Outside in the Circus a large crowd was standing around in the bright sunshine with that air of expectancy that seemed everywhere to-day. A couple of Canadian soldiers were standing – or rather hanging on to – the top of the concrete covering to the Eros statue plinth. Someone was setting off fireworks. Down Lower Regent Street they were gravitating towards the Mall and Trafalgar Square. Most people carried some sort of flag – Union Jacks were predominant – with a sprinkling of rattles and carnival hats. In Trafalgar Square a huge crowd covered every part of the paths, the fountains and the base of the Column. Fireworks were being let off but everything was relatively quiet on the whole.

The Beaver Club was crowded but no excitement abroad.

Towards three o'clock the lounge began to fill up and people quietly took seats before the Premier's broadcast. The windows were open and as Mr Churchill spoke one could see the crowds still parading both towards the Palace and into Trafalgar Square; the VADs were ready on the grass verge. People in the lounge heard the broadcast without a sound or a comment; they stood up for the National Anthem, then filed out quietly.

Trafalgar Square was transformed. The crowd seemed even larger and more dense. From down Charing Cross Rd was crawling a stream of vehicles all covered with a mass of people on the roofs and hanging onto the running boards and anything they could find. From the top of a taxi the place was 'a sea of faces'. There was a surge under Admiralty Arch towards the Mall and Whitehall . . .

In Whitehall the crowd was assembling outside the Ministry of Health building waiting for Mr Churchill's appearance at 5p.m. The balcony was wreathed in bunting, there were several news-reel cars, mostly American and Canadian. In the windows of the buildings opposite were set cameras to take stills of the event. People were sitting on the pavement opposite. Towards 5p.m. the crowd got more dense, several women fainted. The cameramen fiddled with last minute adjustments to their apparatus and an American radio put some alterations in his script. After 5p.m. the crowd began to get impatient, sundry officials who appeared at the balcony for a moment were given a rousing cheer; two girls on the Ministry building getting out on to the balcony and showed a nifty pair of legs got the usual whistle used in those circumstances and some wisecracks. A section of the crowd starting clapping in rhythm, the sound of 'Why are we waiting' drifted along to the tune of 'O Come All ye Faithful', 'One, two, three, four, what the hell are we waiting for?' 'We want Winnie.' Two War Correspondent cameramen behind the columns of the balcony kept the crowd on tenterhooks as they peered into the interior of the building, fiddled with their cameras and damped the cheering as they relaxed into their former positions. People on the roof-tops on the opposite side kept everyone amused by sending paper aeroplanes into the air while the crowd followed their impatient eyes. Two drunken sailors appeared at the door of the Ministry Building and got a huge cheer – the crowd were in a mood to cheer anyone or anything.

Mr Churchill appeared with Mr Bevin and Mr Morrison and several other members of the Cabinet. When the initial cheering had died down the Premier said 'God bless you all' – terrific cheers and applause. He made his speech – more cheers.

Elizabeth Layton remembered:

That night he and members of the War cabinet appeared on a balcony overlooking Parliament Street and Square. Some of us were able to squeeze on to a small part adjoining, to watch the fun. Flags and bunting had been put up, and floodlights were directed upon the balcony. A crowd which some estimated at 20,000 stood below, the roar of their cheering seeming almost to lift one off one's feet. It was just a sea of faces and waving arms. As Mr Churchill emerged, the noise increased almost to deafening point. Microphones were ready. He knew so well what to say. He congratulated the Londoners on their fortitude, saying, 'I always said "London can take it" Were we downhearted?' . . . The response was overwhelming. He mentioned Japan, and the crowd booed happily. Then he began the first few words of 'Land of Hope and Glory', and the multitude took it up with a will.

I shall always remember Mr Churchill as he was at that moment – spick-and-span in black coat and striped trousers, a flower in his buttonhole, his face smooth and pink, a man medium in height and somewhat round in figure, a man whose character contained all the elements of greatness and whose knowledge of human nature made him understand equally the reactions of his valet and the Heads of other States.

That was Mr Churchill's hour. Whatever was to come, nothing could take it from him. The entire nation came forward to show its gratitude and affection for the man whose courage had been an inspiration in its darkest hours. For the next few days he could not move from the office without being mobbed in every street. He took to driving in an open car, so that he could sit in the back and wave his hat to the crowds, who appeared from nowhere wherever he was to be seen. Letters, telegrams and gifts poured into the office from all over the country.

I think he enjoyed it. He knew he deserved it. I expect that, being the old Parliamentarian he is, he knew it could not last.

Already his thoughts were fully enmeshed in the trials that lay ahead; winning the peace might prove more difficult than winning the war . . .

Jean Crossley recorded that:

In the evening Jimmy and I went out and joined the crowds thronging the streets. We made our way down Whitehall and were fortunate enough to arrive opposite the Treasury building just as Winston Churchill appeared on the balcony. He did not make a formal, pompous speech: he just talked to us, allowing us to join in with boos for Hitler's attempts to break us, imitations of Sirens and Flying Bombs and, of course, heart-felt cheers and then we all sang 'Roll Out the Barrel', 'We'll Hang Out the Washing on the Siegfried Line' and other such early war-time favourites. Up and down Whitehall and in Trafalgar Square people were dancing 'The Lambeth Walk' and 'Knees up Mother Brown'. Nobody seemed to be rowdy or violent, nor even very drunk, so far as I can remember. We drifted with the crowd to Buckingham Palace but I do not remember if the King and Queen appeared while we stood there cheering. It did not seem so important to see them as to see Churchill at that moment . . .

Church bells rang, solemn and formal services of Thanksgiving were held, there were Street Parties for children everywhere, Banquets and Speeches galore, but nothing equalled the spontaneous rejoicing in the streets of London on that May evening. I was lucky to have been able to take part in it and to have heard Churchill speak on that occasion. No doubt he had his faults and made mistakes but I feel convinced that without him we should not have won the War. We felt that he understood our fears, our sufferings and our needs. And, whatever his more terrible and pressing responsibilities and anxieties, he never minimised the dangers and the difficulties that faced the country and by calling upon all of us to do more than we thought ourselves capable of, to fight and endure to the last, he gave us courage and enormous pride in ourselves and our country.

Churchill's next task was to attend a conference, to be held in July, in Germany with Stalin and Harry Truman, the former American Vice President who had succeeded Roosevelt on the latter's death in April. This was held in the old royal residence town of Potsdam outside Berlin, and took place in the former home of the German crown prince. This was in a sense the end of Churchill's wartime pilgrimage. He was in the capital city of his enemies. Naturally he was curious to see the sights and an officer recalled being given the duty of showing him around. Berlin was occupied by Russian troops, and movement (even for such an illustrious personage) was subject to restrictions. The Prime Minister was surprised and moved by the warm reception he received from the inhabitants, as recorded by Major ED Bevan:

> Within a day or two of the arrival of the Prime Minister at the Potsdam Conference, I found that he was a keen sightseer. This usually meant that one received about 15 minutes' notice that the P.M., having an hour or two to spare, wished to see the capital's new palace or the Sans Souci Palace or the Prussian Military Academy or what have you. Ringed in as we were by the Russians these expeditions had a distinct air of uncertainty about them; quite apart from this there had been no time to reconnoitre any routes even if one had been permitted to wander round doing so.
>
> The usual hasty assembly of his 'caravan', as he called it, of about 12 vehicles, was followed by our departure on a road which I fondly hoped would lead us to the autobahn into Berlin. We arrived at the Reichstag, where the P.M. alighted only to be mobbed by a crowd of wildly enthusiastic Germans. The news had spread so quickly that I could see thousands of Germans running towards the Reichstag across the flattened Tiergarten [park]. My anxiety deepened rapidly. By this time I had reached the P.M.'s side and we had cleared a small space. Suddenly a man ran towards Mr Churchill with his arm outstretched. I saw the 'headlines' quite clearly and drew my pistol. He stopped, crestfallen; he wanted to shake the P.M.'s hand!
>
> A little later, in the press, the P.M. suggested that I should turn the 'caravan' around! My first problem was to find it, covered as it was with Germans scrambling for better viewpoints! While I was attempting this feat I suddenly realised, from the movement of the crowd, that Mr Churchill was no longer with us. He had simply commandeered the first jeep he saw and, with Mr Anthony Eden, had taken off in it. But where to? I could sense my hair turning grey!
>
> He had gone into the Russian sector. I followed in another jeep.

Though Japan remained a formidable and still-unconquered foe, this moment – as he visited the remains of Hitler's bunker – symbolized the climax of Churchill's wartime leadership. The author of the account on the opposite page is one of the men standing next to him.

Through the Brandenburg Gate into the Unter den Linden, where a crowd of gesticulating Germans gave us the lead we wanted. Then we saw a British jeep outside Hitler's Chancellery and a harassed-looking driver indicated that the P.M. was in there. In we dashed and in a few minutes found the P.M. and Foreign Secretary wandering through the Chancellery followed by a few bewildered-looking Russian troops (no Germans allowed!). We were soon reinforced by other members of the caravan, plus a horde of photographers, and the worst was over.

A famous photograph taken for the *Daily Mail* on this occasion shows Churchill in the khaki uniform of the 4th Hussars, and with a cigar in his mouth, gingerly sitting on a broken Chancellery chair.

11
SHEATHING THE SWORD

World War II had been a war of movement. There were no trenches, and the major fixed defensive position – the Maginot Line – had proved ludicrously ineffectual when the Germans simply went around it. The tactic of *Blitzkrieg*, or 'lightning war', enabled them to conquer their objectives within days.

Aircraft and tanks had improved out of all recognition during the 20 years of peace after the Great War. Dive-bombers could now attack targets with pinpoint accuracy, while paratroops (another new development) could seize strategic positions and hold them until they were relieved by fast-moving armour.

The weapons carried by individual soldiers had become much more powerful. They included hand-held machine-guns, shoulder-fired rocket-launchers (bazookas) and flame-throwers – a Great War invention subsequently refined. While large armies continued to struggle on battlefields, another type of warfare had come into being: small groups of highly trained specialist undercover troops were organized at Churchill's behest to attack enemy targets surreptitiously. These offered a rare opportunity to strike back at the Axis forces occupying Europe. From their beginnings in 1940, special forces became a vital part of many nations' war effort. Commandos, as they were called in Britain, were given the title of Rangers when emulated by America. A further refinement, dating from the desert war, was the Special Air Service, an infiltration and sabotage group that was to become the model for the special forces of other nations.

The air had been the decisive theatre of operations in this war. Bombers, and the loads they carried, became bigger. Flying in huge formations, and in spite of heavy losses, they were able to lay waste to enormous areas of the enemy's hinterland, supply routes and cities. Radar made possible the plotting of an enemy's positions and thus rendered the sky an even more dangerous arena. Aircraft took part in every area of World War II, for airfields could be created, quickly and easily, wherever armies were concentrated. There were even airfields at sea. The aircraft carrier, invented during the Great War, had grown in scale and importance. A number of these, with the planes that flew from them, could dominate an entire region – as the Japanese and then the Americans did in the Pacific. Not only could carrier-launched aircraft fight naval battles, they could also bomb the enemy's homeland.

The jet aircraft made its appearance at the end of World War II, though it was too late to influence the outcome. The remote-control bomb had been a more serious development: the V-1 was destructive but slow and vulnerable to interception; but the V-2, a rocket too fast and silent to be shot down, could have won the war for Germany if introduced earlier. It was extensively studied by both the Western allies and the Soviet Union, becoming the basis for the guided missiles of the Cold War era.

By 1945 British and American scientists had created the atomic bomb. The dropping of this on Japan made further resistance untenable and, in theory at least, made conventional armies obsolete. The potential for nuclear destruction did not, however, put an end to war. The world divided into armed camps – the West, the Eastern bloc, China – and although an uneasy truce existed between these giants, there would be many other outbreaks of conflict after World War II. Satellites of the superpowers fought their wars by proxy, and the rapid break-up of colonial empires brought further strife as indigenous forces fought the occupying power or each other. The British Army was to be involved in this type of operation constantly from the end of the war in 1945 until Churchill's death. The United Nations, established in 1946, likewise did not prevent wars from starting, though it did produce the concept of international police actions using neutral troops that has been used with some success ever since.

VICTORY AND DEFEAT

In July 1945, two months after V-E Day, Lieutenant DGF Gudgeon wrote in his diary:

> Have been listening to Churchill's election speeches on the wireless and was disappointed by them. He seems to have lost interest and his arguments are very feeble. I can't believe it's the same man after hearing some of his fighting speeches. He is definitely a wartime Premier, and [I] don't consider him suitable for peacetime . . .

As soon as Hitler had been defeated, the wartime coalition began to come apart. The immediate danger was over and the British people were impatient to get on with recovery and reconstruction. Churchill had hoped that his unified government – and his personal leadership – could remain until Japan, too, had been dealt with, but that might take another two years and the voters were in no mood to wait. He resigned the premiership and led a caretaker government, pending an election in July.

Preoccupied with the conference at Potsdam, and well aware of the adulation that met him everywhere, he and his circle had virtually no inkling of the revolution that was about to occur. The Conservatives assumed that public gratitude would sweep their leader back into Downing Street without difficulty and they retained this feeling until the results began to come in. Elsewhere, and particularly among the servicemen waiting to come home, the Prime Minister was viewed with a sort of respectful hostility. David Niven had earlier noticed this attitude among the men in his unit:

> **One thing that stuck out a mile in [political] debates – the vast majority of men who had been called up to fight for their country held the Conservative Party entirely responsible for the disruption of their lives and in no circumstances would they vote for it next time there was an election – Churchill or no Churchill.**

The Premier himself had been given some indication, though perhaps he preferred to believe the smiling faces around him rather than the rumours of disquiet that occasionally reached him. He had, for instance, asked Field Marshal Sir William Slim how the troops in the 14th Army would vote, and received the reply: 'Seventy per cent will vote Labour, Sir.' When he asked what the other thirty would do, Slim answered: 'They will abstain from voting at all, Sir, out of affection for you.'

He was probably unaware of it, but one factor that weighed against him with both military and civilian voters was his long-standing hostility towards Russia. Many people believed that he was not the right man to deal with the Soviets and that he might provoke a third world war.

Churchill loved electioneering and, though he had not sought this distraction from the business of rebuilding Europe, he threw himself into it. He was now such a huge celebrity that his presence anywhere would guarantee large crowds. His secretary, Elizabeth Layton, who as a Canadian had not previously experienced a British election campaign, remembered:

There was a tremendous cross-country tour lasting about five days. Sarah drove her father, and Commander Thompson and I preceded them in the loud-speaker car; we could see the smiles that lit up all the faces as they caught sight of him, and hear the continual repetition of 'There he is. There he is' from those lining the route. We stopped about fifteen times during the day, and Mr Churchill spoke on behalf of his candidates.

Little did we guess that this wonderful reception was an expression of thanks for the past rather than an indication of the future. I think it was misleading. Knowing nothing of British elections, I once or twice asked the Private Secretaries what they thought the outcome would be. The answer was 'Probably a reduced majority; however, with elections you never can tell.' All the same, I don't think the possibility of defeat was seriously considered in the office.

However, she added ominously that, during this tour:

Mr Churchill had more heckling than usual, and a day or two later, when he was touring South London, a Labour stronghold, someone threw a stone and hit him. It hurt, I'm sure, not actually but inside. It is not the kind of thing one would have expected from political opponents; the British are not normally stone-throwers. It betokened feelings of which one had previously known nothing.

Miss Nellie Carver, a resident of South London and typical of those whose admiration for his wartime leadership would ensure lasting loyalty, attended a rally at which he spoke a few days before polling began:

July 14th
General election campaign was in full swing & Winston was expected to speak at West Norwood Tram Terminus at 6p.m. Such huge crowds had assembled but Mum was game to risk going so we stood on the island outside the Thurlow Arms & waited for him.

The people were in every spot available – even on top of Woolworth's & other shops with their legs dangling over the sides – most dangerous looking! He has had a most triumphant tour round Britain, winding up with 4 days in London. Don't know what the results may be, but Winston himself is idolized by so many people & followed everywhere. His son-in-law Duncan Sandys is M.P. for Norwood so election fever is very high with our neighbourhood! Some folks think Labour will get in on Housing, but in the meantime it's all very hectic. We are grateful in one way for this Campaign as it has quite absorbed our thoughts & staved off the reaction after the ending of the War. The crowd was jolly & good tempered, singing away as they awaited the arrival of his car. It was 20 mins. late and what a roar went up when it arrived! He chucked his daughter (Mrs Sandys) under the chin, shook hands with our Member & climbed up on a platform. Someone from the Thurlow Arms handed him a tankard - & with every appearance of enjoyment & a most wicked schoolboy smile [he] held it up & drank it in full view of the delighted crowd! How wonderful to be so lacking in self-consciousness & so absolutely natural! He made a fine, fighting speech & in spite of a few interruptions you could feel the grip he has on a crowd. It was worth the heat & squashing to be there – one could understand it all – just to hear him.

Her diary went on to describe the atmosphere in the telegraph office where she worked:

26th July 1945
Election Results. Lots of extra staff on copying table to get out & rush results as they come. The 1st lot came before 11 a.m.! Got a shock as, so far, Labour is leading – it's terrible to think of Winston being put out, after all he has done. Even Norwood has gone over for the first time & poor Duncan Sandys is out! It's a very strange affair as I've seen such a few Labour posters about in our windows.

27th July 1945
Shock and consternation in final result, large Labour majority. Think it must be the Forces vote as cannot [imagine enough civilians] voted Labour! Very depressing, anyway. Fancy Mr Atlee as Prime Minister – am simply furious at the unthinking ingratitude of the public. Don't think this Party has had enough experience & will get us into muddles soon – am sure. Felt so strongly about this that I wrote a letter of thanks to

Mr Churchill – it's the least one can do. I expect he will have thousands.

Labour won 393 seats, the Conservatives 213. It was the most crushing defeat the party had suffered since 1905. For those in the eye of the storm, the trauma was perhaps greatest. Elizabeth Layton recalled the creeping dismay within Number 10:

> I was on duty the morning of that fateful 27th. Mr Churchill seemed much as usual when I went in at 8.30.
>
> Of that horrible day I do not like to think. From unsuspecting confidence we turned to mere hope, from hope to doubt, and from doubt to the certainty of failure. By mid-day we knew for sure that the landslide had taken place, with over 300 Labour victories; they were in and we were out.
>
> The shock and sense of catastrophe were overwhelming. It seemed a lifetime since 8.30 that morning. We began to realize things we had never thought of. We no longer belonged to the Prime Minister's staff. We no longer had the official staff on which to lean. We should have to get ourselves and our belongings out of No 10 and the Annexe, and this pretty quickly. Mrs Hill and I were now Private Secretaries to the Leader of the Opposition.
>
> But the little we felt for ourselves was completely lost in what we felt for Mr Churchill. True, he was, as ever, a tower of strength and self-control. Perhaps his long life had taught him that those who hold high office are for ever open to such disappointments and can never make sure they will not happen. While knowing that the nation was voting out his Party rather than himself, he must still have felt the most terrible, searing hurt, intensified because of the welcome he had received on his tours of the country.

But, she said, it was more than hurt:

> It was not being allowed to lead the Peace, which had been his dream while he was still leading the War. When you have worked for something day in, day out, night in, night out for five years – and held all the strings in your own hand, and seen your carefully planned schemes coming to fruition – then you cannot have that

responsibility snatched away without feeling the gaping hole
it leaves. It seemed particularly cruel that this should happen
at this very moment, as an anti-climax to the climax, without
warning, apparently without cause – and with the war against
Japan still to be finished off. Roosevelt dead, Germany beaten,
Churchill out – how swiftly things can change.

OUT OF OFFICE

The Churchills' initial reaction was to take a holiday – their first since the
war had begun. Winston spent some weeks painting among the Italian
Lakes. Though out of office, he was still Honorary Colonel of his old
regiment and they provided security at Viscount Alexander's villa, in which
he stayed. The regimental history records the arrangements, and suggests
that he was still able to enjoy some pomp:

> Winston Churchill took a holiday in August 1945 and stayed
> at Lake Como. The Regiment had the honour of providing
> an Honorary ADC and a personal guard, which consisted of
> 18 picked men. The Commanding Officer spent a week as the
> Colonel's guest. The guard lived in the lodge of the villa and
> mounted a permanent guard on the only entrance, turning
> out at full strength every day for the Colonel and, when he was
> visiting there, for Field Marshal Viscount Alexander. [The C.O.
> and Guard Commander] accompanied the Colonel on his daily
> excursions by car or speed-boat, when a picnic-lunch was the only
> interlude in a full day of painting. To be able to guard and attend
> the Colonel was a very happy privilege.

Had he been less ambitious, picnics and painting could have remained the
pattern of their lives. Clementine, for whom the war had been a terrible strain,
hoped he would now retire. Few political leaders, after all, had had the chance
to leave office on such a high note. She suggested that his defeat might prove
a blessing in disguise, and received the famous retort that 'At the moment it
seems very effectively disguised.' People all over the world had followed the
election and were shocked by the result. One of the more intriguing reactions
was offered to a journalist who was canvassing opinion among soldiers in
occupied Berlin, and appeared in the *Daily Mail* on 27 July:

> The Germans are just dumbfounded that Britain should have
> deserted Mr Churchill. 'To me it sounds like awful ingratitude

and a mistake,' a retired Wehrmacht officer said to me. 'We Germans think now that Mr Churchill is one of the greatest men in the world, and if he had been our leader we certainly would not have turned him out after what he has done. It's really most puzzling.'

A few weeks later, with some of the old humour now restored, Churchill mentioned that:

A friend of mine, an officer, was in Zagreb when the results of the late general election came in. An old lady said to him, 'Poor Mr Churchill! I suppose now he will be shot.' My friend was able to reassure her. He said the sentence might be mitigated to one of the various forms of hard labour which were always open to His Majesty's subjects.

Ironically, one who would not have been surprised by the result was the late Nazi Minister of Propaganda. A few months earlier, Goebbels had made an entry on this matter in his diary – a 'voice from beyond the grave' indeed:

19 March 1945
. . . it is being indicated to [Churchill] by both Conservative and Labour Party publicity that, although he may be acceptable as a war leader, as a peacetime leader he would be rejected by practically all circles concerned. There is no doubt, therefore, that shortly after the end of the war Churchill will be dispatched to the wilderness. It is, after all, long-established British practice to tolerate men who amass an exaggerated plentitude of power in wartime but in peacetime to cast them off at once.

There was, by and large, nothing personal in the public's rejection of Churchill. They were simply more concerned with domestic issues – above all the desperate shortage of housing – than with further strutting on the world stage. They knew that mundane domestic issues were not of interest to him, and the Conservatives had had nothing original to say about them during the election campaign. For Churchill's party, his image and stature had been their only electioneering device. Labour had won by identifying the voters' concerns and offering new policies that met their expectations. The outcome was a wide-ranging reorganization of the British economy and society.

Churchill continued to be fêted everywhere (his appearance at a theatre would bring the audience to their feet) and he received numerous gifts from abroad. These included 500 cigars from Jamaica and 116 gallons of vintage port from Portugal. Australia gave him a kangaroo and New Zealand offered a kiwi. The French city of Aix-en-Provence even announced that it was changing its name to 'La Ville Churchill'. Nearer home, Churchill was offered Britain's highest honour, the 'Garter.' This order of knighthood, founded in 1348 by King Edward III and the oldest continuously existing order of chivalry in the world, would normally have appealed to his romantic sense of history. He declined it, however, with the sulking comment that there was no point accepting the Order of the Garter when the British people had given him the Order of the Boot. He had also declined the offer of a dukedom (the title Duke of London had been suggested) because he wanted to remain in the Commons. He was still leader of the Conservative Party and Leader of the Opposition. He now had the burning ambition to win his way back to power in a future election. There would be no retirement after all.

Over the following years, as well as leading the Opposition, he travelled extensively, giving speeches and receiving awards. Universities showered him with honorary degrees. Denmark gave him the Order of the Elephant and Holland the Order of The Netherlands Lion. In France he was made a Companion of the Order of Liberation – a rare honour indeed, for all he deserved it. This Order had been founded by General de Gaulle in exile, and membership was limited to 1,053 Companions. When this number was reached, the membership book was closed, apparently for ever. For Churchill, however, it was re-opened so that his name could be the last inscribed.

As well as medals, he received a great deal of money. He was now a best-selling author. Always extremely well paid for his writing, he could now command truly enormous sums. He had two projects in hand. One was his *History of the English-Speaking Peoples*, begun several years before the war but mothballed when hostilities began. The second was his history of the war. As with several other conflicts, he had decided to write a history of it long before it had ended, and in this case, because it was always his instinct to record his involvement in great events, his mind would have been assembling themes and material well before May 1940. Owing to the shrewdness of his literary agent, Emery Reves, he was paid very handsomely for the serialization rights. *The Daily Telegraph* gave him £555,000 and he was offered $1,500,000 by *Life* magazine and the *New*

York Times, while Alexander Korda paid £50,000 for the film rights to *English-Speaking Peoples*.

Churchill was thus, for the first time in his adult life, clear of debt and able to afford outright the lifestyle he had always had to live on a knife-edge to enjoy. He bought 500 acres surrounding Chartwell and went into farming as a serious occupation (his son-in-law, Christopher Soames, ran the estate for him). He bred cattle and racehorses. Coincidentally at this time he was relieved of financial responsibility for Chartwell. A consortium of friends and admirers bought the house for just over £48,000 and enabled the Churchills to live in it for life, after which it would be preserved as a memorial. In the meantime, he also acquired a new London property, buying two adjacent houses in Hyde Park Gate opposite the south side of Kensington Gardens, which became his home and office. Because this was some distance from the House of Commons, he rented a suite at the Savoy as what he called his 'forward headquarters' for entertaining political friends. He travelled, expensively and luxuriously and often at the expense of publishers or wealthy businessmen.

And what of the books that made all this possible? His large historical works were produced, very efficiently, by a team, and they were assembled rather than written. Academics and researchers gathered, sifted and interpreted the raw material; Churchill shaped his conclusions from it, put it into his own words and dictated it to secretaries who, working in relays, scribbled down a torrent of words that often reached 4,000 a day. He would go over these once they were typed up and add further thoughts. It was because he had this staff of helpers that he was able to be an active politician as well as a full-time author.

The History of the Second World War was a six-volume work that appeared between 1947 and 1954. It was the biggest and most important contribution to military history that he made, though like all his books it was entirely subjective. It marked his last involvement with the military world. Though he remained in politics for several more years, he had hung up his sword for good.

When the war against Japan had ended in August 1945, the new Labour Government began their radical overhaul of British life and institutions. Churchill, betrayed but weary, spent his time in painting and travelling and writing. He carried on with a task interrupted by the war: the completion of his *History of the English-Speaking Peoples*, which was to win the Nobel Prize for Literature in 1953. The citation specified that this award was in recognition of his speeches as well as his writings in defence of democracy – but Churchill, for whom too much was never enough, had hoped to be offered the Nobel Peace Prize as well.

There were many other developments. The United Nations was established in 1946. India became independent the following year. Churchill opened the Congress of Europe. China became a Communist country, and the North Atlantic Treaty was signed. The European Coal and Steel Community (the genesis of the European Union) was created. The Korean War began, involving United Nations forces, in May 1951.

By 1946 nothing remained of the wartime alliance between Russia and the West. Suspicion had been manifest since the moment Societ forces met up with Anglo-American troops advancing into Germany, and had hardened into antipathy before the fighting was even over. Stalin's refusal to give up any territory overrun by his forces divided Europe neatly into two camps. Though the two sides co-operated in policing occupied territory and prosecuting war criminals, there was a mutual hostility that made another war seem at best likely and at worst inevitable. It was in this climate that Churchill made one of his most famous speeches at Fulton College in Missouri. Speaking unofficially, he defined the Cold War with these words:

> A shadow has fallen upon the scene so lately lighted by the Allied victory. From Stettin in the Baltic to Trieste in the Adriatic, an iron curtain has descended across the Continent. Behind that line lie all the capitals of the ancient states of central and eastern Europe, Warsaw, Berlin, Prague, Vienna, Budapest, Belgrade, and Sofia, and all these famous cities and the populations around them lie in what I must call the Soviet sphere, all subject to Soviet control. This is certainly not the liberated Europe we fought to build up.
>
> I do not believe that Soviet Russia desires war. What they desire is the fruits of war and the indefinite expansion of their power and doctrine. From what I have seen of our Russian friends and allies during the war I am convinced there is nothing they admire so much as strength and there is nothing for which they have less respect than weakness.
>
> If we adhere faithfully to the Charter of the United Nations, if all British moral and material forces and convictions are joined with our own, the high roads of the future will be clear, not only for our time but for a century to come.

The phrase 'iron curtain' became one of Churchill's most famous utterances. It was not original, having been used earlier by Goebbels in the Nazi newsaper *Das Reich* on 25 February 1945. As one author has said:

If a royalty had to be paid for its use each time by Western publicists and politicians to the original author, the shade of Goebbels would now be the wealthiest shade in Hades.

Churchill was still leader of the Conservative Party, and thus Leader of the Opposition. In October there was a general election and this time the Conservatives won. For the second time he was Prime Minister, at the age of 77. Shortly afterwards the first British atomic bomb was detonated in the Monte Bello Islands, and Eisenhower was elected President of the United States.

Churchill's health was failing. Although he was well enough to help to organize the Coronation of Queen Elizabeth II in June 1953, he suffered a stroke only a few weeks afterwards. He seemed to recover and was able to issue, with President Eisenhower, a joint declaration on foreign policy (the Potomac Charter) in June 1954. His great desire, as the last act of his political life, was to set up a disarmament conference between East and West. In this he was frustrated. The West – Washington – had reservations, while the East felt that the time was not right. Churchill himself was not in any case capable of any further dynamic leadership. He resigned from office as Prime Minister on 5 April 1955 and was succeeded by Anthony Eden, his long-serving (and long-suffering) Foreign Secretary.

The last ten years were quiet for Sir Winston, as he now was (he accepted the Garter the second time it was offered), though not for Britain. His successor involved the country in the Suez Crisis, which proved an international humiliation. The Suez Canal was controlled by Anglo-French interests and when it was abruptly 'nationalized' by Egypt's President Nasser the two powers, together with Israel, landed troops and seized it. They were quickly forced by hostile world opinion to give it back. The Cyprus emergency, in which insurgents on this British-held island sought union with Greece, was only one of several post-colonial conflicts that preoccupied the government and army. He remained an MP until 1964, though he scarcely ever visited the Chamber. By that time he had received the accolade of being created an honorary citizen of the United States. It is often said that he was the only man in history to receive this, though in fact there had been one previous award – to the Marquis de Lafayette.

These were the last prizes. A life spent in single-minded pursuit of renown had succeeded beyond the dreams of the self-assured Harrow schoolboy who had sought to emulate his father but had gone immeasurably further. There had always been about him an uncanny feeling that Fate kept a special eye on him, and that even the ordinary experiences of his life would be different to those of other people. So it was with his death in 1965. He died – several days after a massive stroke – when he had said he would: on 24 January, the exact anniversary of his father's death, which had been 70 years earlier.

The previous year, a tribute had been broadcast on television to celebrate his 90th birthday. He was probably unable to comprehend much of it, but it included the boys of his old school singing the Harrow songs that he had so loved in his youth. The most famous of these, 'Forty Years On', has a chorus that might still have stirred the memory, and the blood, of the elderly listener: 'Follow up, Follow up, Till the field ring again and again, with the shout of the twenty-two men.'

This time, another verse had been added. The boys sang:

> Blazoned in honour, for each generation,
> You kindled courage to stand and to stay,
> You led our fathers to fight for the nation,
> Called 'Follow up', and yourself showed the way,
> We who were born in the calm after thunder,
> Cherish our freedom to think and to do,
> If in our turn we forgetfully wonder,
> Yet we'll remember, we owe it to you.

If he did manages to hear this, there can be no doubt that the famous tears will have flowed.

CHRONOLOGY

1874, Nov 30 Born at Blenheim Palace.

1886 Lord Randolph appointed Chancellor of the Exchequer, but resigned shortly afterwards.

1888 Arrived at Harrow.

1892 Left Harrow to attend an army 'crammer'.

1893 Entered Royal Military College Sandhurst at 3rd attempt.

1894 Passed out of Sandhurst.

1895 Death of Lord Randolph. WSC commissioned into 4th Hussars.

1895, Nov–Dec Went to Cuba to observe Spanish forces, wrote articles for *Morning Post*.

1896 Departed for garrison duty in India with 4th Hussars.

1897, Sep Joined Malakand Field Force on North-West Frontier as correspondent, also served as officer.

1898 Joined expedition to Sudan, commanded by Kitchener, to defeat the Khalifa.

1898, Sep Battle of Omdurman. WSC took part in cavalry charge by 21st Lancers; publication of *The Malakand Field Force.*

1899 Resigned commission. Returned to England.

1899, July Stood unsuccessfully for election as MP in Oldham, Lancashire.

1899, Oct Sent as newspaper correspondent to South Africa where war had broken out between Britain and Boer republics.

1899, Nov Published *The River War.*

1899, Nov 15 Armoured train ambushed by Boers. WSC captured.

1899, Dec 12–23 Escaped from prison camp in Pretoria – made international headlines.

1900 Commissioned in South African Light Horse (unpaid) while remaining correspondent.

1900, Jan 20–22 Battle of Spion Kop.

1900, May Published first volume of Boer War history: *London to Ladysmith via Pretoria.*

1900, June Entered Pretoria with British troops. Liberated his former prison camp.

1900, July Arrived in England.

1900, Oct Elected MP for Oldham; second volume of war history – *Ian Hamilton's March* – published.

1900, Dec Made lecture tours of Britain and North America.

1901, Jan Entered Parliament.

1904, May Switched allegiance from Conservative to Liberal Party.

1906 Published two-volume biography of Lord Randolph; became Under-Secretary of State for the Colonies.

1906, Sep Visited German army manoeuvres.

1908 Published *My African Journey.*

1908 Elected Liberal MP for Dundee.

1909, Sep Revisited German manoeuvres.

1910, Jan Appointed Home Secretary.

1911, Jan 'Battle of Sidney Street'. Supervized soldiers and police while attending siege of anarchists' lair.

1911, Aug Sent for troops to deal with striking railwaymen.

1911, Aug Joined Committee of Imperial Defence. Wrote memo predicting the course of events in a future European war.

1911, Oct 25 Appointed First Lord of the Admiralty. Increased size of naval guns from 13.5 inch to 15 inch. Converted Royal Navy from coal to oil power.

1912 Established Royal Naval Air Service. Initiated experimentation with armoured cars.

1914, June Britain bought control of Persian oil for the Royal Navy at WSC's urging.

1914, July As First Lord refused to allow Home Fleet to disperse, following practice mobilization, owing to international situation.

1914, Aug 1 Sent North Sea Squadrons to battle stations.

1914, Aug 4 Britain declared war on Germany.

1914, Oct Churchill assumed personal command of Allied troops defending Antwerp.

1915, Jan WSC proposed attack on Turkey to relieve pressure on Russia.

1915, Mar Naval operations in the Dardanelles.

1915, Apr 25 Allied landings on Gallipoli peninsula.

1915, May 26 Coalition Government formed. WSC appointed Chancellor of the Duchy of Lancaster.

1915, Nov 11 WSC resigned from the Cabinet. Went to France to serve in the Army as Major.

1915, Nov-Dec Spent one month on Western Front with Grenadier Guards, then promoted to Lt Col commanding 6th Battalion, Royal Scots Fusiliers.

1916, May With amalgamation of battalions, lost post in Royal Scots Fusiliers; returned to England.

1917, July Became Minister of Munitions.

1917, Nov 20 Battle of Cambrai, first effective use of tanks.

1918, Nov 11 War ended with armistice.

1919 Appointed Secretary of State for War and Minister for Air; responsible for demobilization.

1919, June 28 Peace settlement finalized at Versailles.

1922 Lloyd George's Government defeated. WSC resigned as Colonial Secretary.

1923, Apr Published the first 6 volumes of *The World Crisis*, his personal history of World War I (completed 1929).

1924, Oct WSC elected MP for Epping as Constitutionalist (quasi-Conservative).

1924, Nov As full Conservative, appointed Chancellor of the Exchequer.

1930, Oct Published memoir *My Early Life.*

1931 Resigned from Shadow Cabinet.

1931 Coalition Government led by Ramsay MacDonald. WSC objected to their disarmament policy. Began his warnings regarding German re-armament.

1933, Aug Made major speech about German threat.

1933, Oct Published first volume of biography of Duke of Marlborough (completed 1938); WSC predicted that Germany's still-secret air force would equal the RAF in size by 1935.

1935 Joined Committee of Imperial Defence on Air Defence Research.

1938, Sept Neville Chamberlain signed Munich Agreement on behalf of Britain.

1938, Sep 1 German invasion of Poland.

1938, Sep 3 Britain declared war on Germany. WSC appointed First Lord of the Admiralty.

1940, Apr WSC became President of the Military Co-ordination Committee.

1940, Apr 9 German invasion of Norway and Denmark.

1940, Apr Narvik operation – British attempt to forestall German capture of vital Norwegain port. Chamberlain, as Prime Minister, blamed for failure.

1940, May Chamberlain resigned following vote of no confidence.

1940, May 10 Germany invaded France, Netherlands, Belgium and Luxembourg. WSC invited by King George VI to form a Government.

1940, May 13 WSC delivered 'blood, toil, tears and sweat' speech.

1940, May 15 Britain loaned by USA 50 ancient destroyers.

1940, May-June 4 Dunkirk evacuation.

1940, June To bolster French resistance to Hitler, WSC offered confederation that would pool sovereignty between Britain and France. This concept rejected by the French Government.

1940, July 4 WSC ordered Royal Navy to bombard French fleet in the harbour at Oran to prevent its use against Britain. This impressed Roosevelt but made an implacable enemy of Vichy France, with serious consequences.

1940, Aug 20 Speech praising 'the Few' – RAF fighter pilots – for their resistance to the Luftwaffe.

1940, Sep Beginning of the 'Blitz'.

1940, Oct WSC became leader of the Conservative Party.

1940, Dec Lend-lease Bill passed by US Congress.

1941, Mar British troops dispatched to Greece following German invasion.

1941, Jun 22 German armies invaded the Soviet Union. Britain and Russia become allies.

1941, Aug 12 Signing of Atlantic Charter, detailing war aims.

1941, Dec 7 Japanese attack on Pearl Harbor. US entered war.

1942, Feb 15 Fall of Singapore.

1942, Aug 2 WSC travelled to North Africa.

1942, Aug 12 Met Stalin in Moscow.

1943, Jan 12 Casablanca Conference with Roosevelt and French representatives. Agreement to demand unconditional surrender of Germany.

1943, May WSC visited Washington.

1943, Aug Quebec Conference.

1943, Nov Cairo and Tehran Conferences.

1943, Dec WSC ill with pneumonia.

1944, June 6 D-Day. Allied invasion of Europe.

1944, Aug 24 Paris liberated.

1944, Sep Second Quebec Conference.

1944, Oct WSC met Stalin in Moscow.

1944, Dec British troops intervened in fighting in Greece (civil war).

1944, Dec 24 WSC went to Athens to negotiate a peaceful settlement of the conflict.

1945, Feb Yalta Conference.

1945, Apr 12 Death of FDR.

1945, May 8 Unconditional surrender of Germany ('VE Day').

1945, May 23 Resigned as Premier. End of wartime coalition. Acted as 'caretaker' pending General Election.

1945, July 17 Potsdam Conference attended by President Truman. Decision taken to use atomic bomb against Japan.

1945, July 26 General Election resulting in major defeat for Conservatives. WSC out of office, became Leader of the Opposition.

1945, Aug 6 & 9 Atom bombs dropped on Hiroshima and Nagasaki.

1945, Aug 15 Surrender of Japan ('VJ Day')

1946, Mar 'Iron Curtain' speech delivered at Fulton, Missouri.

1948, Jan Published first volume of *History of the Second World War* (completed 1948).

1949, Mar North Atlantic Treaty Organization established.

1951, Oct 26 General Election. WSC again Prime Minister after Conservative win.

1952, Feb 6 Death of King George VI.

1952, Oct 3 First British atomic bomb exploded.

1953, Apr 24 Created Sir Winston Churchill, Knight of the Garter.

1953, June 23 WSC suffered mild stroke.

1953, Oct 15 WSC received Nobel Prize for Literature.

1954, Nov Second stroke.

1954, Nov 30 WSC's 80th birthday.

1955, Apr 5 Resigned Premiership.

1956, Apr Published first two volumes of *History of the English-Speaking Peoples*.

1963, Apr 9 WSC created honorary US citizen.

1964, Sep WSC retired from Parliament.

1964, Nov 30 90th birthday.

1965, Jan 24 Died.

1965, Jan 30 State funeral.

CHURCHILL'S MEDALS

Companion of Honour (1923)
The Order of Merit (1946)
Knight Companion of the Most Noble Order of
the Garter (1954)

The India Medal (1898) with clasp Punjab Frontier
1897-1898
The Queen's Sudan Medal 1896-1898 (1899)
The Queen's South Africa Medal 1899-1902
(1901) with clasps as follows: Diamond Hill,
Johannesburg, Relief of Ladysmith, Orange Free
State, Tugela Heights, Cape Colony
The George V Coronation Medal (1911)
The 1914-15 Star (1919)
The British War Medal 1914-18 (1919)
The Victory Medal (1920)
The Territorial Decoration (1924)
The George V Silver Jubilee Medal (1935)
The George VI Coronation Medal (1937)
The 1939-45 Star (1945)
The Africa Star (1945)
The Italy Star (1945)
The France and Germany Star (1945)
The Defence Medal (1945)
The War Medal 1939-45 (1946)
The Elizabeth II Coronation Medal (1953)

FOREIGN DECORATIONS

The Cross of the Order of Military Merit, Spain
(1895)
The Cuban Campaign Medal 1895-98, Spain
(1899)
The Khedive's Sudan Medal, with clasp
'Khartoum', EgyApt (1899)
The Distinguished Service Medal (Army), United
States (1919)
The Order of Leopold with Palm (Grand Cordon),
Belgium (1945)
War Cross (with Palm), Belgium (1945)
Military Medal, Luxembourg (1945)
The Order of the Lion of the Netherlands (Knight
Grand Cross), Netherlands (1946)
The Order of the Oaken Crown (Grand Cross),
Luxembourg (1946)
Military Medal, France (1947)
War Cross (with Palm), France (1947)
The Royal Norwegian Order of St. Olaf (Grand
Cross with Chain), Norway (1948)
The Order of the Elephant, Denmark (1950)
The Order of Liberation, France (1958)
The Order of the Star of Nepal (First Class), Nepal
(1961)
The High Order of Sayyid Mohammed bin Ali el
Senoussi (Grand Sash), Libya (1962)

BIBLIOGRAPHY AND SOURCES

Alldritt, Keith (1992) *Churchill the Writer*, Hutchinson
30, 138-9
Anonymous *The Harrovian* 55, 58-60, 148-9, 153-4,
163-4, 176-7
Anonymous (1902) *Imperial Yeomanry Training
(Provisional)*, HMSO 82, 104
Anonymous (1906) *The War in South Africa: The
Advance to Pretoria after Paardeberg, the Upper Tugela
Campaign, etc.*, Historical Section of the General
Staff, Berlin, John Murray 165-6, 167, 171
Anonymous (1944) *Brief History of the 11th Sikh
Regiment*, Military Star Press, Nowshera 108-9
Bevan, ED (1964) 'Sight-Seeing with the Prime
Minister from the Potsdam Conference', in
*The Lion and the Dragon: Regimental Gazette of the
King's Own Royal Border Regiment*, Vol. 3, No. 2,
September 1964 294-5
Blood, Sir Bindon (1933) *Four Score Years and Ten*, G
Bell 109-10
Bonham-Carter, Violet (1965) *Winston Churchill as I
Knew Him*, Eyre and Spottiswoode 135, 179, 191,
205-6
Bosanquet, Ben and Douglas, Colin (1991) *West
Indian Women at War*, Lawrence and Wishart,
London 272
Brendon, Piers (1985) *Winston Churchill: An Authentic
Hero*, Methuen
Brighton, Terry (1998) *The Last Charge*, Crowood
Press 126-7, 128-9, 131-2
Buchan, John (1925) *The History of the Royal Scots
Fusiliers (1678-1918)*, Thomas Nelson 216, 224
Burleigh, Bennett (1899) *Khartoum Campaign 1898*,
Chapman and Hall 125-6, 127-8, 131, 135
Byng of Vimy, Viscountess (Evelyn) (1946) *Up the
Stream of Time*, Macmillan, Toronto 173
Chaplin, EDW   (ed.) (1941) *Winston Churchill
and Harrow*, Harrow School Book Shop 46,
48-53, 61, 257
Charmley, John (1993) *Churchill: the End of Glory*,
BCA 238
Churchill, Randolph (1966) *Winston S. Churchill, Vol.
I: Youth, 1874-1900*, Heinemann 41, 43, 54, 61,
63-4, 65-6, 90-1. 101, 111, 118, 128-9, 132-3,
140, 141, 147, 149, 150, 151, 152, 161, 164,
166-7
Churchill, Randolph (1967) *Winston S. Churchill, Vol.
II: Young Statesman*, Heinemann 192
Churchill, WS (1899) *The Story of The Malakand Field
Force*, Longmans, Green 113
Churchill, Winston S (1943) *Unrelenting Struggle:
War Speeches by the Right Hon. Winston S. Churchill*,
Cassell
Churchill, Winston S (1947) *My Early Life: a Roving
Commission*, Odhams Press (1958 printing), ©
Eland 2000 73, 82-3, 112, 138, 150, 152
Churchill, Winston S (1990) *Thoughts and Adventures*,
Octopus Publishing 185-7, 213-16
Cilcennin, Viscount (1960) 'Admiralty House,
Whitehall', in *Country Life*, 1960 10-11, 29
Cole, Howard N (1951) *The Story of Aldershot: a*

History and Guide to Town and Camp, Gale and Polden, Aldershot 81

Cooper, Diana (1960) *Trumpets from the Steep*, Rupert Hart-Davis 20, 277-8

Cooper, Duff (1954) *Old Men Forget: The Autobiography of Duff Cooper (Viscount Norwich)*, Rupert Hart-Davis 250-1

Cowles, Virginia (1953) *Winston Churchill: the Era and the Man*, Hamish Hamilton 31, 43, 44, 104

Croft, WD (1919) *Three Years with the 9th (Scottish) Division*, John Murray 217, 225

Eade, Charles (ed.) (1953) *Churchill: By His Contemporaries*, Hutchinson 16, 28, 241, 246. 251-2, 263-4, 271-2

Fairbanks, Douglas, Jr (1988) *The Salad Days*, Collins 246-7

Fuller, Major-General JFC (1936) *Memoirs of an Unconventional Soldier*, Ivor Nicholson and Watson 199, 226-7

Gibb, AD (Captain X) (1924) *With Winston Churchill at the Front*, Cowans and Gray, Glasgow 217, 221-2, 224-5

Gordon, John (1941) *Culled from a Diary (1867–1939)*, Oliver and Boyd, Edinburgh 201-2

Gough, General Sir Hubert (1954) *Soldiering On*, Arthur Barker 173

Haffner, Sebastian (1996) *Churchill*, Haus Publishing 47

Halle, Kaye (ed.) (1985) *The Irrepressible Churchill*, Robson Books 25, 31-2

Hamilton, Sir Ian (1944) *Listening for the Drums*, Faber and Faber 112, 172, 206-7

Harding Davis, Richard (1897) *Cuba in War Time*, Heinemann 93-5

Horne, Pamela (1992) *High Society: The English Social Elite, 1880-1914*, Sutton Publishing Ltd.

Hume, James C (2003) *Winston Churchill*, Dorling Kindersley 26

James, Colonel Lionel (1929) *High Pressure: Being some Record of Activities in the Service of The Times Newspaper*, John Murray 111, 118-19, 136

Ismay, Lord (1960) *Memoirs of General the Lord Ismay*, Heinemann 102, 260-1

Jones, Lawrence (1956) *An Edwardian Youth*, Macmillan 183-4

Langworth, Richard M (1998) *A Connoiseur's Guide to the Books of Sir Winston Churchill*, Brassey's 139

Laver, James (1954) 'Sir Winston Churchill Sartorially Considered', in *The Ambassador*, No. 11, 1954 20

Leslie, Shane (ed.) (1957) *Edward Tennyson Reed*, Heinemann 185

Lucaks, John (1990) *The Duel*, Bodley Head 252

Lucaks, John (2002) *Churchill: Visionary, Statesman, Historian*, Yale University Press, New Haven, Connecticut

MacLeod, Colonel R (1980) 'Field-Marshal Lord Ironside, GCB, CMG, DSO: His Life and Times', in *Journal of the Royal Artillery*, Vol. CVII, No. 1, March 1980 160

Marchant, Sir James (ed.) (1954) *Winston Spencer Churchill: Servant of Crown and Commonwealth: a Tribute by Various Hands Presented to Him on His Eightieth Birthday*, Cassell

Marsh, Edward (1939) *A Number of People: A Book of Reminiscences*, William Heinemann in association with Hamish Hamilton 179, 203-4

Martin, Ralph G (1972) *Lady Randolph Churchill: a Biography: Volume II*, Cassell 40-1, 43, 75, 87-8

McGowan, Norman (1958) *My Years with Churchill*, Souvenir Press 19, 22, 24-5, 26-8

Menpes, Mortimer (1903) *War Impressions*, 2nd edn, A & C Black 174-5

Meredith, John (1998) *Omdurman Diaries 1898*, Leo Cooper 120-2, 122-3,125, 133

Morris, Jan (1995) *Fisher's Face*, Viking 190-1

Nel, Elizabeth (1958) *Mr. Churchill's Secretary*, Hodder and Stoughton 23, 265-8, 282, 288-9, 293-3, 299, 301-2

Nevitt Dupuy, Trevor (1970) *The Military Life of Winston Churchill of Britain*, Franklin Watts, New York 30, 203

Niven, David (1971) *The Moon's a Balloon*, Hamish Hamilton 298

Paneth, Philip (1943) *The Prime Minister Winston S. Churchill: As Seen by his Enemies and Friends*, Alliance Press 30, 249-50, 255

Paterson, Michael (1998) *Alfred the Little: Great Chart's Poet Laureate*, Great Chart Society 142

Pawle, Gerald (1963) *The War and Colonel Warden* (based on the recollections of Commander CR Thompson), George G Harrap 23, 25, 281-2

Payne, Graham and Day, Barry (1994) *My Life with Noël Coward*, Applause, New York/London 31

Reader's Digest (eds) (1965) *Man of the Century: a Churchill Cavalcade*, Little, Brown and Co., Boston 14-15, 16, 28-9, 232, 240-1, 303, 306

Rose, Norman (1994) *Churchill: An Unruly Life*, Simon and Schuster

Sandys, Celia (1994) *From Winston with Love and Kisses*, Sinclair-Stevenson 42, 56, 57, 65

Scott Daniell, David (1959) *4th Hussar: the Story of The 4th Queen's Own Hussars, 1685–1958*, Gale and Polden, Aldershot 85-6, 137-8, 198, 302

Shepperd, Alan (1980) *Sandhurst: The Royal Military Academy*, Country Life Books 63

Shepperd, GA (1965) 'Sir Winston S. Churchill at Sandhurst', in *The Wish Stream*, Vol. XIX, No. 2, Autumn 1965 68-71

Skeen, General Sir Andrew (no date) *Passing It On: Short Talks on Tribal Fighting on the North-West Frontier of India*, Gale and Polden, Aldershot 106-7, 108

Steevens, GW (1898) *With Kitchener to Khartum*, William Blackwood, Edinburgh 122, 123-4, 129-30

Taylor, Fred (ed.) (1982) *The Goebbels Diaries 1939–41*, Hamish Hamilton 26

Terraine, John (1968) *The Life and Times of Lord Mountbatten*, Hutchinson (© Emberdove

Ltd and the Estate of Lord Terraine 1968, reproduced by permission of PFD (www.pfd.co.uk) on behalf of Emberdove Ltd and the Estate of John Terraine 193–5

Trevor-Roper, H (ed.) (1978) *The Goebbels Diaries* (translated by R Barry), Secker and Warburg, reproduced by permission of PFD (www.pfd.co.uk) on behalf of the Estate of Hugh Trevor-Roper 287–8

Trukhanovsky, VG (1978) *Winston Churchill*, Progress Publishers, Moscow 29, 226, 239, 278, 307

Vanderbilt Balsan, Consuelo (1953) *The Glitter and the Gold,* Heinemann (Harper & Brothers, New York, 1952) 16, 31, 32-3, 35, 164–5

Weidhorn, Manfred (1974) *Sword and Pen,* University of New Mexico Press, Albuqurque 113

Whitworth, RH (1974) *The Grenadier Guards,* (Famous Regiments series), Leo Cooper 213

Wilson, Harold (1977) *A Prime Minister on Prime Ministers*, BCA 103

Wingfield-Stratford, Esme (1945) *Before the Lamps Went Out*, Hodder and Stoughton 133–4

Woods, F (ed.) (1992) *Winston S. Churchill: War Correspondent*, Brassey's 95–8

Yardley, Michael (1987) *Sandhurst*, Harrap 63, 67, 67–8, 72

PERIODICALS

Daily Chronicle 25 April 1918 229
Daily Mail 27 July 1945 302–3
Daily Mirror, 27 January 1965 16
Hansard 13 May 1901, HMSO 177–8
Illustrated London News 6 February 1965, courtesy of the *Illustrated London News* Picture Library 8
New York Times Saturday Review 177
The Times 229–30

CHURCHILL ARCHIVES CENTRE

Churchill College, Cambridge:
CHAR 1/15-16 105
CHAR 2/11/5 Churchill College 136–7
CHAR 2/1/6 Churchill College 137
CHAR 28/12/23-24 54
CHAR 28/16/8-9 55
CHAR 28/17/4 60
CHAR 28/17/6 56
CHAR 28/17/17 61
CHAR 28/17/30
WCHL 2/8 154–8
WCHL 2/5 ACC 538 161–2

IMPERIAL WAR MUSEUM

Department of Documents:
T.M. Allison, 87/14/1 271
Admiral O. Backhouse, 86/31/1
Miss N.V. Carver, 90/16/1 252–4, 259, 288, 299–301
E. Chapman, Con Shelf
Clink Chronicle, Misc 120 (1856) 260–70
T.L. Cook, 99/66/1 282–6
Brigadier-General Ernest Craig Brown, DSO, 92/23/2 67, 72
Mrs. J. Crossley, 04/13/1 255–6. 258, 293
B.W. Downes, 80/43/1
W. Ellams, 99/42/1, by permission of his niece Barbara Ellams 232
Lieutenant R.H.W.M. Empson, 95/16/1 197, 200
Major A.F. Flatow, 99/16/1 275–7
C.A. Gould, 02/56/1 256
Lieutenant G.D.F. Gudgeon, 85/8/1 297
Benny Hobson, 04/19/1, letters presented by his niece, Irene Bell 101-2
Major General F.E. Hotblack, DSO, MC, 76/136/1
[Field Marshal Lord Ironside, GCB,CMG, DSO], quoted in Misc 36 item 664 160
LE Jones 188–9
Nurse Winifred Kenyon, 84/24/1 courtesy of Mrs Ann Mitchell 231–2
Miss L. Lewis, 91/5/1
Capt JA Lloyd 182
Lt. Col. C.E.L. Lyne, 80/14/1 217–18
H. Mellanby, 95/5/1
Mr Nicolson 289–90
Col. Roderick McLeod, Misc 11(221)
Air Commodore J.L. Mitchell, LVO, DFC, AFC, 67/277/1 273–5
W.W. Mitchell, 291–2
Lt. Cdr. E.B. Rhead, DSC, RNR, 99/5/1 280–1
Special Miscellaneous P4 261–2
Cecil Talbot, 81/42/3 192
Gen. Sir Andrew Thorne, KCB,CMG, DSO, DL, Con Shelf & DS/MISC/11
Maj. Gen. Sir Hugh H. Tudor, Misc 175 (2658)
Maj. D.R. Vernon, 90/25/1 286–7
Admiral Sir Algernon Willis, CGB,KBE,DSO,DC, P186 & P186A-B 278–9

IMPERIAL WAR MUSEUM

Department of Printed Books:
Press Cuttings Section of Women's Work Collection

INDEX

Picture Credits